The *New Horizons in Forensic Science* book series aims to provide a comprehensive platform for publishing contemporary developments, emerging technologies, and applied research across diverse domains of forensic science. The series will cover a broad spectrum of topics including forensic biology and serology, forensic DNA profiling, forensic chemistry and toxicology, forensic medicine, cyber forensics, crime scene investigation, forensic physics and ballistics, fingerprinting, questioned document examination, and related interdisciplinary areas.

With rapid advancements in analytical technologies, molecular techniques, and digital tools, forensic science continues to evolve as a multidisciplinary field with growing relevance in criminal investigations, legal systems, and scientific research. This series seeks to bridge the gap between research, laboratory practice, and academic learning by bringing together authoritative volumes that integrate theoretical concepts with practical applications.

The series is intended to serve as a valuable resource for researchers, forensic practitioners, students, law professionals, investigating agencies, and members of the judiciary by providing up-to-date insights into modern forensic methodologies and emerging trends. Guided by an experienced international editorial team and advisory board, the series will promote high-quality scholarly contributions that support innovation, education, and professional practice in forensic science.

Vijay Kumar • Leena Bhardwaj
Tirath Das Dogra
Editors

Forensic Speech Sciences

A Practical Approach

Springer

Editors
Vijay Kumar
Department of Audiology and Speech Language Pathology
Amity Medical School, Amity University Haryana
Gurgaon, Haryana, India

Leena Bhardwaj
Department of Chemistry, Biochemistry and Forensic Sciences
Amity University Haryana
Gurgaon, Haryana, India

Tirath Das Dogra
Department of Forensic Medicine and Toxicology
All India Institute of Medical Sciences
New Delhi, India

ISSN 3120-6719 ISSN 3120-6727 (electronic)
New Horizons in Forensic Science
ISBN 978-981-92-1474-7 ISBN 978-981-92-1475-4 (eBook)
https://doi.org/10.1007/978-981-92-1475-4

This Springer imprint is published by the registered company Springer Nature Singapore Pte Ltd.
The registered company address is: 152 Beach Road, #21-01/04 Gateway East, Singapore 189721, Singapore

Preface

Forensic speech science is recognized as an important interdisciplinary area of research that combines the fields of speech science, linguistics, acoustics, psychology, and law. The increasing use of recorded speech in modern communication systems has made the scientific analysis of voice and spoken language an important area of forensic analysis. The use of telephone records, digital messages, and other speech materials is common in many criminal and civil cases. Thus, there is a growing need to develop knowledge about the scientific analysis of speech and its contribution to the administration of justice.

This edited book attempts to present a comprehensive overview of the principles and applications of forensic speech science. The book includes theoretical and applied knowledge that reflects the analysis of speech characteristics for purposes such as speaker identification, voice comparison, linguistic analysis, and profiling. Human voice is recognized as having important characteristics that can be used to identify speakers. However, it is important to understand that the forensic analysis of voice requires appropriate scientific methodology and awareness of its limitations. The book attempts to introduce readers to the scientific analysis of speech and its use in forensic contexts.

The various chapters included in this book, in total, emphasize different facets of forensic speech science. The chapters included in this book demonstrate that speech analysis is not just limited to acoustic and phonetic analysis, as it requires linguistic, technological, and legal aspects as well. The book includes chapters from different experts in different fields of speech science, and hence, it can be said that this book has attempted to provide an interdisciplinary approach to forensic speech science.

Central Theme of the Book

The central theme of this book is to explore speech and voice as forensic evidence and to understand different scientific approaches to analyse speech and voice. Human speech has different acoustic, physiological, and linguistic aspects, which can be significant in understanding different aspects of human speech. This can be useful in identifying speakers, understanding linguistic aspects, and interpreting speech in different legal scenarios. The book emphasizes different aspects of speech analysis, and one such aspect is that it requires scientific methods to analyse speech evidence. Unlike voice recognition, forensic speech analysis requires different acoustic parameters, comparison, and linguistic analysis as well. The book has discussed how auditory analysis can be used for forensic speech analysis.

Another significant part of this theme is the interdisciplinary character of the field. Forensic speech science incorporates knowledge from phonetics, linguistics, acoustics, engineering, speech pathology, and law. These fields provide unique perspectives and methodologies, which enhance the overall analysis of speech evidence. The book, therefore, indicates how scientific approaches can be used in providing practical solutions in complex crime situations. The book also indicates the relationship between scientific research and the law. *The presentation of speech evidence should meet the requirements of judicial evaluation and expert testimony. The book, therefore, indicates the scientific basis of speech evidence and its relevance to the law.*

Distribution of Chapters

The chapters in this book have been distributed in a manner that gradually takes the reader from basic concepts to perspectives and future developments. The initial chapters introduce the reader to the larger field of forensic speech science and provide an overview of the theoretical foundations. These chapters provide the reader with an understanding of the fundamental principles underlying the analysis of speech and voice. In the following chapters, specialized areas like forensic phonetics and forensic linguistics are discussed. Forensic phonetics and forensic linguistics involve different aspects of speech. Forensic phonetics deals with the acoustic and articulatory characteristics of speech, and forensic linguistics deals with patterns of language use, which may reveal some facts about the speaker.

The chapters include the methodological and technological aspects of speech. The chapters on instrumentation used in voice analysis provide information about the tools used to measure and analyse speech. Other chapters include topics like changes in voices with age, voice matching, and speaker profiling. The following chapters include topics about the role of speech in the court and the social aspects of speech. Topics about the stigma associated with speech disorders and the interpretation of speech are included to provide information about the social aspects. The case studies provide readers with an idea about how the theoretical aspects are used in practical cases. The final chapter provides information about the scope of forensic speech science, including the challenges.

Selection of Contributors

The contributors to this volume have been chosen in a manner that is expected to bring together experts and practitioners in the field who have knowledge in various domains of speech science and its application in the field of forensic science. Forensic speech science is an interdisciplinary field, and therefore needs knowledge from various related disciplines. The contributors are experts in various domains like phonetics, linguistics, speech science, and related disciplines. One of the important considerations in choosing the contributors to this volume is their experience in research and work in the domain of speech analysis. The experience of the contributors is a significant consideration in this volume because their contributions are expected to bring a new perspective based on their research and work in the field of speech analysis.

Another consideration in the choice of contributors is the perspective presented in the volume. The contributors have expertise in various domains, and therefore the volume is expected to bring a comprehensive perspective in the field of forensic speech science. The editors also emphasized the selection of authors who can effectively communicate complex ideas clearly and concisely. This is because the book is intended for a readership with varying academic and professional backgrounds. The collective expertise of the authors ensure that the book is academically sound while being accessible to a wide readership.

Target Readership

The book is intended for a readership with a general interest in the scientific and practical aspects of speech analysis for forensic purposes. One of the primary readers of the book will be individuals with an academic and research interest in the fields of linguistics, phonetics, speech science, and communication studies. For this readership, the book will provide an introduction to the theoretical basis of the methods of forensic speech analysis. The book will also be of interest to legal and investigative professionals. These include lawyers, judges, and law enforcement officials. These individuals often encounter cases where speech and voice comparison play a significant role.

Other professionals who may find the discussions in this book useful include speech-language pathologists and speech scientists. Their understanding of speech production, the nature of speech disorders, and acoustic analysis may be useful in forensic speech science. Other topics, such as voice change across age and speech-related stigmas, may be of interest to them. Other potential readers who may find this book useful include criminologists, forensic scientists, and psychologists. The scope of practice of these professionals are interdisciplinary in nature. They may find the book useful as a reference on speech-based evidence. The book offers a wide range of discussions on theoretical aspects, methodologies, and real-world examples, making it a useful guide for readers interested in forensic speech science.

Gurgaon, Haryana, India — Vijay Kumar
Gurgaon, Haryana, India — Leena Bhardwaj
New Delhi, India — Tirath Das Dogra

Contents

Editors and Contributors

About the Editors

Vijay Kumar is an Associate Professor and Head of the Department of Audiology & Speech-Language Pathology at Amity University Haryana. He is the leading faculty member who established and commenced Audiology & Speech-Language Pathology academic program at Amity University Haryana. He has over 19 years of teaching experience at postgraduate and undergraduate level for ASLP/Psychology/MBA-HR and Forensic science students. He is also supervising six PhD scholars. Forensic Speech Science, Language processing, Cognitive processes, Aphasiology, Language outcome in Cochlear Implantation, etc. are his core research areas. He has received outstanding research scholar award from Ohio University, USA, in 2009. He has published 59 research papers in Scopus/Web of Science and other indexed journals and presented over 52 research papers at national and international conferences such as Academy of Aphasia and Clinical Aphasiology Conference, USA. Besides, he has also published nine book chapters in leading publishers. He is empanelled as the visiting expert of Rehabilitation Council of India, an autonomous body of Govt. of India, since 2014. He is also the Board of Studies and Academic Council member of eight leading Indian universities.

Leena Bhardwaj started her academic career in 2010 from Babu Banarasi das University Lucknow, where she joined as Lecturer in the Department of Oral Pathology and Microbiology. She further strengthened her clinical proficiency by achieving certification at Advanced Proficiency in Laser Dentistry from Arizona, USA, in the year 2011. Further she pursued her academic career in Forensic Odontology and Genomics in Forensic Odontology and Genomics with pioneering scientist and Forensic Pathologist Dr T D Dogra at CFSl, CBI, New Delhi. She explored Cyber Forensics, Forensic Ballistics, and Investigative Psychology. She is a certified Cyber Crime Intervention Officer (CCIO & CPEW) from AICTE, and an Expert in Lean Management Practices certified from IIM Bangalore in collaboration with Japan. Currently she is serving at Amity University Haryana in Amity School of Applied Sciences as an Assistant Professor since 2022. She has published 37 research papers and book chapters in Scopus and other indexed journals in the domain of forensic sciences. She authored two textbooks highlighting teaching-learning practices and cell modelling and genomics. Besides, she has also filled 12 patents in the domain of multidisciplinary bio-medical sciences.

Tirath Das Dogra is a former director of the *All India Institute of Medical Sciences* (AIIMS) New Delhi and an authority on forensic medicine. He was a member of the *Medical Council of India* from December 2013 till its dissolution in September 2018. He was the President of National Medicos Organization Delhi State from 2012 to 2017. He was a member of the TEQ-Equivalence committee and the Administration and Grievance committee of the Medical Council of India. He was a member of the Advisory committee on MOOC's program of University Grants Commission of India New Delhi. He was an emeritus professor of forensic medicine and forensic sciences, professor of Andragogy and educational philosophy and advisor, Internal Quality Assurance Cell (IQAC) at SGT University Gurgaon till January 2022. He is a member of the Rehabilitation Council of India. He has been involved in medico-legal investigations of high-profile cases throughout India.

He has presented his medico-legal opinion in cases concerning to three prime ministers: *Indira Gandhi*, *Charan Singh*, and *Rajiv Gandhi*. He was deposed as a medical witness in the Mahesh Chandra Trial Court for Indira Gandhi's assassination for the prosecution. His areas of interest have been DNA profiling, population genetics, bioethics, medical education, forensic psychiatrics, and crime scene investigations.

Contributors

Emmanuel Kwaku Addo Department of Community Research and Action, Binghamton University, Binghamton, NY, USA

Monika Arora Amity Business School, Amity University Haryana, Gurugram, Haryana, India

Yogendra Kumar Awasthi Electronics and Communication Engineering, Galgotias University, Greater Noida, UP, India

Ruchi Bhandari Department of Otorhinolaryngology, Graphic Era Institute of Medical Sciences and Research Foundation, Dehradun, Uttarakhand, India

Leena Bhardwaj Department of Chemistry, Biochemistry and Forensic Science, Amity University Haryana, Gurgaon, Haryana, India

Priyatam Bhardwaj Indian Law Institute, Delhi, India

Prakash Boominathan Sri Ramachandra Faculty of Audiology and Speech Language Pathology, Sri Ramachandra Institute of Higher Education and Research (Deemed University), Porur, Chennai, Tamil Nadu, India

Sahajiya Farhani Chanda Department of Audiology and Speech-Language Pathology, Amity University Haryana, Gurgaon, Haryana, India

Kamal Chauhan Central Forensic Science Lab, Department of Forensic Science Services, Ministry of Home Affairs, Govt of India, Bhopal, India

Swaril Dania University School of Law and Legal Studies, Guru Gobind Singh Indraprastha University, Delhi, India

Suma R. Devenga Department of Communication Disorders and Sciences, RUSH University Medical Center, Chicago, IL, USA

Tirath Das Dogra All India Institute of Medical Science, New Delhi, India

Rodney Gabel Department of Speech, Language Pathology, Binghamton University, Binghamton, NY, USA

Samiksha Gaur Department of Community Research and Action, Binghamton University, Binghamton, NY, USA

Vijay Kumar Department of Audiology and Speech-Language Pathology, Amity University Haryana, Gurgaon, Haryana, India

Krittika Kunda Department of Community Research and Action, Binghamton University, Binghamton, NY, USA

Vikas Madukar Amity University Haryana, Gurugram, Haryana, India

Srirangam Vijayakumar Narasimhan Department of Speech Language Pathology, JSS Institute of Speech and Hearing, Mysore, India

Kashyap Sahana Department of Speech Language Pathology, JSS Institute of Speech and Hearing, Mysore, India

Gaurav Saxena Electronics and Communication Engineering, Ajay Kumar Garg Engineering College, Ghaziabad, UP, India

Aman Sharma Department of Chemistry, Biochemistry and Forensic Science, ASAS, Amity University Haryana, Gurugram, Haryana, India

Bhavya Sharma Department of Chemistry, Biochemistry and Forensic Science, ASAS, Amity University Haryana, Gurugram, Haryana, India

Himanshi Sharma Department of Chemistry, Biochemistry and Forensic Science, Amity University Haryana, Gurgaon, Haryana, India

Himanshu Singh Department of Physics, Hindu College, University of Delhi, New Delhi, India

Vishwadeep Singh Department of Audiology and Speech-Language Pathology, Amity University Haryana, Gurgaon, Haryana, India

Manoj Kumar Sinha Dharmashastra National Law University, Jabalpur, Madhya Pradesh, India

Krupa Venkatraman Sri Ramachandra Faculty of Audiology and Speech Language Pathology, Sri Ramachandra Institute of Higher Education and Research (Deemed University), Porur, Chennai, Tamil Nadu, India

Bhuvnesh Yadav Department of Chemistry, Biochemistry and Forensic Science, ASAS, Amity University Haryana, Gurugram, Haryana, India

Speech Science: Anatomy, Physiology, and Acoustics

1

Sahajiya Farhani Chanda and Vijay Kumar

Abstract

Speech science is an interdisciplinary field that integrates anatomical, physiological, and acoustic principles to explain how humans produce and perceive spoken language. This chapter provides a detailed account of the structural and functional mechanisms of speech, the theoretical models that describe production processes, and the acoustic properties of speech signals. It begins with an overview of the historical development of speech science and its scope. The anatomy of the respiratory, phonatory, and articulatory subsystems is described in depth, followed by an examination of the physiological processes that govern speech production. The chapter also discusses major theories of speech production, methods for acoustic analysis, and the impact of age, gender, and individual variability on speech characteristics. These foundations have significant implications for clinical practice, linguistic research, and speech technology.

Keywords

Acoustic analysis · Speech science · Speech physiology · Speech production · Vocal anatomy · Voice variation

1.1 Introduction

Speech is one of the most remarkable human capabilities, serving as the primary medium for transmitting ideas, emotions, knowledge, and culture. Unlike other forms of communication, speech requires the precise and dynamic coordination of

S. F. Chanda · V. Kumar (✉)
Department of Audiology and Speech-Language Pathology, Amity Medical School,
Amity University Haryana, Gurgaon, Haryana, India
e-mail: vkumar@ggn.amity.edu

V. Kumar et al. (eds.), *Forensic Speech Sciences*, New Horizons in Forensic Science, https://doi.org/10.1007/978-981-92-1475-4_1

multiple physiological subsystems—respiratory, phonatory, resonatory, and articulatory—along with finely tuned neural control. These processes are underpinned by the principles of anatomy, physiology, and acoustics, making speech science an inherently interdisciplinary field. It integrates knowledge from biology, physics, linguistics, engineering, and clinical sciences to explain how speech is produced, transmitted, and perceived (Kent and Read 2002). Speech science has two primary goals: first, to understand the biological and physical mechanisms that make speech possible and, second, to apply this knowledge in practical domains, including clinical intervention for communication disorders, the development of speech recognition and synthesis systems, and forensic voice identification (Titze 2000).

1.1.1 Historical Background

The scientific curiosity about speech production and perception has deep historical roots. Ancient Greek philosophers such as Aristotle (384–322 BCE) and Galen (129–200 CE) wrote about the voice and its dependence on respiration and the anatomy of the throat. In parallel, Indian scholars such as Pāṇini (circa fourth century BCE) meticulously described the articulation of Sanskrit sounds in terms of place and manner of production—a linguistic framework still relevant to phonetics today. By the Renaissance, anatomical dissections by Vesalius and others provided more accurate depictions of the speech apparatus, although physiological functions remained poorly understood. The eighteenth and nineteenth centuries saw significant advances. For example, Hermann von Helmholtz studied vowel production through resonance cavities, establishing a physical basis for vocal timbre (Helmholtz 1954). Alexander Graham Bell, trained in elocution and speech science, applied his knowledge to invent the telephone, revolutionizing communication technology. Ewald Hering advanced understanding of respiratory physiology, linking breath control to phonation.

The twentieth century marked the transformation of speech science into a rigorous discipline. The invention of the sound spectrograph during World War II allowed visual analysis of speech signals, revealing the complex frequency patterns of vowels and consonants (Potter et al., 1947). The development of high-speed laryngoscopy, X-ray imaging, and, later, magnetic resonance imaging (MRI) further deepened our understanding of vocal tract dynamics (Story et al., 1996). Today, speech science stands as a central pillar in fields as diverse as speech-language pathology, computational linguistics, and neurolinguistics, integrating modern imaging techniques, computer modeling, and machine learning to explore speech production and perception in unprecedented detail (Stevens and Blumstein 1978).

1.1.2 Definition, Incidence, and Prevalence

Speech science can be defined as the systematic study of the anatomical structures, physiological processes, and acoustic principles involved in the generation and perception of human speech. It encompasses:

- Anatomy—the structural framework enabling speech production.
- Physiology—the dynamic functioning of these structures in real time.
- Acoustics—the study of the sound signal's physical properties as it travels from speaker to listener.

By understanding how these components interact, researchers and clinicians can identify normal speech patterns, diagnose deviations, and develop interventions (Zemlin 1998).

Incidence and Prevalence: Communication disorders are widespread and have significant social, academic, and occupational consequences. Epidemiological data indicate that approximately 5–10% of the general population will experience a communication disorder at some point in life (World Health Organization 2021). In preschool-aged children, speech sound disorders affect an estimated 8%, often impacting early literacy development (Wren et al. 2016). Among adults, voice disorders are especially prevalent in professional voice users such as teachers, with estimates reaching up to 20% at any given time (Roy et al. 2004). Neurological disorders such as Parkinson's disease, stroke, or traumatic brain injury can cause motor speech disorders (dysarthria, apraxia of speech) in 25–60% of affected individuals (Duffy 2020). Stuttering affects approximately 1% of adults and up to 5% of children, with variable recovery rates (Yairi and Ambrose 2013). The burden of these disorders is compounded by reduced access to specialized services in many parts of the world. Speech science not only offers the framework for evidence-based assessment and therapy but also contributes to preventive measures, public health policy, and assistive technology design (Kent and Read 2002).

1.1.3 Scope and Relevance

The scope of speech science extends across multiple disciplines and applications:

- Clinical practice: Speech-language pathologists rely on principles of anatomy, physiology, and acoustics to assess and treat disorders of speech, voice, and resonance.
- Technology: Speech recognition systems, voice assistants, and text-to-speech synthesis are built upon acoustic modeling principles derived from speech science.
- Education: Understanding speech production supports language teaching, accent training, and public speaking.
- Forensics: Voiceprints and acoustic profiles are used for speaker identification in criminal investigations (Nolan 2020a).
- Research: Neuroscientists study speech motor control to understand brain-language relationships (Guenther 2016).

The relevance of speech science will continue to grow as societies become more interconnected, requiring effective multilingual communication, and as technology increasingly relies on natural language interfaces.

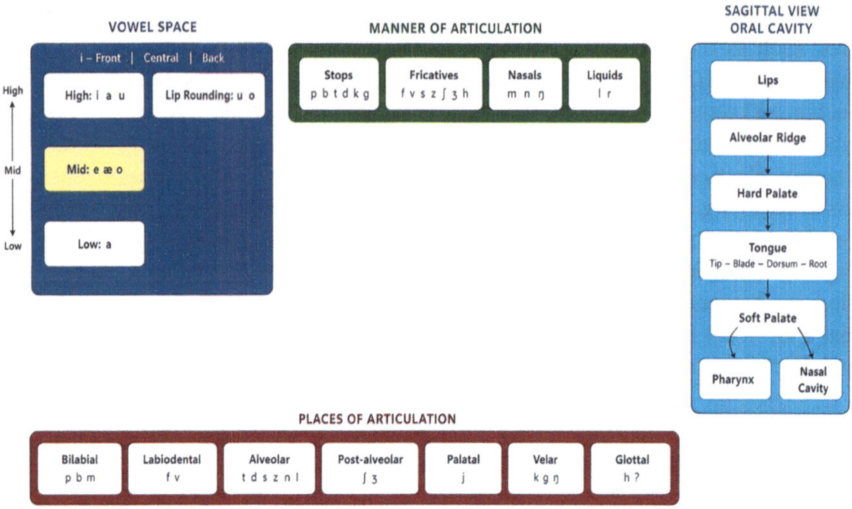

Fig. 1.2 The articulatory-resonatory system (supralaryngeal vocal tract) shapes and filters sound. Movements of the tongue, lips, jaw, velum, and pharyngeal walls modify the vocal tract's shape, altering formant frequencies to produce distinct speech sounds

Key structures include:

- **Oral cavity**—contains the **tongue**, the most versatile articulator, capable of rapid shape changes; the **lips** (for bilabial and rounded vowels); **teeth** (for dental and labiodental consonants); and the **hard palate** and **alveolar ridge** (for alveolar and palatal sounds).
- **Nasal cavity**—coupled to the oral cavity via the **velopharyngeal port**; opened for nasal consonants /m/, /n/, and /ŋ/ and closed for oral sounds.
- **Pharynx**—acts as a resonating chamber, influencing vowel quality.
- **Soft palate (velum)**—raises to block nasal airflow for oral sounds and lowers to allow nasal resonance.

Speech resonance is determined by the vocal tract's length and shape. Altering the cross-sectional area at different points changes **formant frequencies**, which are the primary acoustic cues for vowel identity (Fant 1960). Refer to Fig. 1.2. Clinically, velopharyngeal insufficiency (as in cleft palate) can cause hypernasality, while articulatory imprecision in dysarthria reduces speech clarity. Understanding the anatomy of the articulatory-resonatory system is thus essential for both diagnostic and therapeutic purposes (Yorkston et al. 2010). Refer to Fig. 1.2.

1.3 Physiology of Speech Science

While anatomy describes the structural components of the speech mechanism, physiology explains how these structures function in an integrated manner to produce speech. Speech production is a highly coordinated process involving precise timing, force regulation, and sequence control across the respiratory, phonatory, and articulatory systems. It is regulated by the central and peripheral nervous systems, which ensure rapid adjustments in muscle activity to meet linguistic and prosodic demands (Zemlin 1998; Hixon et al. 2014).

1.3.1 Respiratory Physiology in Speech

In speech breathing, **inspiration** is rapid and deep enough to generate the lung volume required for extended utterances. The **diaphragm** contracts and flattens, while the external intercostal muscles elevate the ribs, expanding the thoracic cavity. The **elastic recoil** of the lungs and chest wall, along with controlled activity of the internal intercostals and abdominal muscles, maintains a steady subglottal pressure during **expiration**. For conversational speech, subglottal pressure is typically maintained at 5–10 cm H_2O, whereas singing or loud speech may require pressures exceeding 15 cm H_2O (Hixon et al. 2014). Fine control is achieved by balancing passive recoil forces with active muscular effort. This allows speakers to adjust loudness, sustain phonation, and modulate pitch across sentences. Respiratory physiology is critical in clinical contexts. For instance, individuals with **spinal cord injury** may lack voluntary control over expiratory muscles, compromising speech volume and phrase length. In contrast, hyperfunctional breathing patterns, often seen in hyperkinetic dysarthria, can result in irregular pressure pulses that disrupt speech rhythm (Duffy 2020).

1.3.2 Phonatory Physiology

The physiology of phonation involves the conversion of aerodynamic energy into periodic acoustic energy via vocal fold vibration. This is best explained by the **myoelastic-aerodynamic theory** (Van den Berg, 1958; Titze, 2000). According to this model:

1. **Muscle activity** adducts the vocal folds via the lateral cricoarytenoid and interarytenoid muscles.
2. **Subglottal pressure** builds beneath the closed folds.
3. When this pressure exceeds the resistance of the folds, they are pushed apart.
4. Airflow through the glottis accelerates, reducing pressure (Bernoulli effect), which, along with tissue elasticity, brings the folds back together.

This cycle repeats hundreds of times per second, generating a **fundamental frequency (F_0)**.

Pitch control is achieved by varying the length and tension of the folds, primarily through cricothyroid activity. Loudness increases are produced by increasing subglottal pressure and medial compression of the folds. Physiological efficiency in phonation is influenced by **laryngeal resistance** and **glottal closure patterns**. Incomplete closure leads to breathy voice quality, while hyperadduction causes strained or pressed phonation (Boone et al. 2014). Voice therapy often targets these physiological patterns to restore balance between airflow and fold vibration.

1.3.3 Articulatory and Resonatory Physiology

Articulatory physiology concerns the coordinated movements of the tongue, lips, jaw, soft palate, and pharyngeal walls to create specific speech sounds. These movements are rapid, precise, and often overlapping in time—a phenomenon known as **coarticulation** (Kent and Read 2002). For oral sounds, the velum elevates to close the velopharyngeal port, preventing nasal airflow. For nasal consonants, the velum lowers to couple the nasal and oral cavities. Tongue positioning changes the shape and length of the oral cavity, directly influencing formant frequencies. The jaw's vertical movement adjusts oral cavity volume, contributing to vowel height distinctions. Resonatory physiology modifies the acoustic signal by selectively amplifying or dampening certain frequencies. Movements of the articulators continually adjust the vocal tract's resonant characteristics, allowing rapid shifts between vowels and consonants. Disorders affecting articulatory physiology include **dysarthria**, where neuromuscular weakness or incoordination reduces precision, and **velopharyngeal insufficiency**, which leads to inappropriate nasal resonance. Both conditions significantly impact intelligibility and require targeted therapeutic strategies (Yorkston et al. 2010).

1.3.4 Neural Control of Speech Physiology

Speech physiology is under tight neural control involving cortical, subcortical, cerebellar, and brainstem structures. The **primary motor cortex** plans and executes voluntary speech movements, while the **supplementary motor area** coordinates complex sequences. The **basal ganglia** regulate movement initiation and smoothness, and the **cerebellum** fine-tunes timing and force. Motor commands travel via **corticobulbar pathways** to cranial nerve nuclei in the brainstem, activating muscles of respiration (via the phrenic nerve), phonation (via the vagus nerve branches), and articulation (via cranial nerves V, VII, IX, X, and XII). Sensory feedback from auditory and somatosensory systems ensures accuracy and adaptability (Hixon et al., 2014). Damage to these control systems can cause motor speech disorders. For example, **Parkinson's disease** often leads to reduced loudness and monotony due to basal ganglia dysfunction, while **cerebellar lesions** produce scanning speech with irregular prosody (Duffy 2020).

1.4 Theory of Speech Production

Speech production is a complex biomechanical and acoustic process, and over the decades, several theoretical models have been developed to explain how humans transform linguistic representations into spoken output. These models differ in their emphasis on physiological, acoustic, and perceptual factors, but together they provide a framework for understanding the interaction between anatomy, physiology, and acoustics in speech (Kent and Read 2002; Titze 2000).

1.4.1 Source-Filter Theory

The **Source-Filter Theory**, first formalized by Gunnar Fant, is one of the most influential frameworks in speech science. It posits that speech production can be conceptualized as two functionally independent stages:

1. **Source**—the vocal folds generate a periodic sound wave during voiced sounds, characterized by a fundamental frequency (F_0) and its harmonics.
2. **Filter**—the supralaryngeal vocal tract modifies this sound through resonance, shaping it into specific speech sounds by amplifying certain frequencies (formants) and attenuating others.

In this model, changes in pitch are controlled by the source (laryngeal function), while changes in vowel quality result from alterations in the filter (vocal tract configuration). This separation is particularly useful in acoustic analysis, where source and filter characteristics can be studied independently. Clinical and technological applications are numerous. Voice therapy may aim to modify the source (e.g., reducing hyperfunction) or the filter (e.g., increasing oral resonance). In speech synthesis, manipulating source and filter parameters allows for highly natural artificial speech production (Titze 2000). Refer to Fig. 1.3.

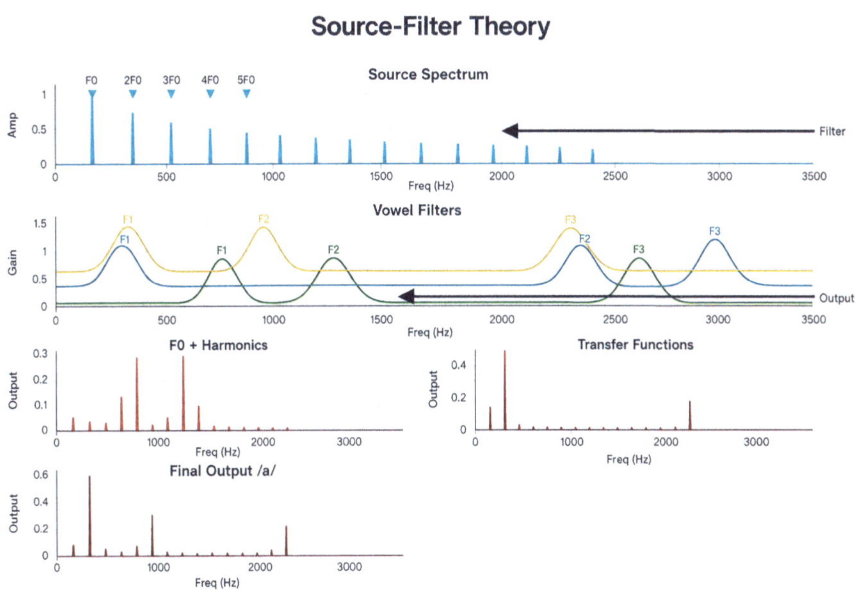

Fig. 1.3 Source-Filter Model: The vocal folds (source) produce a periodic sound wave (characterized by F_0 and harmonics), which passes through the supralaryngeal vocal tract (filter). The tract's resonances (formants) amplify or attenuate frequencies to yield distinct vowels and consonants

1.4.2 Myoelastic-Aerodynamic Theory

Although primarily a physiological model, the **Myoelastic-Aerodynamic Theory** is foundational to speech production theory because it explains the initiation and maintenance of phonation (Titze 2000; Van den Berg 1958). It states that vocal fold vibration results from the interaction of:

- **Myoelastic properties**—elasticity and tension of vocal fold tissue.
- **Aerodynamic forces**—subglottal pressure and the Bernoulli effect.

This theory provides a mechanistic explanation for how a steady airstream from the lungs can produce a self-sustaining oscillation in the vocal folds, which then acts as the source in the Source-Filter framework.

1.4.3 Motor Theory of Speech Perception and its Link to Production

The **Motor Theory of Speech Perception** suggests that speech perception is closely tied to the processes of speech production. It posits that listeners perceive spoken sounds not as abstract acoustic patterns but as intended articulatory gestures (Liberman et al. 1967). Although primarily a perceptual model, it has implications for production because it assumes a direct mapping between motor commands and acoustic output. From a production standpoint, this theory emphasizes the role of **articulatory invariance**—the idea that different acoustic signals can be recognized as the same sound if they result from the same underlying articulatory movement. This aligns with the notion of coarticulation, where contextual variations in sound production still yield stable perceptual categories (Kent and Read 2002). Refer to Fig. 1.4.

1.4.4 Acoustic Invariance Theory

The **Acoustic Invariance Theory** (Stevens and Blumstein 1978) argues that certain acoustic properties of speech sounds remain constant across different contexts and speakers. For example, stop consonants exhibit stable patterns in their burst spectra, regardless of the preceding vowel. This theory is valuable in speech recognition technology and forensic phonetics, as it supports the idea that consistent acoustic cues can be extracted even in noisy environments. In production, this suggests that speakers may aim to maintain these invariant cues through precise motor control, ensuring intelligibility despite variability in speaking rate, loudness, or coarticulatory influence.

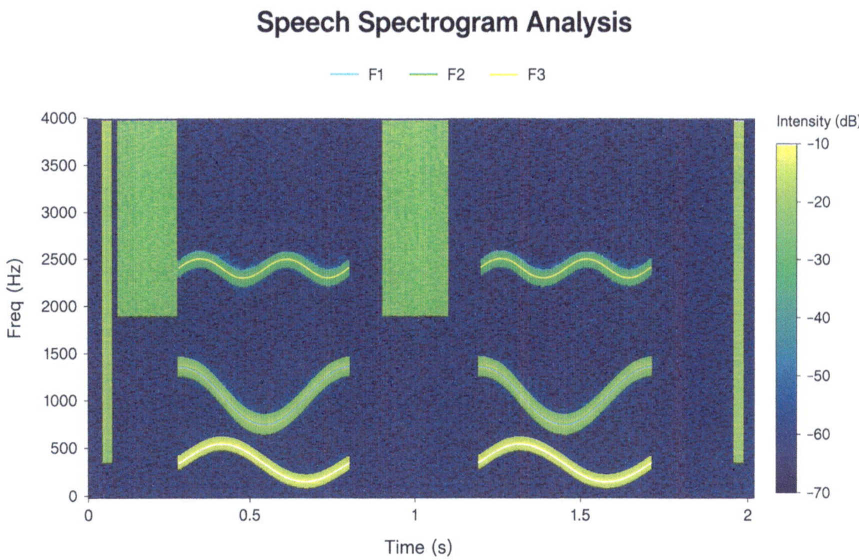

Fig. 1.4 **Spectrogram:** An example spectrogram image (time vs. frequency vs. amplitude) is shown. Wideband spectrograms (left) highlight formant structures (dark bands for vowels), and narrowband spectrograms (right) highlight harmonic structure (horizontal harmonics of F_0). This visual representation is fundamental in acoustic speech analysis

1.4.5 Gestural Phonology and Articulatory Phonology

Gestural Phonology and its related **Articulatory Phonology** framework propose that speech is organized as a sequence of overlapping articulatory gestures rather than discrete phonemes (Browman and Goldstein 1992). These gestures are units of both motor action and linguistic representation. In production, this means that movements of the tongue, lips, jaw, and velum are planned and executed as coordinated patterns, often overlapping in time to achieve fluency and efficiency. This perspective aligns well with findings from kinematic studies showing that articulators begin moving toward a target well before the preceding sound is completed.

1.4.6 Relevance to Clinical and Technological Applications

Understanding these theories has direct clinical relevance:

- In **voice disorders**, therapy may target the **source** (e.g., optimizing vocal fold vibration) or **filter** (e.g., improving resonance).
- In **apraxia of speech**, articulatory gesture sequencing (as described in Gestural Phonology) is disrupted, guiding motor-planning-based interventions.
- In **speech synthesis and recognition**, algorithms often incorporate Source–Filter models and acoustic invariance principles to improve naturalness and accuracy.

Technological applications include speech coding for telecommunications, forensic voice identification, and articulatory-based synthetic voice design for augmentative and alternative communication (AAC) systems.

1.5 Acoustic Analysis of Speech

Acoustic analysis is the examination of the measurable physical properties of speech sounds, typically in terms of frequency, intensity, and temporal characteristics. It serves as a bridge between the physiological processes of speech production and their perceptual outcomes. In speech science, acoustic analysis is essential for both research and clinical applications, as it allows objective documentation of speech parameters, monitoring of changes over time, and evaluation of intervention outcomes (Kent and Read 2002; Titze 2000).

1.5.1 Fundamental Frequency (F_0)

Fundamental Frequency refers to the rate of vibration of the vocal folds, measured in Hertz (Hz). It is determined primarily by vocal fold length, mass, and tension and secondarily by subglottal pressure. Typical adult male F_0 ranges from 85 to 155 Hz, while adult female F_0 ranges from 165 to 255 Hz, and children often exhibit values above 300 Hz (Titze 2000). F_0 is a primary acoustic correlate of pitch. Clinical changes in F_0 may indicate laryngeal pathology, neurological impairment, or hormonal influence. For example, a persistently elevated F_0 in adult males may signal falsetto voice or incomplete vocal fold adduction, whereas a reduced F_0 in females could result from androgenic hormonal changes (Boone et al. 2014).

1.5.2 Formant Frequencies

Formants are resonant frequencies of the vocal tract that shape vowel quality. The first formant (F_1) corresponds inversely to vowel height, while the second formant (F_2) correlates with tongue advancement. For example, the vowel /i/ has a low F_1 (~300 Hz) and a high F_2 (~2200–2500 Hz), reflecting a high, front tongue position (Fant, 1960). Formant analysis is critical in evaluating articulatory precision and resonance patterns. Abnormal formant values can signal structural or functional changes, such as reduced F_2 in /s/ production in cases of anterior tongue placement, or abnormal F_1-F_2 spacing in dysarthric speech (Kent and Read 2002).

1.5.3 Intensity

Speech intensity, measured in decibels (dB SPL), is related to the amplitude of the acoustic waveform and is primarily controlled by subglottal pressure and vocal fold adduction. Conversational speech averages around 65–70 dB SPL at 1 meter, while shouting can exceed 90 dB SPL (Hixon et al. 2014). Intensity analysis is important for assessing hypophonia in Parkinson's disease, hyperfunctional loudness in vocal abuse, and overall projection in professional voice users.

1.5.4 Temporal Measures

Temporal analysis examines speech timing, including segment duration, speech rate, and voice onset time (VOT). VOT is the interval between the release of a stop consonant and the onset of voicing—a key cue for distinguishing voiced and voiceless stops (Lisker and Abramson 1964). Slowed speech rate, prolonged vowel duration, and abnormal VOT patterns may indicate motor speech disorders such as apraxia or dysarthria. These parameters are also sensitive to linguistic influences, such as syllable structure and stress patterns.

1.5.5 Spectrographic Analysis

A **spectrogram** is a visual representation of speech, plotting time on the horizontal axis, frequency on the vertical axis, and amplitude as darkness or color intensity.

- **Wideband spectrograms** reveal formant structures and are useful for vowel analysis.
- **Narrowband spectrograms** highlight harmonic structure, aiding in pitch and voice quality assessment (Kent and Read 2002).

Spectrographic patterns help in differentiating normal and disordered speech. For example, in velopharyngeal insufficiency, formant bandwidths may be wider due to nasal coupling, and in spastic dysarthria, formant transitions may appear flattened. Refer to Fig. 1.5.

1.5.6 Jitter, Shimmer, and Harmonics-to-Noise Ratio

Advanced acoustic measures include:

- **Jitter**—cycle-to-cycle variability in F_0, indicating instability in vocal fold vibration.
- **Shimmer**—cycle-to-cycle variability in amplitude.
- **Harmonics-to-noise ratio (HNR)**—the proportion of periodic energy to aperiodic noise in the voice signal.

Elevated jitter and shimmer, and reduced HNR, are common in pathological voices such as those with vocal fold lesions or neurological impairments (Titze 2000).

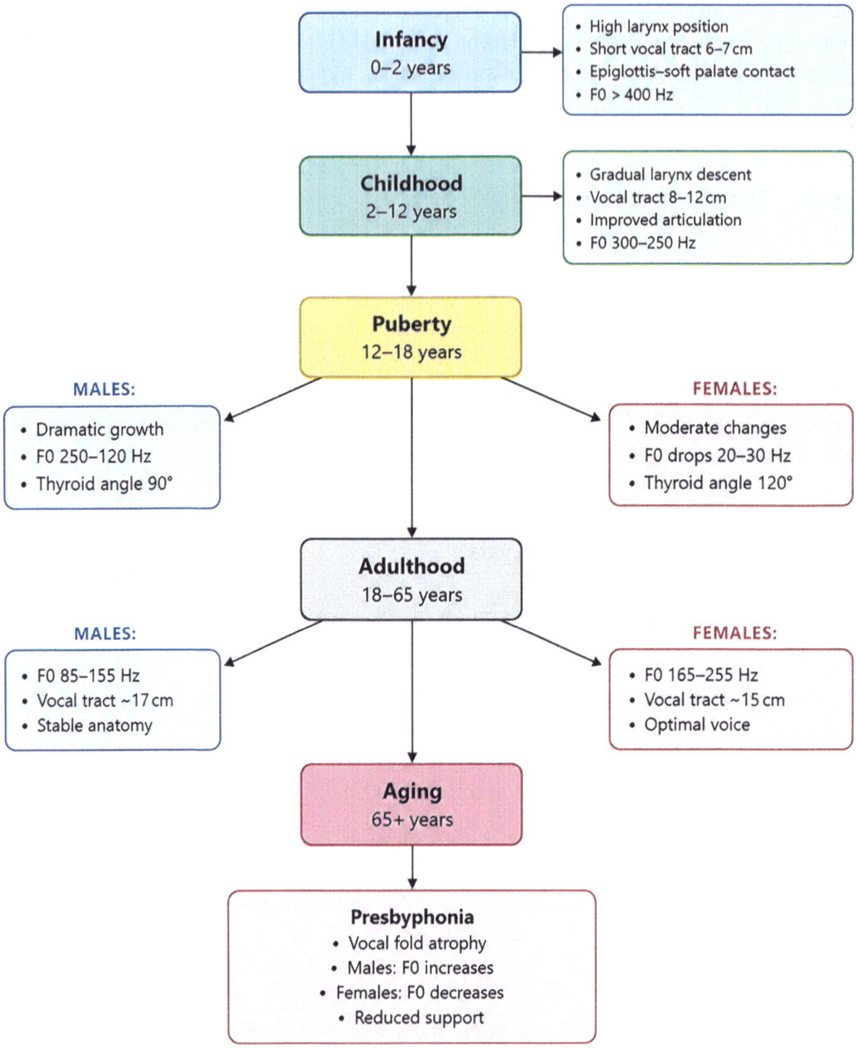

Fig. 1.5 Infant vs. Adult Vocal Tract: A side-by-side outline of an infant's and an adult's head. Infants have a shorter vocal tract and a higher laryngeal position, which limits their phonetic range and yields a higher pitch. The infant's epiglottis and soft palate are closely approximated for airway protection

1.5.7 Instrumentation for Acoustic Analysis

Common tools for acoustic analysis include:

- **Praat**—open-source software widely used for pitch, formant, and intensity tracking.
- **KayPENTAX CSL**—for real-time and multi-dimensional voice analysis.

- **LingWAVES**—for professional voice and speech signal assessment.

These instruments provide objective measurements that complement perceptual evaluation, enabling evidence-based diagnosis and treatment planning.

1.6 Anatomy, Physiology, and Acoustic Variation across Age and Gender

Speech production is not static across the human lifespan. Anatomical structures, physiological functions, and acoustic characteristics undergo continuous change from infancy through old age, and these changes differ significantly between males and females due to hormonal, developmental, and genetic factors (Zemlin 1998; Hixon et al. 2014). Understanding these variations is essential for differentiating normal from pathological changes in clinical assessment.

1.6.1 Developmental Anatomy and Physiology

In **infancy**, the vocal tract is shorter, and the larynx is positioned higher in the neck, allowing simultaneous breathing and swallowing—an adaptation for feeding. The epiglottis and soft palate are in close approximation, limiting the range of possible speech sounds but optimizing airway protection (Kent and Read 2002). The vocal folds are small and lack the differentiated layered structure seen in adults, resulting in higher pitch and less stable phonation (Titze 2000). During **childhood**, rapid growth of the vocal tract and maturation of neuromotor control enable increased articulatory precision. The descent of the larynx increases the pharyngeal cavity length, contributing to changes in resonance patterns and formant frequencies (Vorperian et al. 2005). Refer to Fig. 1.5.

1.6.2 Pubertal Changes and Gender Differences

Puberty brings dramatic **sex-specific anatomical changes**, particularly in the larynx and vocal folds.

- **Males** experience significant enlargement of the laryngeal cartilages and lengthening and thickening of the vocal folds, typically lowering F_0 by about one octave (from ~250 Hz in prepubertal boys to ~120 Hz in adult men).
- **Females** also experience some vocal fold lengthening, but to a lesser extent, leading to a smaller pitch drop (~20–30 Hz on average) (Titze 2000).

The **thyroid angle** in males becomes more acute (~90°) compared to females (~120°), creating the visible "Adam's apple." Hormonal influences—particularly testosterone—drive these morphological changes, affecting both pitch and voice quality.

1.6.3 Adult Anatomy and Physiological Stability

In healthy adults, the speech mechanism is structurally stable, but variations exist in vocal tract length, vocal fold mass, and resonance characteristics. These differences underlie natural variations in voice timbre and pitch among individuals. Gender differences in formant frequencies are partly due to average differences in vocal tract length—typically ~17 cm in males and ~ 15 cm in females. Physiologically, adults exhibit efficient respiratory-phonatory-articulatory coordination, enabling a wide range of prosodic and stylistic speech variations. Acoustic measures such as jitter and shimmer are minimal in healthy adult voices.

1.6.4 Age-Related Changes (Presbyphonia)

With **aging**, anatomical and physiological changes occur in all subsystems:

- **Respiratory system**—reduced vital capacity and elastic recoil result in decreased subglottal pressure, often affecting loudness.
- **Phonatory system**—vocal fold atrophy ("bowing"), reduced muscle bulk, and ossification of laryngeal cartilages lead to changes in vibratory patterns.
- **Articulatory system**—reduced range and speed of movement may affect clarity, though compensatory strategies often maintain intelligibility (Linville 2001).

Acoustically, older males often experience an **increase** in F_0 due to vocal fold thinning, while older females may exhibit a **decrease** in F_0 after menopause due to hormonal changes that thicken the vocal folds (Kent and Read 2002). Voice quality may become breathier or rougher, and perturbation measures (jitter, shimmer) often increase.

1.6.5 Clinical and Acoustic Implications

Recognizing age- and gender-related norms is critical in differentiating between expected physiological changes and pathological conditions. For example:

- A lower-than-expected F_0 in a young adult female could indicate hormonal imbalance or vocal fold mass lesions.
- Higher-than-expected jitter in an elderly speaker may be within normal aging limits but should still be compared to normative data for that demographic.

Acoustic analysis tools, such as **longitudinal F_0 tracking** and **formant dispersion measures**, are particularly useful for quantifying these variations over time.

1.7 Individual Anatomical and Physiological Variation (Adults' Perspective)

Even within the adult population, there is significant **inter-speaker variability** in the structure and function of the speech production mechanism. These differences are influenced by genetic factors, lifestyle, occupation, health status, and learned speech habits. From a speech science perspective, understanding these variations is important for establishing normative ranges, customizing clinical interventions, and developing speaker-specific voice and speech technologies (Kent and Read 2002; Titze 2000).

1.7.1 Anatomical Variations

Anatomical variability among adults includes differences in:

- **Vocal tract length**—typically ~17 cm in males and ~ 15 cm in females but can vary ±1–2 cm, affecting resonance and formant frequencies (Fant 1960).
- **Vocal fold size and mass**—larger or denser folds typically produce lower F_0, while thinner folds produce higher F_0.
- **Laryngeal cartilage shape and angle**—subtle differences in thyroid cartilage angle or cricoarytenoid joint orientation can influence voice quality and pitch range.
- **Oral cavity structure**—variations in palate arch height, dental alignment, or jaw size can affect articulation patterns and resonance.

Such structural differences can be purely anatomical or the result of surgical interventions, trauma, or congenital differences (Zemlin 1998).

1.7.2 Physiological Variations

Functional capacity also varies significantly between individuals:

- **Respiratory support**—lung capacity, expiratory control, and chest wall mechanics differ based on fitness, posture, and health.
- **Laryngeal control**—intrinsic muscle coordination, tension control, and reflex responsiveness can differ, affecting vibratory stability.
- **Articulatory agility**—rate and precision of tongue, lip, and jaw movements may vary due to neuromotor efficiency or learned habits.

For example, professional singers or actors often exhibit enhanced respiratory control and greater laryngeal flexibility compared to the general population, while sedentary lifestyles may reduce respiratory endurance.

1.7.3 Acoustic Consequences

These anatomical and physiological differences manifest acoustically as variations in:

- **Fundamental frequency (F_0)**—individual pitch ranges can differ by more than an octave, even within the same gender.
- **Formant spacing**—vocal tract length and shape affect vowel quality, which can serve as a "vocal fingerprint."
- **Voice quality**—differences in glottal closure patterns and resonance result in perceptually unique timbres (e.g., breathy, pressed, resonant).
- **Perturbation measures**—jitter, shimmer, and harmonics-to-noise ratio vary with neuromuscular stability and tissue properties.

These acoustic markers are the basis of **forensic speaker identification** and are increasingly used in personalized speech synthesis and speaker-adaptive recognition systems (Nolan 2020b).

1.7.4 Clinical Implications

Clinically, recognizing individual variability is crucial to avoid overpathologizing normal differences. For example, a naturally high-pitched male voice may reflect shorter vocal folds rather than a functional disorder. Similarly, slight nasality may be a normal resonance feature in some speakers due to structural anatomy rather than velopharyngeal insufficiency. Therapeutic approaches, particularly in **voice therapy**, **accent modification**, and **speech motor training**, should be tailored to an individual's anatomical and physiological profile to maximize effectiveness (Boone et al. 2014). From a clinical perspective, appreciating these normal variations is essential to prevent misdiagnosis and to design individualized intervention plans. From a technological standpoint, these insights fuel advances in speech synthesis, recognition, and forensic identification. Ultimately, a comprehensive understanding of speech science fosters more accurate assessment, more effective therapy, and more sophisticated voice technology.

1.8 Conclusion

Speech science integrates anatomy, physiology, and acoustics to explain how humans transform thought into spoken language. The structural framework—from the respiratory apparatus to the articulators—provides the physical basis for speech, while physiological processes coordinate muscle activity, airflow, and resonance to achieve precise and intelligible communication (Kent and Read 2002; Duffy 2020). Theoretical models, such as the **Source-Filter Theory** and **Myoelastic-Aerodynamic Theory**, offer conceptual clarity, linking biological mechanisms to acoustic output. Acoustic analysis bridges production and perception by quantifying measurable parameters like **fundamental frequency**, **formants**, **intensity**, and

temporal patterns. These measures not only support clinical diagnosis and monitoring but also enhance our understanding of speech variability across individuals, ages, and genders (Titze 2000; Fant 1960). Developmental changes—from infancy through senescence—and gender-specific anatomical differences underscore the dynamic nature of the speech mechanism. Likewise, individual variations in vocal tract dimensions, neuromuscular control, and resonance patterns highlight the uniqueness of each voice.

References

Boone DR, McFarlane SC, Von Berg SL, Zraick RI (2014) The voice and voice therapy, 9th edn. Pearson, Boston

Browman CP, Goldstein L (1992) Articulatory phonology: an overview. Phonetica 49(3–4):155–180

Duffy JR (2020) Motor speech disorders: substrates, differential diagnosis, and management, 4th edn. Elsevier

Fant G (1960) Acoustic theory of speech production. Mouton, The Hague

Guenther FH (2016) Neural control of speech. MIT Press. Speech Motor Control

Helmholtz HLF (1954) On the sensations of tone as a physiological basis for the theory of music (trans: Ellis AJ). Dover Publications. (Original work published 1863)

Hixon TJ, Weismer G, Hoit JD (2014) Preclinical speech science: anatomy, physiology, acoustics, and perception, 2nd edn. Plural Publishing, San Diego

Kent RD, Read C (2002) The acoustic analysis of speech, 2nd edn. Singular/Thomson Learning, San Diego

Liberman AM, Cooper FS, Shankweiler DP, Studdert-Kennedy M (1967) Perception of the speech code. Psychol Rev 74(6):431–461

Linville SE (2001) Vocal aging. Singular/Thomson Learning, San Diego

Lisker L, Abramson AS (1964) A cross-language study of voicing in initial stops: acoustical measurements. Word 20(3):384–422

Nolan F (2020a) Forensic phonetics. In: Damico JS, Ball MJ (eds) The SAGE encyclopedia of human communication sciences and disorders, vol 2. SAGE Publications, pp 784–788

Nolan F (2020b) Forensic speaker identification and the search for consistency in the voice. Speech Comm 122:56–66

Voice Disorders in TeachersRoy N, Merrill RM, Thibeault S, Parsa RA, Gray SD, Smith EM (2004) Prevalence of voice disorders in teachers and the general population. J Speech Lang Hear Res 47(2):281–293

Stevens KN, Blumstein SE (1978) Invariant cues for place of articulation in stop consonants. J Acoust Soc Am 64(5):1358–1368

Titze IR (2000) Principles of voice production. National Center for Voice and Speech, Iowa City

Van den Berg J (1958) Myoelastic–aerodynamic theory of voice production. J Speech Hear Res 1(3):227–244

Vorperian HK, Kent RD, Lindstrom MJ, Kalina CM, Gentry LR, Yandell BS (2005) Development of vocal tract length during early childhood: A magnetic resonance imaging study. J Acoust Soc Am 117(1):338–350

World Health Organization (2021) World report on hearing

Wren Y, Miller LL, Peters TJ, Emond A, Roulstone S (2016) Prevalence and predictors of persistent speech sound disorder at eight years old: findings from a population cohort study. J Speech Lang Hear Res 59(4):647–673

Yairi E, Ambrose N (2013) Epidemiology of stuttering: 21st century advances. J Fluen Disord 38(2):66–87. Stuttering (Fluency Disorders)

Yorkston KM, Beukelman DR, Strand EA, Hakel M (2010) Management of Motor Speech Disorders in children and adults, 3rd edn. Pro-Ed, Austin

Zemlin WR (1998) Speech and hearing science: anatomy and physiology, 4th edn. Allyn & Bacon, Boston

2 Forensic Phonetics: Speech Variability

Prakash Boominathan and Krupa Venkatraman

Abstract

This chapter examines speech variability as a central issue in forensic phonetics, particularly in relation to speaker identification, speaker profiling, and voice verification in legal settings. The chapter examines the evolution of forensic phonetics as an interdisciplinary field, drawing on the study of linguistics and speech-language pathology, as well as the development of speech science technology. It also, from a practical point of view, emphasises the contributions of speech-language pathologists (SLPs) in the forensic linguistic and phonetic literature, having demonstrated utility of a range of behavioural responses using their considerable knowledge of both speech disorders and voice disguise. SLPs can often assess voice disguise from a relationship of normal to abnormal, making clear distinctions based on acoustic measures and perceptual judgements. The chapter acknowledges the complexities of speaker variance (due to linguistic diversity) and speaker comparisons, which are posed by cross-language differences, while also exploring current developments in Automatic Speaker Recognition (ASR) systems, including their weaknesses associated with synthetic speech or deepfake sources. Finally, the chapter summarises opportunities for greater collaboration between disciplines to improve and add rigour to the methods used, along with considering pragmatic ethical reflections that support vocally based evidence. The chapter utilises selected case studies and technology comparisons to demonstrate the progression of forensic phonetics from a realm of caution to a more robust, scientifically defensible domain, capable of contributing to the complexities of speech evidence presented in a judicial context.

P. Boominathan (✉) · K. Venkatraman
Sri Ramachandra Faculty of Audiology and Speech Language Pathology, Sri Ramachandra Institute of Higher Education and Research (Deemed University), Porur, Chennai, Tamil Nadu, India
e-mail: prakash_boominathan@sriramachandra.edu.in; krupa.v@sriramachandra.edu.in

V. Kumar et al. (eds.), *Forensic Speech Sciences*, New Horizons in Forensic Science, https://doi.org/10.1007/978-981-92-1475-4_2

Keywords

Forensic phonetics · Speech variability · Speaker identification · Acoustic analysis · Perceptual analysis · Automatic speaker recognition

2.1 Introduction

Human vocalisation serves an essential purpose as a marker of identity. In a forensic situation, these qualities are more critical, as the human voice can give evidence, connecting an audio recording to a speaker or speakers. Forensic phonetics is a field of forensic linguistics that involves the careful analysis of auditory evidence, as seen in investigations and in court. A trend within present criminal justice systems is the provision of audio evidence, which may include, but is not limited to, extortion calls, bogus messages, threats, and tape interceptions of conversations, thereby increasing the need for careful interdisciplinary approaches to the analysis of vocal data (Nolan 1983; Gold and French 2011).

At the heart of forensic phonetics is speech variability, that is, the natural variation that occurs in speech in both space and time, and between different or even the same speaker. This variability poses two challenges for forensic analysts: it can hinder direct comparisons of spoken samples, but it can also provide valuable information regarding speaker characteristics, such as indicators of deception or specific clinical speech conditions (such as stuttering). Speech variability can arise from many sources and can occur in the same speaker due to factors such as different dialectal constituencies, speech pathology, emotional states, and recording situations. Generally speaking, forensic analysts try to resolve these nuances with functional acoustic and perceptual parameters. Overcoming the complexities of speech variability is necessary to achieve reliable conclusions when evaluating speakers in forensic contexts. Past forensic contexts have primarily involved normative speakers. The real world often involves speakers with atypical speech, multiple languages, or speakers who actively modify their voice (French and Harrison 2007; Ladefoged 2003; Gibbons 2003). To effectively address this question, a synthesis of expertise and knowledge from linguists, speech-language pathologists (SLPs), and technologists is warranted.

In recent years, forensic phonetics research has expanded significantly in India, driven by advances in detection technology and an increased awareness of the importance of speech evidence in criminal investigations. Perceptions of speaker-specific acoustic variability in Indian languages such as Hindi, Tamil, Kannada, Telugu, and Urdu have provided critical benchmarks for forensic practitioners dealing with multilingual projects (Ridha 2014; Jyotsna 2011; Suresh 2015; Chandrika 2015; Zakia 2014). Some collaborations between academic institutions and law enforcement have developed a local database, shaped analytical procedures, and paid serious attention to the regional phonetic diversity. In India, there is a large number of languages and significant language switching, which often pose challenges for forensic analysts in accounting for language-related variability as opposed to speaker-based characteristics.

This chapter discusses speech variability through the approach of three domains. First, a chapter-level historical overview will be provided for this domain. It will be presented under a set of theoretical underpinnings that inform the study of variation in general. The study of these varieties will use material from the literature and unpublished research projects to discuss how speech variability has been described in terms of phonetic properties, how it can be quantified and analysed, and how it varies in social and clinical contexts. As we navigate through this chapter, we aim to:

- Illuminate the historical development and foundational principles of forensic phonetics.
- Articulate the mechanisms and indicators of speech variability.
- Foster the integration of linguistic, clinical, and technological methodologies in forensic practices.
- Advocate for ethical, standardised, and context-sensitive approaches to speaker identification.

Nolan (1983) classifies speaker variations into two essential domains: segmental and suprasegmental, thus delving into phonological constructs and their contextual occurrences. This specific categorisation functions as a foundational element for interpreting forensic linguistic artefacts, yielding significant revelations in the domains of linguistic research, clinical applications, and advancements in technology. With this typology, academics and practitioners can skilfully evaluate the diversity in speakers, thereby bolstering the dependability and thoroughness of forensic linguistic research. This chapter ultimately presents a cross-disciplinary model for scholars, healthcare providers, and legal experts, emphasising the importance of scientific analysis of speech in promoting just and efficient legal systems, particularly as society becomes increasingly reliant on audio-based evidence.

2.2 Historical Context and Theoretical Underpinnings

2.2.1 Early Developments and Milestones

The examination of the human voice in the legal realm has a surprisingly long history. The seventeenth-century records of court proceedings already show witnesses using auditory recognition to identify speakers, as in the case of the trial of Charles I of England. These proceedings, with their reliance on the listener's regard for the voice, were often haphazard and heavily dependent on a single person's testimony, where the speaker's voice in the courtroom had begun but was firmly rooted in a tradition where voice could potentially serve as legal evidence.

The mid-twentieth century was a watershed moment for human voice work with the advent of "voiceprint" techniques, where speech was visually represented as voiceprints using spectrograms. At Bell Laboratories, it was demonstrated in the 1960s that they could identify individual voices using various spectrographic tools and that individual voices could be recognised through repeating patterns of frequency and amplitude. These concepts came to life with the work of Oscar Tosi and colleagues and reignited discussion regarding the potential of using acoustic evidence in court (Gold and French 2011) for causes of identity. While there is confusion and critique of voiceprints (particularly regarding inter-rater reliability and subjective interpretation of acoustics), these innovations have opened a vast research field into voice as applied to legal proceedings. Around the same time in the USA, Harry Hollien from the University of Florida came up with a methodical way to merge phonetic science with forensic work. His work, *The Acoustics of Crime*, underlined the need for precise techniques, explicit reporting of mistake sources, and meticulous separation of auditory and acoustic evidence. Hollien's groundbreaking research helped the field move toward more scientifically sound methods rather than deciding based on "voiceprints" predominantly. This laid the framework for the professionalisation of forensic phonetics.

The 1970s marked the beginning of a significant evolution in this field, where semi-automated systems and algorithms were being developed to perform speech and voice recognition tasks, most notably the Semi-Automatic Speaker Identification System (SAUSI). SAUSI is a blended early computational technique with forensic applications (French and Harrison 2007). Concurrently, scholars in Europe began to enhance spectrographic analysis by establishing standardised protocols and providing expert training. As a result, the cautious but increasing acceptance of these methods in courtroom settings emerged during the 1980s and 1990s.

These refined techniques have brought a newer perspective to the field, making it more insightful and accurate. Later, statistical models such as i-vectors, x-vectors, and Probabilistic Linear Discriminant Analysis (PLDA) provided a way to measure the degree of similarity between two recordings. These tools form the basis of many of today's automatic voice recognition systems (Ladefoged 2003; Gibbons 2003).

In India, dedicated forensic phonetics units began emerging in the early 2000s, with government laboratories such as the Central Forensic Science Laboratories (CFSL) and State Forensic Science Laboratories (SFSL) initiating voice comparison services. Academic partnerships, particularly with the All India Institute of Speech and Hearing (AIISH), Mysuru, played a significant role in developing indigenous benchmarks for forensic phonetics (Ridha 2014; Jyotsna 2011; Suresh 2015; Chandrika 2015; Zakia 2014).

2.2.2 Contributions of Key Researchers

Several stalwarts have shaped forensic phonetics into a robust, interdisciplinary field of study. Peter French, based in the UK, is notable for his efforts to professionalise forensic phonetics through JP French Associates, focusing on expert witness testimony grounded in empirical research. His team helped codify best practices in auditory and acoustic analysis (French and Harrison 2007).

Francis Nolan co-authored *The Phonetic Bases of Speaker Recognition*, a foundational text that emphasises both the theoretical and applied aspects of speaker comparison. Nolan argued that speech should be analysed probabilistically, taking into account intra-speaker variability and channel effects.

Ton Broeder highlighted the critical scrutiny of expert evidence. He warned against over-reliance on auditory judgements and called for methodological validation (Broeders 2001).

More recently, Geoffrey Morrison and William Thompson have advanced the likelihood ratio framework for speaker comparison, advocating for statistical transparency and legal admissibility. Their work has informed international guidelines and set benchmarks for evaluating forensic voice evidence (Morrison and Thompson 2017).

Jessen (2010) and Lindh (2017) produced materials that integrated spectrographic analysis with perceptual and articulatory phonetics, aiming to support consistent interpretation across experts (Jessen 2010; Lindh 2017).

In India, scholars from the All India Institute of Speech and Hearing (AIISH), Mysuru, including Nataraja, Savithri, Sridevi, Yashoda, Jayakumar, and Rajasudhakar have contributed essential insights. Their research has described acoustic and phonetic variation across Hindi, Kannada, Tamil, Telugu, Malayalam, and Urdu, linking linguistic features to their potential role in speaker identification (Ridha 2014; Jyotsna 2011; Suresh 2015; Chandrika 2015; Zakia 2014).

2.2.3 Theoretical Frameworks of Speech Variability

In forensic phonetics, variability in speech is unavoidable and arises from both physiological and social factors. It is often categorised into:

- **Inter-speaker variability**: Differences in vocal tract anatomy, dialect, age, gender, and sociophonetic backgrounds contribute majorly to inter-speaker variability. Inter-speaker variability refers to the distinctiveness across individuals, which forms the basis of speaker identification. Differences in vocal tract anatomy, articulatory habits, dialect, gender, age, and sociolinguistic background all contribute to this kind of variability. These differences can be leveraged in both human (auditory) and automatic (computational) analysis systems. However, the degree of inter-speaker variability is not uniform. Some individuals, such as identical twins or siblings raised in the same environment, may have highly similar speech characteristics. Likewise, individuals from the same dialect region may exhibit overlapping acoustic patterns, increasing the possibility of confusion between speakers. Research indicates that unfamiliar voices are difficult to identify, especially under time pressure or in poor recording quality. In forensic settings, this raises concerns about the weight that can be placed on eyewitness testimony.
- **Intra-speaker variability**: These are primarily variations noticed within a speaker due to emotion, fatigue, health, disguise, or context (e.g. formal vs. casual speech). Even within the same person, voice changes with mood, health, and context. Stress or fatigue may shift pitch and rhythm, while illness can alter

resonance. Health conditions such as the common cold or vocal strain can affect resonance and clarity. Situational context also matters: a person might speak more formally in court than on a phone call, or they may speak faster when agitated, etc. Technical aspects such as microphone type, recording quality, background noise, and channel mismatch (e.g. landline vs. mobile phone) further affect the captured speech signal and its quality, sometimes leading to distortions that mimic genuine speaker differences.

To further elucidate the sources and types of speech variability, Nolan (1983) proposed a framework that categorises variation into segmental and suprasegmental strands. This model offers a fine-grained understanding of the phonetic factors contributing to both inter- and intra-speaker variability.

At the segmental level, Nolan identifies four primary contributors listed below. We provide some examples from an Indian context also to illustrate the segmental-level differences:

- Systemic differences, such as phonemic inventory contrasts (e.g. a greater number of rounded vowels in Assamese compared to Kannada).
- Phonotactic differences, for instance, the tendency to release word-final stops in Indian English versus elision in British English.
- Stress patterns, which differ across languages in terms of predictability (e.g. contributing to the rhythm in the spoken utterance; the rhythm structure in Dravidian languages is syllable or mora timed, as opposed to English, which is stress-timed languages), and placement (e.g. contributing to assigning word categories, emphasis and implied meanings, etc.).
- Realisation rules and allophones encompass context-driven phonetic alternations, such as vowel reduction or assimilation. For instance, the English phoneme /t/ exhibits distinct realisations contingent upon contextual factors: it may manifest as an aspirated [tʰ] in the word top, an unreleased [t̚] in the term cat, a flap [ɾ] in water (as observed in American English), or even as a glottal stop [ʔ] in butter (in particular British dialects). In Tamil, voicing is allophonic, the stop often is pronounced as voiced when followed by a nasal consonant, otherwise can be pronounced as voiceless. This allophonic variation illustrates how a single underlying segment can assume multiple surface manifestations, thereby introducing variability inherent within individual speakers, which may prove misleading in forensic comparisons if not duly considered.

At the suprasegmental level, variability is shaped by:

- Nucleus types and integration rules, influencing syllabic structure and rhythm.
- Physiological constraints, such as laryngeal size or vocal tract configuration, that affect formant structure and fundamental frequency (F0).
- Cognitive and affective intent, including mood, attention, and mental state, which may influence prosody and timing.

- Social and stylistic variation encompasses shifts in speech style, register, and identity markers across various communicative contexts.

Nolan's framework thus complements the inter–/intra-speaker distinction by offering a linguistically grounded taxonomy of the articulatory and prosodic dimensions of speech variability, making it particularly relevant for forensic phonetic analysis involving multilingual and cross-linguistic populations.

Nolan's framework is most useful in practice when applied to measurable cues. For instance, vowel formants, particularly F1 and F2, reflect the shape of the vocal tract and are usually consistent for a speaker, though higher formants tend to vary more (Martínez et al. 2014; Cenceschi et al. 2021). Segmental cues such as vowel formants (especially F1 and F2) reflect vocal-tract configuration and are relatively speaker specific, though not immune to style or phonetic context; F1 is typically more repeatable across sessions, whereas higher formants (F3–F4) show greater dispersion [1819]. Laryngeal or voice-quality cues, including jitter, shimmer, and harmonics-to-noise ratio (HNR), measures of phonatory control and indices of pathology (eg., Dysphonia Severity Index - DSI, Cepstral Peak Prominence - CPP) can effectively separate pathological from typical phonation, however, these are highly sensitive to the quality of sample analysed (Kavanagh 2012; Chan 2023). Prosodic and temporal measures such as F0 level and range, rhythm metrics, and speech rate capture register, affect, and task demands thus contribute substantially to within-speaker variability and the risk of false exclusions if not modelled (Parllaku et al. 2020). In practice, analysts should (i) prioritise parameters with proven test-retest reliability under channel constraints (e.g. F1 over F3, HNR under matched bandwidth) and (ii) treat intra-speaker variance from style, affect, and channel as a separate component in statistical modelling, for example, through likelihood-ratio estimation (Rose 1998; Broeders 2001; Morrison and Thompson 2017). Evidence from Indian laboratories, such as AIISH datasets on typical and disordered phonation across Kannada, Hindi, and Tamil, reinforces these stability rankings and highlights how retroflex articulation and syllable-timed rhythm interact with formant dispersion and timing measures in multilingual settings (Ridha 2014; Jyotsna 2011; Suresh 2015; Chandrika 2015; Zakia 2014). Indian cross-linguistic studies further highlight distinctive features, such as retroflex consonants, systematic vowel centralisation, and language-specific formant distributions, in Dravidian versus Indo-Aryan languages (Jyotsna 2011; Suresh 2015; Chandrika 2015), underscoring the need to incorporate language-specific phonetic profiles into forensic models for improved speaker discrimination accuracy.

Eriksson (2003) reminds us that speaker identity is probabilistic: no two utterances by the same person are identical. Forensic analysis, therefore, requires models that accommodate variability instead of seeking perfect matches. The likelihood ratio (LR) framework is a statistical method that evaluates the likelihood of the evidence under two competing hypotheses: that the questioned and known samples are from the same speaker versus different speakers. LR framework supports transparency and reproducibility and is recommended by international forensic standards (Broeders 2001).

More recently, scholars such as Fairclough (2023) have drawn on Third Wave sociophonetics to show that speakers actively shape their speech through style and interaction. For forensic work, this means that code-switching or shifts in register can easily be misinterpreted as a change in identity, especially in multilingual contexts (Fairclough 2023).

2.2.4 Definition, Incidence, and Prevalence

Forensic phonetics is defined as the scientific analysis of speech and voice recordings for use in legal proceedings. It encompasses tasks such as speaker identification, profiling, transcription of disputed utterances, voice authentication, and evaluation of communicative competency. Analyses typically use a combination of auditory-perceptual judgements, acoustic measurements, and automated systems.

Quantifying the exact incidence of forensic phonetics usage is challenging due to variations in jurisdiction. In the UK, approximately 60–70% of forensic audio investigations involve phonetic assessments (Rose 1998). In continental Europe, particularly in Germany and the Netherlands, expert-based auditory-acoustic approaches remain the standard. In contrast, the USA applies stricter admissibility criteria, limiting expert testimony unless backed by robust validation studies (Morrison and Thompson 2017).

In India and parts of Southeast Asia, forensic phonetics is an emerging domain. The multilingual context introduces additional complexity, as regional dialects and speech styles significantly affect analysis. Increasingly, academic institutions in India are collaborating with law enforcement agencies to develop protocols for multilingual forensic analysis (Ortega-García et al. 1999). Recent postgraduate research in India reports that a significant proportion (approximately 25–35%) of forensic voice analysis requests involve multilingual speakers, often engaging in code-switching between Indian languages and English (Sommers and Barcroft 2006). Kaur et al. (2023) further note that urban casework increasingly features non-native English accents, necessitating specialised analytical approaches for robust speaker identification (Kaur et al. 2023).

Prevalence also extends to voice disguise and deepfake technologies. Mopas (2023) and others warn of a rise in cases where synthetic voices or altered recordings are submitted as legal evidence. These cases demand sophisticated forensic techniques to identify deception or fabrication (Mopas 2023).

2.3 Linguist Perspectives

2.3.1 Nature and Types of Speech Variability

Linguists in forensic phonetics often distinguish between inter-speaker and intra-speaker variation. Inter-speaker variation reflects the differences that naturally occur between people, shaped by vocal tract anatomy, articulatory habits, social background, and language experience. These differences show up in vowel formants, voice quality, pitch, and speaking rate.

Intra-speaker variation, on the other hand, captures the changes in a single person's voice across contexts. Emotional states such as stress or anger can raise pitch or disrupt rhythm, while fatigue or illness may reduce clarity. In India, these fluctuations are often intensified by code-switching. Many speakers routinely move between Hindi, Tamil, Urdu, English, or other languages, which alters vowel space and consonant precision in ways that sometimes resemble inter-speaker differences (Rose 1998; Munson 2007). Unless accounted for, such variation can lead to mistaken exclusions in forensic comparison (Chan 2023).

2.3.2 Dialectology and Sociophonetics

Sociolinguistic variation adds another dimension. Speakers of the same language may differ in dialect, accent, or register, and these differences can provide critical forensic cues. Features such as r-lessness in particular English dialects, glottalisation patterns, tonal contrasts, or aspiration distinctions often signal regional or social identity. For example, aspiration is not phonemic in Tamil but is contrastive in Hindi, which makes it a useful diagnostic feature (Kavanagh 2012). Still, analysts must use dialect profiling cautiously. Code-switching, accommodation, or style-shifting can blur dialectal markers. If treated as static, these shifts risk being misinterpreted in forensic contexts (Parllaku et al. 2020).

2.3.3 Linguistic Methodologies

Linguists draw on both perceptual and instrumental approaches to analyse voice data. Perceptual analysis depends on trained phoneticians listening for fine-grained segmental and suprasegmental patterns. Acoustic analysis, often performed using software such as Praat or Wavesurfer, measures parameters including F0, formants, intensity, and duration.

Transcription systems, particularly the International Phonetic Alphabet (IPA), allow precise labelling of variation and are often combined with acoustic data. This dual approach ensures that subtle cues, which might go unnoticed by untrained listeners, are documented for forensic comparison (Soh et al. 2019; Torres et al. 2023).

2.3.4 Cross-Linguistic Variation

Forensic analysis becomes especially complex in multilingual settings, where phonological systems, prosody, and phonotactic rules differ sharply across languages. Tamil, for instance, has voiced retroflex stops that are absent in English, while Arabic includes emphatic consonants and pharyngeals. Such language-specific traits often hinder the transfer of automatic speaker recognition (ASR) systems trained on Western languages (Fairclough 2023; Huilgol et al. 2019).

Second-language (L2) speakers also bring transfer effects from their first language, which must be distinguished from genuine inter-speaker differences. Stress-timed languages, such as English, tend to reduce vowels, increasing variability, while syllable-timed systems, like Tamil, maintain clearer vowel quality and a more regular rhythm. Dravidian retroflexion and Hindi aspiration likewise influence how Indian English is produced (Table 2.1). If these system-specific features are overlooked, analysts may mistake code-switching or transfer effects for evidence of a different speaker (Cenceschi et al. 2021; Kavanagh 2012).

In practical casework, analysts should (i) normalise variation within the phonological expectations of a speaker's L1 (e.g. treat retroflex drift in Indian English as baseline rather than anomaly); (ii) model code-switching explicitly, since acoustic trajectories across Hindi↔English or Tamil↔English reset vowel centroids and rhythm metrics over short spans; (iii) privilege invariants under transfer, such as F1 anchoring for /a/ or retroflex burst spectra, which are more robust than global prosody; and (iv) document phonotactic repairs like epenthetic vowels in consonant clusters, as these reflect speaker-habituated yet language-licensed behaviours that remain probative when consistently observed (Rose 1998; Cenceschi et al. 2021; Chan 2023; Lakshmi and Savithri 2009).

Table 2.1 Examples of some comparative cross-linguistic features relevant to forensic phonetics

Language	Segmental features	Suprasegmental features	Forensic implications	References
English	Vowel reduction, glottal stops	Stress-timed rhythm	Stable ASR resources; high style-driven variance in F0/rate	Rose (1998) and Jessen (2010)
Tamil (Dravidian)	Retroflex /ʈ, ɖ/, nasalisation	Syllable-timed rhythm	L1 → L2 transfer of retroflex; robust cluster epenthesis in English	Jyotsna (2011)
Hindi (indo-Aryan)	Aspirated vs. unaspirated stops; vowel length	Mixed rhythm in L2 English	VOT bimodality; aspiration under disguise is confusable with the channel	Ridha (2014) and Morrison and Thompson (2017)
Indian English	Retroflex-like [t, d], non-rhoticity	Predominantly syllable-timed	Epenthetic vowels in clusters; segmental duration skew	Lindh (2017), Cenceschi et al. (2021), Kaur et al. (2023)
Arabic	Pharyngeals, emphatics	Variable pitch accents	Place-dependent spectral peaks; cross-dialect confounds	Fairclough (2023)
German	Final devoicing; fricative voicing split	Falling intonational contours	Dialect labelling aids exclusion/triage	Lindh (2017) and Eriksson (2005)

Abbreviations: *L2* second language, *ASR* automatic speaker recognition

This linguistic diversity necessitates culturally and linguistically informed forensic strategies. Failure to account for such system-specific articulatory and prosodic variation can lead to unreliable conclusions in multilingual speaker comparison. The forensic implications of English as a second language in India include phonotactic transfers, such as the insertion of epenthetic vowels in consonant clusters, which can introduce identifiable speech patterns while also increasing intra-speaker variability (Cenceschi et al. 2021). This linguistic diversity necessitates that forensic practitioners adopt culturally and linguistically informed strategies in their analysis. Failure to account for language-specific articulatory settings or dialectical variation can lead to unreliable conclusions in speaker comparison.

2.4 Speech-Language Pathologists' Perspectives

Based upon a conceptual understanding of how speech is variable both between and within speakers, we now examine what that variability means in a practical context, particularly for clinical practitioners. Having had daily interactions with people who have atypical speech, speech-language pathologists (SLPs) are uniquely positioned to comment on forensic situations involving errors of speech and voice pathology.

Nolan (2010) offers a more specific categorisation of within- and between-speaker differences. Segmental elements relate to systemic differences (e.g. deficits within phonemic inventories), phonotactic differences, stress differences, and realisation rules. Suprasegmental elements include types of nuclei, physical limitations, cognitive-affective intention, and social-stylistic variation. This creates a structure for subsequent analytic protocols.

2.4.1 Clinical Contributions to Forensic Analysis

Speech-language pathologists (SLPs) have long contributed to the understanding of human communication disorders; however, their role in forensic phonetics is increasingly being acknowledged and systematised. The clinical expertise of SLPs in diagnosing, characterising, and treating voice and speech disorders positions them uniquely to contribute to forensic investigations, especially when questions involve disordered or atypical speech. Clinical case data from Indian speech-language pathology practice, such as acoustic profiling of cleft palate speech and dysarthric speech in multilingual speakers, provide valuable reference points for forensic evaluation, particularly when pathological speech is encountered in suspects or witnesses (Kavanagh 2012; Chan 2023).

The ability to differentiate pathological variation from typical intra- or inter-speaker variability is critical in forensic contexts. Speech pathologists offer insights into deviations that may not reflect deception, disguise, or identity concealment but rather underlying speech, voice, or neurological disorders. For example, hoarseness due to vocal fold paralysis may result in decreased harmonic-to-noise ratios (HNR),

2.4.3 Cross-Cultural Considerations in Disordered Speech

Disordered speech manifests differently across languages and dialects, requiring forensic speech-language pathologists (SLPs) to be sensitive to phonological, prosodic, and morphophonemic characteristics of regional and non-dominant languages. For instance, Tamil speakers with velopharyngeal dysfunction may adopt compensatory retroflex articulations not typically seen in English. In contrast, Hindi speakers with cleft-related hypernasality may be mistaken for producing disguised voices if nasalance is not measured objectively (Kavanagh 2012; Chan 2023; Fairclough 2023; Huilgol et al. 2019). Similarly, in Bengali, where nasalisation is lexically robust, hypernasal resonance may be judged "normal" unless contrasted with controlled oral targets; conversely, in languages without phonemic nasality, similar resonance is rapidly marked as "pathological" or "disguised." These examples underscore that forensic evaluation must normalise samples both to the language's phonological system and to the speaker's clinical presentation.

Phonological expectations, therefore, shape how disordered speech is perceived in forensic contexts. Retroflex errors in cleft palate speech may be misread as L2 English transfer, while pharyngeal constriction in Arabic-influenced speech may be misinterpreted as pressed phonation. Such misattributions are avoidable if analysts systematically benchmark against language-specific norms and supplement auditory impressions with acoustic evidence such as nasalance, HNR, and burst spectra (Ridha 2014; Jyotsna 2011; Suresh 2015; Chandrika 2015; Zakia 2014; Yeshoda and Jayaram 2011). Table 2.3 illustrates these cross-cultural diagnostic differences.

In addition to phonology, socio-cultural norms of acceptable pitch ranges, speech rates, and prosodic styles will also mediate perceptions of what constitutes "natural" versus "abnormal" speech. For instance, Indian female groups have been known to have a higher mean pitch, while courtroom speech uses a slower and more formal register. Without an understanding of these norms within the sociolinguistic aspects of forensic analysis, the possibility exists that cultural variation will be attributed to disguise or pathology. In best practice, forensic voice analysts should (i) use language-matched wordlists that also have oral-nasal minimal pairs; (ii) use samples that consist of sustained vowels, as well as connected speech so that source versus filter factors can be separated; and (iii), where resonance is an issue, could be supported by instrumental measures (e.g. nasometry). By explicitly describing these socio-cultural baselines in forensic report writing, it will help inform adjudicators (and forensic experts) and explain why "naturalness" cannot be used as a universal comparator (Ridha 2014; Jyotsna 2011; Suresh 2015; Chandrika 2015; Zakia 2014; Chan 2023).

2.4.4 Legal and Ethical Roles

SLPs may serve as expert witnesses in both civil and criminal cases involving communicative competence, speaker identification, and the capacity to give testimony. In the forensic domain, ethical concerns arise in multiple ways:

Table 2.3 Examples of some cross-cultural considerations in disordered speech for forensic contexts

Language	Disordered feature	Likely forensic misinterpretation	Implication for protocol	References
Tamil	Retroflex articulation errors in cleft speech	L2 English retroflex transfer	Compare Tamil→Tamil tokens; inspect burst spectra	Sreedevi (2007)
Hindi	Hypernasality; vowel centralisation	Disguise; ASR mis-ID	Include nasalance or HNR; avoid denoising that elevates nasal poles	Ridha (2014) and Aparna and Savithri (2010)
Bengali	Extensive lexical nasalisation	Disguise-induced nasality	Use controlled oral targets; track vowel F1 bandwidth	Kavanagh (2012) and Chan (2023)
Arabic	Pharyngealisation/uvularisation	"Hoarseness" judgement	Separate spectral tilt from place-specific peaks	Fairclough (2023)
Japanese	Mora timing; devoicing	Phonological disorder	Evaluate rate within the mora framework; avoid WPM comparators	Lindh (2017)

1. **Consent and Recording Use**: Voice samples collected in clinical settings are protected under health privacy laws, e.g. HIPAA (Health Insurance Portability and Accountability Act–USA), GDPR (General Data Protection Regulation–European Union), and the DPDPA (Digital Personal Data Protection Act–India). Their forensic use must follow strict legal frameworks.
2. **Bias in Interpretation**: SLPs must recognise and mitigate confirmation bias, mainly when employed by prosecution or defence.
3. **Testimony Limitations**: The forensic speech language pathologist's role is to present probabilities, not certainties. This aligns with best practices in evidence-based practice.

Cases such as the US Supreme Court's decision in Daubert v. Merrell Dow Pharmaceuticals (Morrison and Thompson 2017) established the importance of peer-reviewed methods and known error rates for admissibility. SLP testimony must meet similar scientific standards to be accepted. Ethical codes from professional bodies such as ASHA and RCSLT recommend impartiality, transparency, and data sharing as cornerstones of forensic SLP practice. The Indian Speech-Language and Hearing Association (ISHA) does not offer any guidelines as on date for forensic speaker identification; however, this does not limit SLPs in India from practising in this domain. In 2022, the Directorate of Forensic Science Services (DFSS), a government agency in India, released a working procedural manual for speaker identification and audio-video analysis. This manual outlines the procedural aspects required to handle audio and video samples during forensic analysis and reporting for speaker identification.

Smart Box 2.1 A: DFSS (2022) Working Procedure Manual for Speaker Identification and Audio-Video Analysis

The Directorate of Forensic Science Services (DFSS), Government of India, issued this manual in 2022 as the national guideline for handling, analysing, and reporting speaker identification and audio-video evidence.

- **Evidence Handling**: Maintain chain of custody, use write-protected copies, and preserve original recordings without alteration.
- **Recording Quality**: Document medium, mode (telephone, digital, analogue), and background noise; enhance only for audibility, not alteration.
- **Analytical Protocols**: Combine **auditory-perceptual** (ear-based phonetic judgements) and **instrumental-acoustic** analyses (formants, pitch, spectrograms).
- **Specimen Collection**: Ensure comparable speaking style, language, and conditions between questioned and reference recordings.
- **Evaluation Categories**: Conclusions reported as *positive identification*, *probable identification*, *inconclusive*, *probable elimination*, or *elimination*.
- **Reporting Standards**: Final opinions must be cautious, evidence based, and explicitly acknowledge limitations (e.g. sample duration, quality, disguise).

Readers are encouraged to consult the full DFSS manual for detailed procedural guidance.

2.4.5 Case Reports Involving Pathological and Atypical Voices

Real-world forensic cases demonstrate how speaker variability complicates identification due to factors such as pathology, disguise, stress, and poor audio quality. However, the right acoustic and perceptual cues can provide valuable evidence. For example, in a Dutch case involving threat calls, experts verified an answering-machine recording against a prison sample using spectrographic analysis and vowel formant measurements, leading to court-admissible conclusions despite the poor quality (Corthals et al. 2011).

In cases of obscene calls, Grigoras (2005) found that systematic measurements of vowel distributions revealed differences between the caller and a suspect, although casual listeners perceived them as similar. This demonstrates the effectiveness of formant analysis. Stress can significantly affect a speaker's characteristics. In one robbery case, the fundamental frequency (F0) of an offender increased from 140 Hz to approximately 228 Hz under duress (Boss 2013), highlighting how emotional state influences voice and why additional context is necessary. Disguises, like glottal fry, also complicate analysis. Hirson (1993) noted that while short-term voice measures were affected, long-term features, such as formant trajectories, provided reliable distinctions.

Research such as the Dynamic Variability in Speech (DyViS) project has shown that formant dynamics are strong indicators of speaker identity (McDougall 2006). Similarly, Zhang et al. (2019) found that bi-dialectal Mandarin speakers maintained distinct voiced-interval patterns across dialects. These findings highlight the need for a multi-cue, probabilistic approach to speech analysis. Although unusual speech patterns can make it harder for automated speech recognition (ASR) systems to understand what's being said, we can still interpret these speech instances effectively when we consider the subtle acoustic details and the clinical background.

Stress and disguise effects inflate intra-speaker differences, requiring analysts to model variability rather than treat cues like F0 as static identifiers. Formant-based and dynamic measures consistently show greater resilience across conditions, supporting their central role in forensic speaker comparison.

By embedding clinical knowledge of pathology with empirical evidence from threat, ransom, and obscene-call cases, forensic phonetics demonstrates its strength: the ability to transform variability from a confound into an evidential resource. This section bridges naturally to the subsequent discussion of technological systems, where automatic methods seek to formalise these insights within reproducible, statistical frameworks.

2.5 Technologists' Perspectives

2.5.1 Introduction to Technological Advances

Forensic phonetics has progressively embraced technology to enhance the objectivity, scalability, and validity of speaker identification. While this domain involves complex computational and statistical methodologies, speech-language pathologists (SLPs) must grasp foundational concepts that bridge clinical phonetics and forensic applications. This section provides an accessible overview of key technological milestones and their practical implications in the forensic arena.

2.5.2 Evolution of Forensic Speech Technologies

The journey of forensic phonetic technology began with the analogue sound spectrograph, developed in the 1940s by Bell Labs. Initially used for linguistic research, it became instrumental in generating visual representations of speech known as "voiceprints". Though the reliability of voiceprints was later questioned, they marked the transition from subjective auditory analyses to semi-objective methodologies (Hollien 1990).

By the 1990s, the field had moved toward digital signal processing and the integration of basic computational models such as Mel Frequency Cepstral Coefficients (MFCCs) and Gaussian Mixture Models (GMMs), which enabled structured comparisons between known and unknown speakers (Kumar et al. 2015; Reynolds and Rose 1995). These early models formed the basis of automatic speaker recognition (ASR) systems.

2.5.3 Practical Technologies in Forensic Phonetics

Modern forensic phonetics increasingly relies on neural networks and probabilistic algorithms to enhance the accuracy of speaker recognition. Among the most widely used tools are i-vectors and x-vectors, which embed a speaker's acoustic traits into low-dimensional vectors. These embeddings condense information from thousands of acoustic cues, pitch, timing, and resonance, into a format optimised for rapid comparison across speech samples (Dehak et al. 2011). From a clinical perspective, the value lies less in computation than in appreciating what these systems capture: patterned acoustic behaviour that distinguishes typical from atypical voices.

In India, forensic laboratories now adapt automatic speaker recognition (ASR) systems to local linguistic contexts, training models on datasets that reflect regional accents, phonotactic norms, and multilingual speech (Huilgol et al. 2019). Such adaptation is essential in a setting where code-switching and cross-linguistic transfer are common. Importantly, these technologies are also applied to challenging materials, such as pathological voices, disguised speech, or disfluencies, where embedding-based models still capture usable traces of speaker-specific variability. For speech-language pathologists (SLPs), understanding how these computational tools interpret atypical signals helps bridge the gap between clinical expertise and forensic application.

Box 2.1 A—From i-vectors to ECAPA-TDNN: What an SLP Needs to Know (with Indian Context)

- **MFCC + GMM-UBM:** classical baseline that models average spectral envelopes. Strengths: interpretable, works with small datasets. Weakness: channel- and language-mismatch sensitive (Kumar et al. 2015).
- **i-vectors + PLDA:** compress utterances to low-dimensional identity vectors; robust to moderate channel variation; still sensitive to language/task mismatch (Dehak et al. 2011).
- **x-vectors / ECAPA-TDNN**: deep embeddings capturing long-range spectral-temporal patterns; best current accuracy, but opaque; need domain-matched training (Chan 2023; Torres et al. 2023).
- **Indian adaptation:** Labs increasingly fine-tune models on regional, multilingual data; performance lifts are largest when training covers the test dialects and pathological voice types (Arjun and Rajasudhakar 2016; Sharma et al. 2017; Radha and Bansal 2023; Rizvi et al. 2022).
- **For testimony:** report training data composition, error rates by condition (noisy phone vs. studio), and language coverage; avoid black-box claims without these caveats (Gold and French 2011; French and Harrison 2007; Morrison and Thompson 2017).

2.5.4 Acoustic Features Relevant to Clinicians

Speech-language pathologists are trained in analysing voice, segmental, and suprasegmental features; in forensic contexts, these same variables are systematically quantified by algorithms. The most operationally sound features are those familiar to clinicians and simultaneously exploited by ASR systems:

- Fundamental frequency (F0): reflects pitch, gender, and affective state.
- Formant frequencies (F1, F2): map articulatory settings and vowel quality.
- Voice onset time (VOT): indexes stop consonant timing.
- Jitter, shimmer, and harmonics-to-noise ratio (HNR): indicate phonatory stability and quality.

These parameters, which have long been used in clinical diagnostics, become evidentiary when consistently extracted from forensic recordings. For example, elevated jitter and shimmer may indicate laryngeal dysfunction but, if uncorrected for channel artefacts, can also mimic deliberate disguise. Similarly, F0 and formants form a robust bridge: they are interpretable clinically yet also serve as anchors in ASR back-ends. HNR corresponds to perceptual measures of breathiness or strain (e.g. GRBAS), while perturbation metrics align with cycle-level irregularities indirectly encoded in vector-based systems.

Table 2.4 Examples of some acoustic measures for forensic profiling with Indian benchmarks

Feature	Clinical relevance	Forensic application	Indian benchmarks	References
F0	Gender/age, affect	Profiling: Stress/ disguise inference	M: 110–140 Hz; F: 200–240 Hz	Chan (2023)
Formants (F1/F2)	Articulation; VPI effects	Accent/dialect; ID anchors	See Table 2.2	Lakshmi and Savithri (2009)
Jitter/ shimmer	Dysphonia severity	Disguise vs. disorder	See Table 2.2	Soh et al. (2019), Torres et al. (2023)
HNR (dB)	Breathiness/ strain	Modal vs. non-modal separation	15–25 dB (modal)	Sreedevi (2007)
Rate/ pausing	Fluency; motor planning	Stress vs. impairment	Report task-bound	Jessen (2010), Bradshaw et al. (2020)

Indian benchmarks now provide contextual baselines for these variables. For instance, normative data from AIISH cohorts show overlapping ranges for F0 and perturbation metrics across typical and pathological voices (Table 2.4), highlighting the need for multivariate rather than single-feature interpretation (Ridha 2014; Jyotsna 2011; Suresh 2015; Chandrika 2015; Zakia 2014; Kavanagh 2012; Chan 2023; Soh et al. 2019; Torres et al. 2023; Lakshmi and Savithri 2009). SLPs, therefore, can advise whether acoustic deviations are more consistent with clinical pathology or with deliberate disguise.

If F0 and HNR simultaneously deviate from normative corridors and perturbation measures are elevated, a clinical aetiology is more plausible than deliberate disguise; conversely, isolated F0 elevation with stable HNR and formants points to state-driven or strategic change. Always contextualise with recording metadata (microphone, codec, noise reduction), which can invert these signatures.

2.5.5 Limitations and Cautions

Despite its advancements, forensic technology is not infallible. Algorithms are only as practical as the data on which they are trained. A system trained predominantly on native English male speakers may struggle with Tamil-accented female voices. Similarly, disordered speech, such as dysarthria, apraxia, or cleft-related anomalies, can introduce variability that impairs system accuracy (Becker and Jessen 2020). In India, the absence of a large-scale pathological and multilingual voice database hampers the training of robust ASR systems. Dialectal variation within languages further complicates modelling without substantial cross-dialect data (Hema 2016). Moreover, forensic systems do not inherently "understand" speech pathology. SLPs, therefore, play a crucial role in flagging potential clinical influences that could impact speaker identification outcomes. This multidisciplinary cooperation enhances the validity of forensic interpretations.

2.5.6 Technological Integration in Legal Settings

The legal admissibility of technological evidence in forensic phonetics is often scrutinised under standards such as the Daubert ruling (Morrison and Thompson 2017). The technology used must be peer reviewed, have known error rates, and demonstrate general acceptance among the relevant scientific community. From a clinical perspective, this necessitates understanding not only whether a technology works but also under what conditions it may fail to work.

SLPs involved in forensic teams or courtroom testimonies must advocate for:

- Use of normative and pathological voice datasets.
- Transparent explanation of error margins.
- Highlighting when voice differences arise from clinical conditions rather than criminal intent.

2.5.7 Cross-Training and Continuing Education

Given the intersection of technology and speech science, continuing education modules focused on forensic phonetics and acoustic technology could significantly empower SLPs. Topics might include:

- Basics of ASR systems.
- Interpretation of spectrograms.
- Voice database design for disordered populations.

Technological advances have undeniably refined the process of forensic speaker identification. However, their appropriate use demands interdisciplinary collaboration. Speech-language pathologists, with their expertise in voice, fluency, and speech variability, can play a pivotal role in ensuring that technological tools are used ethically and accurately (Fig. 2.1a, b). By understanding the clinical significance behind acoustic parameters, SLPs can help bridge the gap between digital analysis and human interpretation in forensic settings (Jessen 2010; Lindh 2017).

2.6 Conclusion and Future Directions

The domain of forensic phonetics, particularly the study of speech variability, stands at the intersection of linguistics, clinical speech-language pathology, and technological innovation. As this chapter has illustrated through multiple disciplinary lenses, speech variability is not merely a source of analytical complexity but also a reservoir of diagnostic and identificatory richness. Whether viewed through the phonological patterns of language users, the diagnostic perspectives of speech-language pathologists, or the acoustic precision of forensic technologies, variability

a)

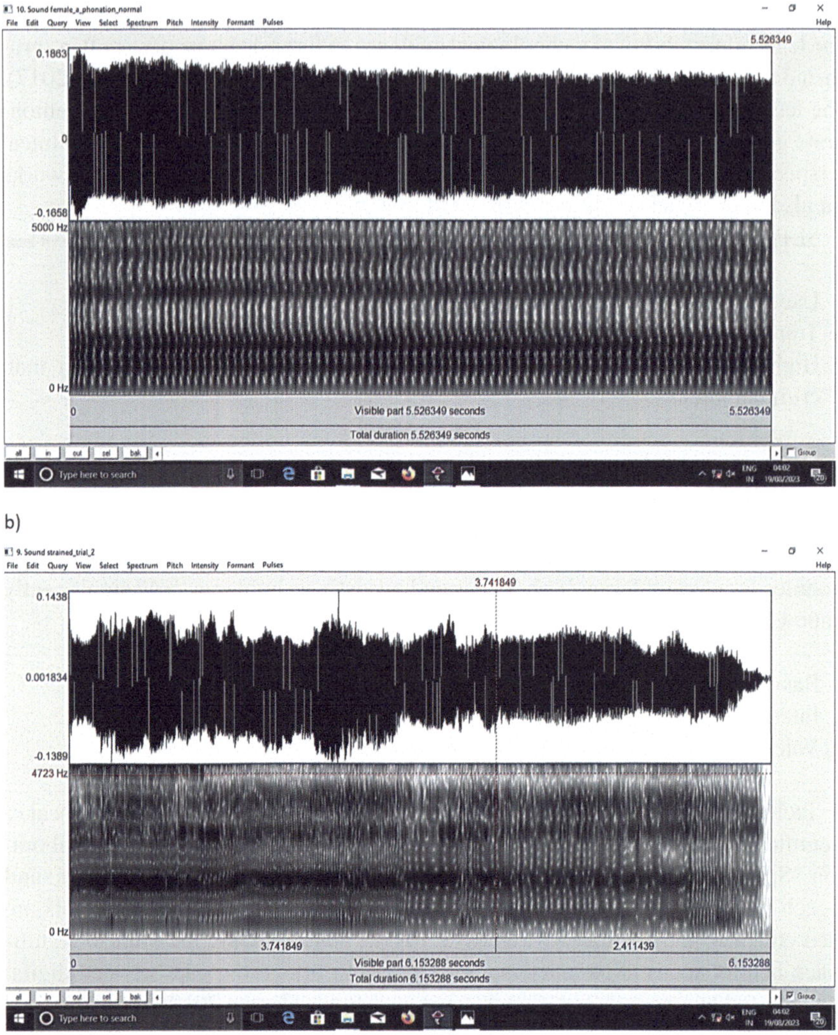

Fig. 2.1 Spectrographic display of (**a**) normal phonation of /a/ versus (**b**) disguised (strained) phonation of /a/ [Figure showing differences in formant clarity between typical and disguised voice samples]

in speech emerges as both a challenge and a resource in forensic contexts (Nolan 1983; French and Harrison 2007; Hollien 1990).

From a historical perspective, forensic phonetics has evolved from rudimentary auditory analyses and court-based voice identifications to sophisticated multimodal approaches combining auditory-perceptual, acoustic-phonetic, and automatic speaker recognition methods. Key researchers such as Hollien, Nolan, and French have significantly shaped this trajectory by advocating for empirical rigour and standardisation in practice. Technological advancements, including spectrographic voiceprints, machine learning models such as i-vectors and x-vectors, and the growing use of artificial intelligence in speech analysis, characterise this evolution (Ridha 2014; Jyotsna 2011; Suresh 2015; Chandrika 2015; Zakia 2014; Chan 2023; Eriksson 2005).

The theoretical underpinnings of speech variability, anchored in sociophonetics, motor speech control, and acoustic phonetics, underscore the complexity of speaker identity. Variability is influenced by a multitude of factors, including anatomical differences, developmental trajectories, emotional states, health conditions, and cultural and linguistic backgrounds. Understanding these influences is critical not only for linguistic theorists but especially for forensic practitioners seeking to distinguish between speaker-specific traits and context-driven fluctuations (Ridha 2014; Jyotsna 2011; Suresh 2015; Chandrika 2015; Zakia 2014; Soh et al. 2019; Torres et al. 2023).

This chapter stressed that forensic phonetics must incorporate clinical perspectives from speech-language pathology. The clinical profiles of difficulties in speech production, dysarthria, apraxia, speech disorders arising from cleft behaviours, and psychogenic voice disorders, demonstrate how pathological speech characteristics converge with the forensic interpretation. Speech-language pathologists (SLPs) possess a unique ability to inform legal actors and forensic analysts on the characteristics and implications associated with pathological speech. SLPs have a clinical knowledge base in measuring, in an acoustic sense, various parameters in speech such as jitter, shimmer, pitch, and formants, which can be used to help differentiate whether a voice anomaly is due to a severe speech disorder or a conscious or deliberate camouflaging of voice (Munson 2007; Stevens 1996; Broeders 2001; Morrison and Thompson 2017; Jessen 2010). In addition, from a linguistic perspective, we gain insights into dialectal variation, prosodic markers, and code-switching from a speech context, especially as it relates to forensic contexts that are inherently multicultural. Similarly, the presence of regional accents, sociolects, dialects, and bilingualism complicates speaker comparisons and programmatically inserts the necessity for culturally competent analyses. Collectively, these analytical perspectives will establish a holistic, ethically responsible approach to forensic phonetics (Lindh 2017; Martínez et al. 2014; Cenceschi et al. 2021; Kavanagh 2012).

Future Directions

Several promising avenues exist for advancing the field of forensic phonetics and refining our understanding and application of speech variability in legal settings:

1. **Interdisciplinary Cooperation:** Collaboration between linguists, SLPs, technologists, and legal experts should be improved. This multidisciplinary perspective enables a more comprehensive assessment of speaker samples, thereby enhancing the reliability of forensic conclusions.
2. **Voice Databases with Inclusivity**: Future research that quenches a thirst for database research should create inclusive databases to evaluate voices that exhibit vocal pathology, multilingual speakers, dialectal variation, etc. Research

in these areas would enable the greater generalisability of forensic technologies used in diverse populations.

3. **Modules for Training SLPs and Linguists:** Continuing education that familiarises clinical and academic professionals with forensic principles/practices, like likelihood ratio frameworks, Automatic Speech Recognition (ASR) system interpretation, courtroom testimony, etc., will broaden the pool of experts available for forensic consultations.
4. **Ethical Assurances and Legal Changes:** As forensic phonetic practices become a larger part of the legal landscape, ethical assurances will need to adapt. Privacy, consent, data security, and wrongful conviction are areas that need to be addressed in proactive ways.
5. **Technological Transparency and Explainability:** Given that deep learning models are likely going to become the problematic technique of choice for forensic approaches—something that prevents the rigour of necessity to support systems' transparency of decision-making for officials or non-experts; unintentionally designed decision-making systems that cannot be used by officials as a black box (without any human oversight) will compromise judicial transparency.
6. **Case-Based Research and Best Practice Guidelines**: Publishing detailed case studies, especially those involving disordered speech, multilingualism, or child speakers, will contribute to a corpus of real-world examples that can inform forensic best practices. Professional bodies should consider developing guidelines that explicitly include provisions for analysing non-standard and clinically atypical speech.
7. **Public and Legal Literacy**: Increasing awareness among legal professionals, judges, and the public about what forensic phonetics can and cannot do is vital. This would prevent over-reliance on technology or misinterpretation of acoustic evidence in high-stakes legal contexts.

In conclusion, the intricacy of human speech, its variability, individuality, and adaptability, are both the foundation and the dilemma of forensic phonetics. This chapter hopes (at least in part) to make that complexity less complex, providing a basis for linguists, clinicians, and non-legal professionals to reflect and work together. Ultimately, while technology may play an integral role in our future, it will be based on our ability to integrate empirical science, clinical experience, and ethical practice as a unified foundation in the world of forensic science.

Appendix A: Extended Acoustic Parameters and Measurement Notes

Source Dynamics and Spectral Shape

- Spectral tilt (A-weighted slope) and cepstral peak prominence (CPP) track breathiness/pressed voice; useful in dysphonia and disguise detection but are processing sensitive (denoisers may flatten tilt, inflate CPP). Report FFT size/windowing and any noise reduction (Chan 2023; Soh et al. 2019).

- Long-term average spectrum (LTAS) summarises vocal tract filtering over continuous speech, stabilising idiolectal tendencies; compare only like tasks (read→read) and matched bandwidth.

Laryngographic/EGG-Derived Measures

- Contact quotient (CQ) and open quotient (OQ) disentangle source-filter trade-offs; depressed OQ with high HNR suggests pressed phonation as opposed to nasalance changes.

Temporal Metrics

Researchers frequently employ measurements such as %V and nPVI (pairwise variability index) to investigate speech rhythm. To avoid misleading comparisons between different speakers, these metrics must be interpreted in light of the type of language, whether stress timed (like English) or syllable timed (like Spanish) (Ridha 2014; Jyotsna 2011; Suresh 2015; Chandrika 2015; Zakia 2014; Rose 1998; Kavanagh 2012). Similarly, where and how long someone pauses while speaking can indicate if they are organising their ideas or having problems making a speech. To accurately comprehend these patterns, consider how the same person communicates in different contexts.

Measurement Protocol

- Collect sustained vowels ($\geq$ 3 s) and connected speech ($\geq$ 30 s) per condition; note codec, sampling rate, device; run analyses at the narrower bandwidth when channels differ.
- Avoid aggressive spectral subtraction before perturbation/HNR; use matched filtering and report any processing.
- In multilingual cases, segment by language window; do not pool across code-switching boundaries during feature aggregation (Ridha 2014; Jyotsna 2011; Suresh 2015; Chandrika 2015; Zakia 2014; Cenceschi et al. 2021; Fairclough 2023).

References

Aparna VS, Savithri SR (2010) Benchmark for speaker identification using glottal source parameters in Hindi speakers. MSc Dissertation. University of Mysore, AIISH

Arjun MS, Rajasudhakar R (2016) Benchmark for speaker identification using linear prediction coding (LPC) on vowels preceding nasal continuants in Kannada. J Acoust Soc India 43(2):97–107

Becker T, Jessen M (2020) Limitations of automatic speaker recognition with non-standard speech. Int J Speech Lang Law 27(1):57–82. https://doi.org/10.1558/ijsll.40785

Boss D (2013) The problem of F0 and real-life speaker identification: a case study. Int J Speech Lang Law 3(1):155–163. https://doi.org/10.1558/ijsll.v3i1.155

Bradshaw L, Hughes V, Chodroff E (2020) Investigating the forensic applications of global and local temporal representations of speech for dialect discrimination. Speech Prosody 2020. https://doi.org/10.21437/SPEECHPROSODY.2020-130

Broeders T (2001) Forensic speech and audio analysis forensic linguistics 1998–2001. In: paperssrncom https://papers.ssrn.com/sol3/papers.cfm?abstract_id=2870568

Cenceschi S, Meluzzi C, Trivilini A (2021) The variability of vowels' formants in forensic speech. IEEE Instrum Meas Mag 24(4):56–61. https://doi.org/10.1109/MIM.2021.9345600

Chan R (2023) Evidential value of voice quality acoustics in forensic voice comparison. Forensic Sci Int 348:111725. https://doi.org/10.1016/j.forsciint.2023.111725

Chandrika T (2015) Benchmark for speaker identification using nasal continuants in Telugu. Unpublished Dissertation

Corthals P, Van Borsel J, Van Lierde K (2011) Een gevalsstudie in forensische fonetiek. Ghent University, Belgium. Available: https://biblio.ugent.be/publication/1957852/file/1991624.pdf. Accessed 26 Aug 2025

Dehak N, Kenny PJ, Dehak R et al (2011) Front-end factor analysis for speaker verification. IEEE Trans Audio Speech Lang Process 19:788–798. https://doi.org/10.1109/tasl.2010.2064307

Eriksson A (2005) Tutorial on forensic speech science. Part I: forensic phonetics. In: Interspeech/Eurospeech 2005, Lisbon, 4–8 September, pp 4–8

Fairclough L (2023) Towards methodological and theoretical synergies between forensic phonetics and third wave sociophonetics. Mod Lang Open. https://doi.org/10.3828/mlo.v0i0.452

French P, Harrison P (2007) Position statement concerning use of impressionistic likelihood terms in forensic speaker comparison cases. Int J Speech Lang Law 14. https://doi.org/10.1558/ijsll.v14i1.137

Gibbons J (2003) Forensic linguistics: an introduction to language in the justice system. Blackwell, Malden

Gold E, French P (2011) International practices in forensic speaker comparison. Int J Speech Lang Law 18. https://doi.org/10.1558/ijsll.v18i2.293

Grigoras C (2005) A case for formant analysis in forensic speaker identification. Speech Lang Law 12(2):143–163. https://doi.org/10.1558/sll.2005.12.2.143

Hema N (2016) Effect of noise reduction technique on speaker identification. In: AIISH research fund (ARF) project report. All India Institute of Speech and Hearing, Mysore

Hirson A (1993) Glottal fry and voice disguise: a case study. Forensic Sci Int 61(1):13–26. https://doi.org/10.1016/0379-0738(93)90115-F

Hollien H (1990) The Acoustics of Crime. https://doi.org/10.1007/978-1-4899-0673-1

Huilgol S, Baik J, Shattuck-Hufnagel S (2019) A framework for labelling speech with acoustic cues to linguistic distinctive features. J Acoust Soc Am 146(2):EL184. https://doi.org/10.1121/1.5121717

Jessen M (2010) The forensic phonetician. In: Coulthard M, Johnson A (eds) The Routledge handbook of forensic linguistics. Routledge, pp 517–531

Jyotsna P (2011) Benchmark for speaker identification using Tamil nasal continuants in live and mobile network recordings. Unpublished Dissertation

Kaur J, Juglan KC, Sharma K, Sharma V (2023) An acoustic analysis of fluctuations for inter- and intra-speaker variability in speech sounds. J Forensic Sci Med 9(1):38–43. https://doi.org/10.4103/jfsm.jfsm_7_22

Kavanagh C (2012) New consonantal acoustic parameters for forensic speaker comparison. J Acoust Soc Am 132(3):1948

Kumar A, Raj A, Shee A, Kumar K, Nagarathna R (2015) Speaker identification based on voice samples using MFCC and GMM. Int J Sci Res Dev 3(3):72–81

Ladefoged P (2003) Phonetic data analysis: an introduction to fieldwork and instrumental phonetics. Blackwell, Oxford

Lakshmi R, Savithri SR (2009) Benchmark for speaker identification using vector F1=F2. [AIISH dissertation]

Lindh J (2017) Forensic comparison of voices, speech and speakers: tools and methods in forensic phonetics. In: Mešički CI (ed) Forensic phonetics and speaker identification

Martínez MH, Blanco AM, Palacios G (2014) Speech pattern recognition for forensic acoustic purposes. Rev Esp Doc Cient 37(1)

McDougall K (2006) A forensic phonetic study of dynamic sources of variability in speech: the DyViS project. Proc Speech Sci Technol 17:74–79

Mopas M (2023) Hearing voices: forensic speaker identification technology and expert listening in the American courtroom. Sound Stud 9(2):209–232. https://doi.org/10.1080/20551940.2023.2232186

Morrison GS, Thompson WC (2017) Assessing the admissibility of a new generation of forensic voice comparison testimony. Sci Technol Law Rev 18(2):326–434. https://doi.org/10.7916/stlr.v18i2.4022

Munson B (2007) The acoustic correlates of perceived masculinity, femininity, and sexual orientation. Lang Speech 50(1):125–142

Nolan F (1983) The phonetic bases of speaker recognition. Cambridge University Press

Ortega-García J, Cruz-Llanas S, González-Rodríguez J (1999) Speech variability in automatic speaker recognition systems for forensic purposes. Proc IEEE Carnahan Conf Secur Technol, pp:31–36. https://doi.org/10.1109/CCST.1999.797932

Parllaku F, Choi J, Shattuck-Hufnagel S (2020) Cue-dependent processing in an automatic acoustic cue analysis system for detecting atypical speech. J Acoust Soc Am 148:2808. https://doi.org/10.1121/1.5147821

Radha K, Bansal M (2023) Closed-set automatic speaker identification using multi-scale recurrent networks in non-native children. Int J Inf Technol 15:1375–1385. https://doi.org/10.1007/s41870-023-01224-8

Reynolds DA, Rose RC (1995) Robust text-independent speaker identification using Gaussian mixture speaker models. IEEE Trans Speech Audio Process 3:72–83. https://doi.org/10.1109/89.365379

Ridha F (2014) Benchmark for speaker identification using nasal continuants in Hindi (direct and mobile recordings). Unpublished Dissertation

Rizvi A, Jamata A, Rudrapal D, Chakma K, Gambäck B (2022) Cross-lingual speaker identification for Indian languages. In: Proceedings recent advances natural language processing (RANLP), pp 979–987

Rose P (1998) A framework for forensic speaker comparison. Int J Speech Lang Law 5(1):1–26

Sharma S, Jain SK, Sharma RM (2017) Characterization of temporal and acoustic parameters for speaker identification in disguised speech. J Forensic Sci Crim Invest 4(5):555651

Soh C, Talkar T, Choi J, Shattuck-Hufnagel S (2019) Alignment of canonical and realised acoustic cue labels for modification patterns in speech analysis. J Acoust Soc Am. https://doi.org/10.1121/1.5137281

Sommers M, Barcroft J (2006) Stimulus variability and the phonetic relevance hypothesis: effects of variability on spoken word identification. J Acoust Soc Am 119(4):2406

Sreedevi N (2007) Tamil (retroflex cleft): AIISH cleft palate articulatory datasets (a case study)

Stevens KN (1996) Acoustic phonetics. MIT Press

Suresh S (2015) Benchmark for speaker identification using nasal continuants in Kannada. Unpublished Dissertation

Torres D, Choi J, Shattuck-Hufnagel S (2023) Development of an algorithm for characterizing speech production patterns as context-based cue production profiles. J Acoust Soc Am. https://doi.org/10.1121/10.0018884

Toscano JC (2011) Perceiving speech in context: compensation for contextual variability during acoustic cue encoding and categorization. PhD Dissertation, University of Iowa. https://doi.org/10.17077/ETD.QUE83ZKA

Yeshoda K, Jayaram M (2011) Importance of some spectral and temporal parameters for speaker identification. Doctoral Thesis. University of Mysore, AIISH

Zakia S (2014) Benchmark for speaker identification using nasal continuants in Urdu under direct and mobile conditions. Unpublished Dissertation

Zhang Y, He L, Dellwo V (2019) Speaker individuality in the durational characteristics of voiced intervals: the case of Chinese bi-dialectal speakers. Phonetica 76(4):261–284. https://doi.org/10.5167/UZH-177495

Forensic Linguistics

3

Ruchi Bhandari, Vijay Kumar, and Suma R. Devenga

Abstract

Language is the fundamental architecture of the legal system, yet it requires scientific decoding to ensure judicial truth. Forensic linguistics (FL) emerges as a vital discipline, bridging raw communication and the law by applying a scientific lens to how meaning is constructed and manipulated. The scope of forensic linguistic centers on the "linguistic fingerprint"—the unique, subconscious idiolect every individual possesses through specific sentence structures and semantic habits. These patterns serve as critical tools for authorship attribution and identifying forged texts. In current practice, forensic linguistics is vital in the courtroom for analyzing the power dynamics of interrogations, distinguishing voluntary confessions from linguistic coercion. Furthermore, the field integrates clinical expertise to protect individuals with language disorders, ensuring cognitive barriers are not mistaken for deception. By applying scientific rigor to human behavior, forensic linguistics provides a humanizing safeguard, ensuring the law listens to every voice with precision and maintains the integrity of the judicial process.

R. Bhandari
Department of Otorhinolaryngology, Graphic Era Institute of Medical Sciences an Research Foundation, Dehradun, Uttarakhand, India

V. Kumar (✉)
Department of Audiology and Speech-Language Pathology, Amity Medical School, Amity University Haryana, Gurgaon, Haryana, India
e-mail: vkumar@ggn.amity.edu

S. R. Devenga
Department of Communication Disorders and Sciences, RUSH University Medical Center, Chicago, IL, USA

V. Kumar et al. (eds.), *Forensic Speech Sciences*, New Horizons in Forensic Science, https://doi.org/10.1007/978-981-92-1475-4_3

Keywords

Authorship attribution · Forensic linguistics · Linguistic coercion · Linguistic fingerprint · Idiolect

3.1 The Forensic Linguist: An Introduction

The forensic linguist explores how language operates within legal contexts through systematic, ethical, and scientifically grounded analysis (Coulthard and Johnson 2007). In forensic linguistics, language is not treated as an abstract system but as real-world data produced by individuals in high-stakes situations. The forensic linguist applies tools from phonetics, morphology, syntax, semantics, pragmatics, and discourse analysis to explain how meaning is constructed, misunderstood, or manipulated within the justice system (Olsson 2008). This applied orientation distinguishes forensic linguistics from purely theoretical approaches and places responsibility on clarity, transparency, and methodological rigor. A core concern across forensic linguistic work is context. Legal interactions are shaped by power imbalance, institutional norms, and emotional pressure, all of which influence language production and interpretation (Gibbons 2003). Forensic linguists therefore examine not only what was said or written but how, why, and under what conditions it was produced. This includes attention to wording choices, structural patterns, interactional dynamics, and the potential for ambiguity (McMenamin 2002). Examples from police interviews, written statements, contracts, threats, and digital communication illustrate how small linguistic features can carry significant legal consequences.

Methodology is central to credible forensic linguistic practice. Analyses are comparative, data driven, and probabilistic rather than absolute. Linguists avoid claims of certainty and instead explain likelihoods, patterns, and limitations. Ethical responsibility is emphasized, particularly when findings may influence judicial outcomes. The expert's duty is to the court, not to either party, and conclusions must be expressed in accessible language (Tiersma and Solan 2012). From a speech-language pathology perspective, these principles intersect with concerns about communicative competence, vulnerability, and accessibility. Individuals with language disorders, limited literacy, or second-language status may be disadvantaged in legal settings. Integrating linguistic and clinical insight supports fairer procedures (Kniffka 2007).Overall, the forensic linguist serves as a bridge between linguistic science and the justice system, ensuring that language is interpreted accurately, fairly, and contextually. SLP's contribution supports transparency, reduces miscommunication, and helps prevent miscarriages of justice.

3.2 Historical Perspective and Evolution of Forensic Linguistics in the Courtroom

3.2.1 Development of the Discipline Since the Mid-twentieth Century

The development of forensic linguistics as a recognized discipline is relatively recent, although language has always played a central role in legal processes. Early legal systems relied heavily on oral testimony, written documents, and formalized language, yet systematic linguistic analysis was largely absent. It was only in the latter half of the twentieth century that linguistics began to be formally applied to legal problems (Svartvik 1968). The emergence of forensic linguistics is closely associated with scholars who demonstrated how linguistic expertise could clarify legal issues. Early cases involving disputed confessions, ambiguous legal language, and authorship attribution highlighted the need for trained linguists in the courtroom. Over time, courts began to recognize that linguistic analysis could provide insights comparable to other forensic sciences (Levi 1994).

3.2.2 Key Milestones: Recorded Interviews and Authorship Analysis

One major turning point was the increasing use of recorded police interviews and written confessions. Linguists revealed how coercive questioning techniques, leading questions, and pragmatic misunderstandings could result in false confessions (Shuy 2006). These findings challenged traditional assumptions about the reliability of verbal evidence.

Another historical development was the analysis of authorship and speaker identification. Linguistic features such as vocabulary choice, syntax, spelling patterns, and discourse structure were shown to reveal individual variation. This led to the acceptance of linguistic evidence in cases involving anonymous letters, threats, and digital communication.

In more recent decades, forensic linguistics has expanded to address issues such as courtroom discourse, jury instructions, legal translation and interpretation, and the rights of vulnerable populations. The discipline has also adapted to technological advances, including text messaging and online communication. Today, forensic linguistics is increasingly recognized as a valuable support discipline within the legal system. Its historical development reflects a growing awareness that justice depends not only on facts but also on how language is used, interpreted, and understood.

3.3 Linguistic Frameworks: Components of Language—Form, Content, and Use

3.3.1 Language Form: Structure, Phonology, and Syntax

Form, content, and use of language (components of language) explores how language operates within legal contexts through systematic, ethical, and scientifically grounded analysis. In forensic linguistics, language is not treated as an abstract system but as real-world data produced by individuals in high-stakes situations. Language can be understood through three interconnected components: form, content, and use (Bloom and Lahey 1978). These components are particularly important in forensic contexts, where subtle differences in language may carry legal significance. Form refers to the structural aspects of language, including phonology, morphology, and syntax. In forensic analysis, form may be examined to identify speaker characteristics, dialectal features, or grammatical patterns. For example, sentence structure and pronunciation may provide clues about a speaker's regional background or level of education.

3.3.2 Language Content: Semantics and Legal Homonyms

Content relates to semantics or meaning. In legal settings, meaning must be interpreted with extreme care, as legal consequences often depend on how words and phrases are understood (Crystal 2018). Ambiguity, polysemy, and legal homonyms can lead to misunderstanding. Forensic linguists analyze content to determine what was said, what was meant, and how meaning may shift across contexts.

3.3.3 Language Use: Pragmatics and Social Interaction

Use refers to pragmatics, or how language is used in social interaction. This includes speech acts, conversational implicatures, turn-taking, and politeness strategies (Levinson 1983). Pragmatics is especially relevant in analyzing threats, confessions, consent, and interrogation practices. What appears to be a simple question may function as a command, depending on context and power relationships. For speech-language pathologists, understanding these components is essential when evaluating individuals involved in legal proceedings. Communication disorders may affect form, content, or use, leading to misinterpretation. A forensic approach to language recognizes that all three components interact and must be considered together to ensure fair and accurate legal interpretation.

3.3.4 Language as Evidence vs. Physical Evidence (DNA)

Unlike static physical evidence like DNA, linguistic evidence is interpretive and context dependent. Specialized analysis is required to ensure nuances are not misinterpreted, helping the court distinguish between genuine threats and frustrated remarks. While DNA provides a statistical rarity of one in millions, ill-defined language can erroneously lead a jury to view forensic findings as a definitive statement of identity rather than a correspondence. Linguistic evidence is highly variable, shifting across different audiences, situations, and emotional states, which makes its conclusions probabilistic rather than absolute. Because words are dynamic, they require the deconstruction of the surrounding situation and the speaker's intent to reveal the "linguistic friction" that physical evidence lacks. Ultimately, treating the written or spoken word with the same scientific scrutiny as DNA ensures a more accurate and equitable path to justice.

3.4 Individual Variation in Pragmatics (Authorship Attribution)

3.4.1 The Idiolect and Unique Habitual Patterns

Individual variation in language use serves as the cornerstone of authorship attribution within the field of forensic linguistics (Finegan 2014). While speakers of the same language share a common foundation of grammatical rules, every person develops unique, habitual patterns of language use. This concept is often referred to as a linguistic fingerprint. These habits are most visible at the pragmatic level, which involves how we use language to achieve specific goals or navigate social interactions. Because these patterns are deeply ingrained, they provide a stable basis for identifying a writer's identity. Pragmatic variation includes a wide range of personal preferences. These may include a person's favorite expressions, their use of discourse markers like actually or basically, and their specific strategies for showing politeness. It also involves how an individual chooses to structure information within a paragraph or an argument. Most of these features are entirely unconscious. Because they are not part of our active focus when writing, they are incredibly difficult to disguise or change consistently over a long period. In a legal case involving authorship attribution, a forensic linguist carefully compares a questioned text such as an anonymous threat with known samples from a suspect. The goal is to assess the likelihood that the same person produced both sets of writing.

Contrary to what is often shown in popular media, authorship attribution is never based on a single smoking gun feature. It is not about one specific word or a single typo. Instead, the process relies on a complex combination of linguistic cues. Experts look at lexical choices, which refers to the specific vocabulary a person uses. They also analyze sentence complexity, such as a preference for short, punchy sentences versus long, winding ones. Punctuation habits, like the frequent use of semicolons or a specific way of using ellipses, also play a major role (Kredens

2002). By layering these pragmatic conventions together, the linguist builds a profile. However, this analysis is always probabilistic rather than absolute. It acknowledges that language is a human behavior, not a fixed physical science, and respects the limits of linguistic evidence.

3.4.2 Digital Fingerprints: Emojis, Abbreviations, and Messaging

In the modern world, digital communication has made pragmatic variation even more noticeable. The way we text or email provides a wealth of data for forensic analysis. Choices regarding abbreviations, the frequency of certain emojis, and variations in spelling can reflect deeply rooted individual habits. Even the physical structure of a message such as whether a person sends one long paragraph or several short burst messages can be a distinguishing trait. These digital habits are particularly useful when trying to tell the difference between a genuine message and one created by an impersonator. An impersonator might get the facts right, but they often fail to mimic the subtle pragmatic rhythm of the person they are trying to copy.

3.4.3 Identifying Individual vs. Borrowed Text (Plagiarism and Fraud)

Distinguishing between individual and borrowed text is an important task in forensic linguistics, particularly in cases involving plagiarism, fraud, or disputed authorship. Individual text reflects an author's unique linguistic habits, while borrowed text originates from external sources. The critical challenge of distinguishing between individual and borrowed text requires a deep understanding of how human beings naturally communicate versus how they mimic others. In the field of forensic linguistics, this distinction serves as the backbone for resolving high-stakes legal disputes, particularly in cases of plagiarism where creative property is stolen, or fraud where documents are manipulated for deceptive gains.

At the heart of this investigation is the reality that individual text serves as a mirror for an author's unique linguistic habits, reflecting a personal style that is almost impossible to fully hide. On the other hand, borrowed text stands out because it originates from external sources, often creating "linguistic friction" where the tone, complexity, or vocabulary suddenly shifts away from the writer's natural voice.

When experts tackle cases of disputed authorship, they don't just look for surface-level similarities; they dig into the underlying patterns and the frequency with which a person uses certain expressions. By mapping the distribution of features across various documents, analysts can see if a writer's "vocal fingerprint" remains steady or if it has been artificially patched together. Borrowed text may be copied verbatim, paraphrased, or subtly modified. Forensic linguists examine patterns of consistency and inconsistency within a document to identify sections that diverge from an author's typical style. Sudden changes in vocabulary, syntax, or tone may indicate borrowing.

3.4.4 Distinguishing Personal Identity from Social/ Regional Background

To ensure scientific accuracy, the process of forensic linguistic analysis moves beyond simple similarity by recognizing that different individuals often share common linguistic features due to shared social or regional backgrounds. Rather than looking for mere resemblances, experts identify unique identities by examining patterns that reveal a writer's habitual tendencies and measuring the frequency of specific markers to determine if they are statistically significant. This data is further strengthened by analyzing the distribution of features across multiple samples to see if these habits remain constant over time.

Furthermore, the analysis must account for various contextual factors that might alter a person's natural style, such as the specific genre of the writing, which dictates formal or informal rules, and the overall purpose of the message that influences the tone and vocabulary used. By linking these analytical methods, forensic experts can distinguish between coincidental overlaps and a truly unique individual style.

In both academic and legal environments, the ability to separate a person's original voice from borrowed content carries significant ethical and legal implications. Forensic linguistics offers a rigorous scientific approach to settle these disputes by using systematic methods based on measurable data, ensuring that conclusions are rooted in linguistic theory rather than subjective judgment. When looking at this through educational and clinical perspectives, it becomes clear that communication is not a one-size-fits-all process. It is vital to acknowledge that language proficiency and writing skills vary wildly depending on a person's background and experience. Analysts must engage in careful interpretation to avoid unfair conclusions, especially when working with second-language users or individuals with communication difficulties whose unique speech patterns might be misinterpreted.

From the perspective of a speech-language pathologist (SLP), it is vital to remember that pragmatic abilities are not uniform. These skills vary greatly across individuals due to developmental, cognitive, or neurological factors. For example, a person on the autism spectrum or someone who has survived a stroke may have very different pragmatic patterns than a neurotypical individual. In a forensic context, these variations must be interpreted with extreme caution. An investigator who does not understand these underlying clinical factors might mistake a symptom of a communication disorder for a sign of guilt or deception. Ultimately, authorship attribution shows how our individuality is woven into every sentence we write. It demonstrates that language can serve as powerful evidence in a court of law (Coulthard 2004). However, because language is so personal and complex, this field also emphasizes the need for a cautious and ethical approach. By balancing linguistic science with an understanding of human diversity, experts can ensure that

Because words can shift in meaning based on where, when, and how they are used, they require specialized analysis to ensure that the subtle nuances of human communication are not overlooked or misinterpreted by the courts.

3.6.2 Pragmatic Context and Message Interpretation

This specialized field covers a wide array of materials, including high-stakes threats, formal confessions, complex legal contracts, and the vast world of digital messages. In many cases, the literal words on the page are only half the story. The true meaning of such evidence often hinges on pragmatic context, which is the specific situation that surrounds the conversation, as well as the speaker's actual intent and how a listener might reasonably interpret the message (Haworth 2006). Forensic linguists act as essential translators in these scenarios, working to clarify the hidden dimensions of a conversation. By looking past the surface level of the text, they help the legal system understand the difference between a genuine threat and a frustrated remark, or a voluntary admission of guilt and a coerced statement. This careful deconstruction of language ensures that the complexities of human interaction are handled with scientific accuracy and fairness (Heydon 2005).

3.6.3 Challenges in Reliability and Legal Outcomes

One challenge in using language as evidence is variability. Language changes across situations, audiences, and emotional states. Therefore, forensic conclusions are typically probabilistic rather than definitive. Despite these challenges, linguistic evidence plays a crucial role in modern legal systems. Clear analysis can reveal coercion, deception, or misunderstanding, contributing to fairer outcomes. For speech-language pathologists, language as evidence highlights the importance of communication competence and accessibility within legal processes. Linguistic investigation provides an objective framework for understanding how language functions as evidence (Fraser 2003).

3.7 Uniqueness in Text Messaging

3.7.1 Distinctive Patterns in Digital Communication

In the modern era, text messaging has evolved into a vital source of linguistic evidence that offers a window into an individual's private and social world. Despite the seemingly informal and spontaneous nature of digital chats, these messages display consistent individual patterns that contribute significantly to forensic analysis. Because texting is often less filtered than formal writing, it provides a more authentic representation of a person's natural communication style (Snow and Powell 2012). Uniqueness in digital communication is frequently observed through specific spelling variations and the unique way a person uses abbreviations or punctuation. These habits, alongside specific emoji preferences and the overall structure of a message, serve as digital fingerprints that reflect both personal habits and deeply rooted social identity (LaVigne and Van Rybroek 2011). When an analyst looks at these features, they are seeing the subconscious choices a writer makes every time they hit send.

3.7.2 Interactional Dynamics and Temporal Factors

Forensic analysis of these messages extends beyond the words themselves to consider both linguistic and contextual factors. The timing of a message, the speed of response patterns, and the overall interactional style provide a narrative of how the individuals relate to one another. These elements help investigators understand the power dynamics or the level of intimacy within a conversation.

3.7.3 Social Conventions and Clinical Perspectives

However, experts must approach this data with a high degree of caution, as texting conventions evolve at an incredibly rapid pace and are constantly reshaped by social trends. A forensic linguist must be skilled enough to distinguish between a person's unique individual habits and shared conventions, slang or styles that are common to a specific generation or online community (Handy et al. 2020). From an educational and clinical perspective, text messaging offers a fascinating look into functional language use and pragmatic competence. For speech and language professionals, these digital interactions reinforce the relevance of texting in forensic contexts, as they demonstrate how effectively an individual can navigate social rules and convey intent in a real-world, fast-paced environment.

3.8 The SLP as Expert Witness

3.8.1 The SLP's Role in Determining Legal Competency

In the complex machinery of the modern courtroom, justice is often served through the medium of language. We operate under the fundamental assumption that every participant, whether a defendant, a witness, or a victim, can understand the gravity of what is being said and express their own truth with clarity. However, for many individuals, the legal system is a bewildering labyrinth of inaccessible jargon and high-pressure communication that they are simply not equipped to navigate. This is where the speech-language pathologist (SLP) steps in, transitioning from a clinical setting to the witness stand to serve as a vital bridge between human vulnerability and the rigid, often-unforgiving requirements of the law (Snow and Sanger 2011). When an SLP acts as an expert witness, they do much more than defining a medical condition; they are interpreting a person's ability to exist and function within a legal framework. Legal proceedings are notorious for their dense and confusing nature. For a neurotypical adult, the reading of Miranda rights or the intensity of a cross-examination can be intimidating. For a child, an elderly person with early-onset dementia, or an individual with a traumatic brain injury, these same situations can be entirely incomprehensible. The SLP's primary role in these moments is to determine competency. They ask the hard questions that the court might overlook: Can this person truly grasp the gravity of the oath they are taking? Do they understand the questions being fired at them, or are they simply nodding along to please an authority figure? By assessing language comprehension and pragmatic competence, the SLP ensures that the court does not mistake a disability for a lack of cooperation or, even worse, evidence of guilt.

3.8.2 Evaluation Processes and Interdisciplinary Collaboration

The core of an SLP's forensic work lies in a meticulous evaluation process that looks far beyond the surface of mere "talking." They examine the underlying cognitive processes that allow a human being to process and produce information (Gupta et al. 2019). This involves a deep dive into expressive language evaluating if an individual can narrate events chronologically and accurately and receptive language, which tests whether a person can understand complex "if-then" sentences or specialized legal terminology. Furthermore, they evaluate pragmatic competence, which is the ability to understand social cues, sarcasm, or the subtle nuances of a lawyer's tone. Once these findings are gathered, the SLP must perform a secondary, equally difficult task of translation. A judge or jury doesn't need a lecture in phonology or syntax; they need to understand how a specific communication barrier affects the case at hand (Snow 2019). The SLP must explain these clinical limitations in a way that is accessible, objective, and grounded in evidence. In this high-stakes environment, their professional ethics are their most valuable currency. They are not there to "win" a case for one side but to provide an unbiased clinical lens that ensures the person's communication profile is accurately understood. Justice is rarely a solo endeavor, and one of the most significant developments in modern forensics is the partnership between SLPs and forensic linguists (Danielewicz-Betz 2012). While these two roles might seem overlapping, they offer different, essential pieces of the puzzle. A forensic linguist might analyze a ransom note or a recorded confession to look at dialect, word choice, and specific grammar patterns. In contrast, the SLP provides the necessary insight into the biological and cognitive capacity of the person who produced that speech. When these two disciplines collaborate, they create a 360-degree view of the evidence. The linguist tells the court what was said and how it was structured, while the SLP explains why it might have been said that way based on the speaker's neurological profile. This synergy is a powerful tool for dismantling the communication barriers that lead to wrongful convictions or the silencing of victims (Snow and Powell 2008).

3.8.3 Statistical Fallacies and Linguistic Reporting in Case Law

Ultimately, the presence of a speech-language pathologist in the legal realm is a testament to the idea that the law should be accessible to everyone, regardless of their communicative ability. By protecting the voices of those who struggle to speak for themselves, SLPs do more than just provide expert testimony; they safeguard the integrity of the judicial process itself. They remind us that for justice to be truly blind, it must first be willing to listen to every voice, no matter how quiet or unconventional is it (Brennan 1999). The critical importance of this precision is further illuminated by legal cases where the failure to maintain clear linguistic and statistical boundaries led to significant judicial challenges.

In the US Supreme Court case of McDaniel v. Brown (2010), the forensic investigation centered on DNA evidence recovered from a victim's clothing that matched the profile of the defendant. During the trial, a criminalist reported the frequency of this specific DNA profile as one in three million; however, a significant linguistic error occurred when the prosecutor and the expert witness converted this frequency into a "source probability." They erroneously claimed there was a 99.999967% likelihood that the DNA in the evidence belonged to the defendant, a transposition known as the "prosecutor's fallacy." This case highlights how ill-defined language can mislead a jury into believing forensic evidence is a definitive statement of identity rather than a statistical rarity. Similarly, in Griffith v. State (1998), the investigation involved a DNA match used to support a charge of sexual assault against a patient in a psychiatric hospital. The forensic expert used a "paternity index" and assumed a "neutral" 0.5 prior probability to conclude that the probability of paternity was greater than 99.99%. The defense argued that this approach attempted to legitimate an "inverse fallacy" by turning a likelihood ratio into a posterior odds ratio through an arbitrary assumption not based on the actual evidence. The court's defense of this method underscored a widespread confusion between percentages and probabilities, demonstrating that without standardized linguistic reporting, forensic findings can be misinterpreted as definitive proof of an act rather than a scientific correspondence.

3.9 Forensic Investigation of Text

3.9.1 Foundations of Forensic Text Analysis

In the intersection of law and linguistics, the forensic investigation of text serves as a sophisticated tool. It uncovers truth within written communication through a scientific lens. This field does not rely on simple intuition. Instead, it uses a systematic examination of written language to answer critical legal questions (Boenninghoff et al. 2019). These cases often involve identifying the anonymous author of a harassing email. They might also involve assessing the true danger in a written threat or finding signs of fabrication in a statement. Forensic text analysis provides a structured way to interpret human expression. It is a deep dive into the unique "linguistic fingerprint" that every writer leaves behind (Grant 2013).

3.9.2 Data Collection and Feature Comparison

The process begins long before any words are analyzed. It starts with careful data collection and a thorough look at the context. For an investigator, the environment of the text is just as vital as the words themselves. They must consider the platform used and the intended audience. Once the data is secured, the investigator identifies and compares linguistic features. This might include looking at unique spelling habits or specific word choices and also examine the way a person structures their sentences (Kelcher 2021). By comparing a questioned text against a known sample, the investigator finds patterns that others might miss.

3.9.3 Scientific Rigor and Legal Scrutiny

What sets this work apart is its focus on rigor and transparency. These findings often serve as key evidence in court. Therefore, they cannot be based on mere opinion. Every conclusion is framed using probability. This acknowledges that language is a fluid human behavior. Every claim must be backed by a clear trail of evidence, and this scientific approach ensures the analysis is reproducible (Etaywe 2024). It must be able to withstand intense scrutiny from a legal defense. The goal is to offer a measured assessment of the facts based on hard data. This disciplined approach highlights the scientific nature of forensic linguistics. It shows how the field contributes to a fair justice system. For speech-language pathologists, this work shows the value of language analysis outside of a clinic. The same tools used to treat communication disorders are useful in the legal world. Analyzing syntax and semantics can help protect public safety. By bridging the gap between clinical expertise and the law, text investigation ensures the written word is treated with care. It treats language with the same level of scrutiny as DNA or physical evidence. This ultimately leads to a more accurate and equitable path to justice.

3.10 Conclusion

At present, forensic linguistics has changed the way the legal system looks at words. Instead of just guessing what someone meant, we now use science to look for a "linguistic fingerprint." This has helped solve cases by proving who wrote a certain text or showing when a police confession was actually forced. One of the best things happening today is how linguists work with speech therapists. This ensures that someone with a brain injury or a speaking disorder isn't seen as "guilty" just because they talk differently. It's about making the law more fair and human.

Looking ahead, the future of this field will be all about technology. With AI like ChatGPT becoming common, forensic linguists will be the ones to figure out if a message was written by a real person or a computer. We will also start looking closer at how we use emojis and how fast we text to help identify people. As more people move around the world, the field will also need to get better at helping people who don't speak the local language well. In the end, the goal of forensic linguistics will stay the same: making sure every voice is heard correctly and that technology never gets in the way of the truth.

References

Bloom L, Lahey M (1978) Language development and language disorders. Wiley

Boenninghoff B, Hessler S, Kolossa D, Nickel RM (2019) Explainable authorship verification in social media via attention-based similarity learning

Brennan M (1999) The discourse of denial: cross-examining child victim witnesses. Open University Press. (Explores the SLP's role in safeguarding the integrity of the judicial process by protecting the voices of those who struggle to speak)

Chaski CE (2001) Empirical assessments of authorship. Forensic Linguistics 8(1)

Coulthard M (2004) Author identification and idiolect. Appl Linguis 25(4)

Coulthard M, Johnson A (2007) An introduction to forensic linguistics. Routledge

Crystal D (2018) How language works. Overlook Press

Danielewicz-Betz A (2012) Language and the law: global perspectives in forensic linguistics. City University of Hong Kong Press. (Specifically addresses the multidisciplinary partnership between clinical speech experts and linguists)

Etaywe A (2024) Unmasking malicious stance indicators and attitudinal priming: an 'evaluative textbite' approach to identity attacks in violent extremist discourse. Corpus Pragmat 8(3):359–390. https://doi.org/10.1007/s41701-024-00172-3

Finegan E (2014) Language: its structure and use. Cengage Learning

Fraser H (2003) Issues in Transcription. Forensic Linguistics 10(2)

Gibbons J (2003) Forensic linguistics: an introduction, Blackwell

Grant T (2010) Text messaging forensics. Int J Speech Lang Law

Grant T (2013) TXT 4N6: method, consistency, and distinctiveness in the analysis of SMS text messages. J Law Policy 21(2):467–508

Grieve J (2007) Quantitative authorship attribution. Literary Linguistic Comput

Griffith, State (1998) 976 S.W.2d 241

Gupta SK, Venkatesan S, Goswami SP, Kumar R (eds) (2019) Emerging trends in the diagnosis and intervention of neurodevelopmental disorders. IGI Global (This source discusses the neurocognitive markers and underlying processes of language production and processing essential for forensic evaluation)

Handy L et al (2020) SLPs in the justice system. J Law Med

Haworth K (2006) The dynamics of the police interview. J Pragmat

Heydon G (2005) The language of police interviewing. Palgrave Macmillan

Juola P (2008) Authorship attribution. Found Trends Inf Retr

Kelcher, F. J. (2021). Imitation and anonymity in linguistic identity disguise

Kniffka H (2007) Working in forensic linguistics. Peter Lang

Kredens K (2002) The concept of idiolect. Int. J Speech Lang Law

LaVigne M, Van Rybroek GJ (2011) Breakdown in the language zone. UC Davis J

Levi JN (1994) Language as evidence. Forensic Linguist 1(1):1–26

Levinson SC (1983) Pragmatics. Cambridge University Press

McDaniel, Brown (2010) 558 U.S. 120 (2010). https://supreme.justia.com/cases/federal/us/558/120/
McMenamin GR (2002) Forensic linguistics: advances in forensic stylistics. CRC Press
Olsson J (2008) Forensic linguistics. Bloomsbury Academic
Shuy RW (2006) Linguistics in the courtroom. Oxford University Press
Snow PC (2019) Speech-language pathology and the youth justice system: 21st-century challenges. Journal of clinical practice in speech-language. Pathology 21(1):31–36. (Focuses on translating complex phonological/syntactic data into actionable insights for legal professionals)
Snow PC, Powell MB (2008) Oral language competence, social skills and behaviour problems in vulnerable young people. Oral Language Competence and Outcome 10:18–24. (Discusses using linguistic synergy to prevent the "silencing" of communicatively vulnerable individuals)
Snow PC, Powell MB (2012) Youth justice and communication. ACQuiring Knowledge
Snow PC, Sanger DD (2011) Restorative justice conferences: the importance of speech, language, and communication. J Forensic Pract 13(2):101–109
Svartvik J (1968) The Evans statements: a case for forensic linguistics. Gothenburg
Tiersma PM, Solan LM (2012) The Oxford handbook of language and law, Oxford
Zheng R et al (2006) Authorship analysis of online messages. JASIST

4 Instrumentation for Forensic Voice Analysis

Vishwadeep Singh and Vijay Kumar

Abstract

Forensic speech analysis involves the scientific examination of speech recordings to assist legal investigations, commonly through speaker identification, authentication, and acoustic comparison. With technological advancement, software-based analysis has become a cornerstone of forensic phonetics, enabling precise measurement of acoustic parameters such as fundamental frequency, formants, pitch, jitter, shimmer, and voice quality indices. This chapter explores the evolution, types, applications, and challenges of forensic speech analysis software. It outlines the historical development of speech analysis tools, reviews widely used software systems, and explains their role in court-admissible forensic investigations. The chapter further discusses the reliability, validity, and standards required for legal acceptance, along with the difficulties posed by poor audio quality, linguistic diversity, and ethical considerations. Finally, it highlights emerging opportunities including artificial intelligence, machine-learning-based speaker recognition, and multilingual forensic datasets. The content aims to guide students, researchers, and forensic practitioners in understanding both the scientific and technological frameworks of speech analysis tools and the future directions in forensic voice technology.

Keywords

Acoustic analysis · Forensic phonetics · Forensic speech analysis · Speaker identification · Voice authentication

---

V. Singh · V. Kumar (✉)
Department of Audiology and Speech-Language Pathology, Amity Medical School, Amity University Haryana, Gurgaon, Haryana, India
e-mail: vkumar@ggn.amity.edu

V. Kumar et al. (eds.), *Forensic Speech Sciences*, New Horizons in Forensic Science, https://doi.org/10.1007/978-981-92-1475-4_4

4.1 Introduction

Speech is an acoustic signal generated by the coordinated action of the respiratory system, larynx, and articulators, such as the tongue, lips, and jaw, to produce audible language (Tiwari 2012). Speech is a complex human behavior comprising phonetic, articulatory, and acoustic components. In forensic contexts, speech becomes evidence used to identify speakers, authenticate recordings, or evaluate disputed utterances. Forensic speech analysis is an interdisciplinary field combining phonetics, acoustics, linguistics, and technology. This chapter introduces key concepts, explains why software analysis is essential, and sets the foundation for modern forensic practices.

Fundamental frequency (F0) represents the vibration rate of the vocal folds, determining pitch perception in voiced sounds. Formants (F1–F3) are resonant frequencies of the vocal tract that shape vowel quality and timbre. Intensity measures amplitude variations linked to loudness, while temporal features like duration and rhythm capture timing, pauses, and speech rate. Speech signals also fluctuate due to intrinsic factors like age, emotion, and health conditions (e.g., neurogenic disorders in Parkinson's), as well as extrinsic ones such as language dialect, recording environment noise, or deliberate alterations like disguise (Drygajlo et al. 2015).

This method involves extracting and comparing phonetic features such as vowels, consonants, and prosody between a questioned speech sample and a known reference using auditory and instrumental analysis. Experts identify segmental (e.g., formant patterns) and suprasegmental (e.g., intonation) traits to assess similarity, often quantifying differences via metrics like F0 range or formant dispersion (Eriksson 2005). Spectrograms visualize frequency, intensity, and time domains of speech, enabling detailed examination of patterns like formant trajectories, frication noise, or voice onset time. Forensic examiners overlay questioned and suspect spectrograms to detect matches or discrepancies in unique speaker traits, such as laryngeal mechanisms or articulation habits.

Trained phoneticians provide auditory evaluations of voice quality, accent, and idiosyncrasies, calibrated against known samples to form subjective similarity scores. This complements instrumental methods but requires validation to minimize bias, often integrated into a holistic case assessment. Quantitative models also compute likelihood ratios (LR) by modeling feature distributions under same-source (H1) versus different-source (H2) hypotheses, using techniques like Gaussian mixture models on F0, formants, and spectral coefficients. Background data from speaker corpora calibrate LR values, providing probabilistic strength of evidence for judicial use while accounting for variability.

Speech is an acoustic signal generated by coordinated actions of the respiratory system, larynx, and supra-laryngeal articulators like the tongue, lips, and jaw. This process follows the source-filter theory, where pulmonic airflow powers vocal fold vibration (source) filtered by the vocal tract to produce distinct sounds.

1. **Fundamental Frequency (F0):** Fundamental frequency (F0), or pitch, arises from periodic vocal fold vibrations during voiced speech, typically ranging 80–250 Hz for adults. It determines perceived pitch height and conveys prosody, intonation, emotion, and speaker identity, with harmonics at integer multiples of F0 enriching the spectrum (Tiwari 2012).
2. **Formants (F1–F3):** Formants F1, F2, and F3 represent resonant frequencies of the vocal tract filter, shaped by articulator positions, with F1 around 500–800 Hz for vowel height and F2 (800–2500 Hz) for front-back placement. These lower formants dominate vowel timbre; F1 rises with jaw opening, F2 shifts with tongue advancement.
3. **Intensity:** Intensity measures signal amplitude or loudness, reflecting subglottal pressure and glottal flow, varying 40–70 dB in speech. It modulates stress, emphasis, and phonation type, with higher values in loud speech due to increased airflow and radiation efficiency.
4. **Temporal Features:** Temporal features encompass duration (segment/syllable length), rhythm (beat patterning), and timing like voice onset time. Longer durations signal stress or vowels, while rhythm—alternating stressed-unstressed syllables—defines prosodic languages; disruptions indicate disorders. These features underpin speaking rate (3–6 syllables/sec) and fluency.

Speech varies across multiple intrinsic and extrinsic factors, impacting its acoustic and phonetic properties in forensic analysis (Paver 2020).

1. **Age Effects:** Aging alters vocal fold elasticity and vocal tract dimensions, lowering fundamental frequency (F0) and formant frequencies over time, with more pronounced changes after age 50. Children exhibit higher F0 and formants due to smaller larynges, while elderly speakers show slower speaking rates and reduced intensity.
2. **Emotional Influences:** Emotions modify prosody: anger raises F0 and intensity, fear shortens durations and increases variability, and sadness lowers pitch and slows rhythm. These shifts challenge speaker matching, as stress-induced changes mimic disguises in forensic recordings.
3. **Health Conditions:** Health issues like colds, fatigue, or neurological disorders (e.g., Parkinson's) disrupt phonation, raising jitter, shimmer, or altering formants via swollen tissues or weakened musculature. Intoxication slurs speech, prolonging durations and reducing F0 control.
4. **Language and Dialect:** Language-specific phoneme inventories, intonation patterns, and rhythms create inter-speaker variability; dialectal accents shift formants and temporal features. Code-switching adds intra-speaker variation in multilingual contexts.
5. **Recording Conditions:** Noise, reverberation, channel distortion (e.g., telephone bandwidth limits), and distance degrade signals, compressing formants and masking F0 harmonics. Poor quality amplifies extrinsic mismatches between suspect and crime-scene samples (Cenceschi et al. 2021).
6. **Intentional Disguise:** Speakers falsetto-shift F0, whisper to eliminate periodicity, or alter articulation to warp formants and rhythm, complicating comparison

but often revealing inconsistent "vocal signatures" in transitions. Forensic experts target dynamic features less affected by short-term disguise.

Forensic speech analysis follows established scientific principles to compare questioned speech samples against known references, evaluating evidence strength via the likelihood ratio (LR) framework under propositions like same-speaker (H1) versus different-speaker (H2). This integrates multiple methods to account for speech variability from factors like age, disguise, or recording conditions discussed previously.

4.1.1 Acoustic-Phonetic Comparison

Acoustic-phonetic comparison extracts segmental (e.g., vowel formants F1-F3, consonants) and suprasegmental features (e.g., F0, intensity) from both samples, quantifying similarities in phonetic realization and prosody. Experts segment speech, measure parameters like formant trajectories, and assess typicality against population norms, often combining auditory validation for robust LR computation.

Background noise can affect the accuracy of these analyses. Noise cancellation techniques improve the quality of voice samples, making it easier for forensic experts to identify and profile speakers. Using software like PRAAT, analysts can focus on various features such as vowel duration, pitch, dialect, and voice quality to enhance the reliability of voice evidence. This study shows that noise cancellation methods significantly improve the precision of voice identification in forensic science (Kersta 1962).

4.1.2 Spectrographic Analysis

Spectrographic analysis visualizes frequency, intensity, and time via spectrograms, overlaying tracings of matching words/phrases from questioned and suspect samples to compare patterns like formant bands or fricative noise. It highlights idiosyncrasies in voice quality or articulation but requires phonetic transcription for interpretation, historically termed "voiceprint" despite not being unique fingerprints. The "spectrographic identification" method of voice identification is based on visually comparing spectrograms of words or phrases that occur in both the questioned-speaker recordings and known-speaker recordings. The practitioner visually compares the questioned-speaker recordings and known-speaker recordings in search of similarities in voice spectrograms that they would expect if the two recordings were produced by the same speaker but not if they were produced by different speakers and in search of differences in voice spectrograms that they would expect if the two recordings were produced by different speakers but not if they were produced by the same speaker.

The basis for the use of spectrograms in speaker identification in forensic settings is derived from the work of Lawrence Kersta and Oscar Tosi (Tosi et al. 1972). Interestingly, Kersta, (Kersta 1962) who was the first person to testify as a voice identification "expert" in 1966, did not utilize aural comparisons in his work and, incorrectly, claimed that the accuracy of voiceprints was comparable to that of fingerprints. In the forensic setting, spectrographic identification is different from fingerprint identification. This is because, in spectrographic identification, comparisons of spectrograms involve finding sufficient similarities, while fingerprints always have exactly the same pattern (Jain et al. 2024). The individual differences in the spectrograms, caused by intra-speaker variation, make it the examiners task to subjectively determine if a match exists (Mnesota Law Review Editorial Board 1972).

4.1.3 Perceptual Judgment

Perceptual (aural) judgement relies on trained experts' listening to detect holistic voice traits like timbre, accent, or speaking style, integrated within the auditory-acoustic framework (AAF). Multiple sessions reduce bias, with findings calibrated qualitatively or scored for LR, emphasizing long-term features resistant to disguise. The forensic practitioner noted auditory perceptual similarities between the pronunciation of particular Swedish vowel and consonant sounds and particular words in the questioned-speaker recordings and in the known-speaker recordings. He also noted: similar use of filler words and of a grammatically incorrect phrase; similarities in tempo and intonation; and that the voices were somewhat nasal and had a raised laryngeal setting that the speakers mixed languages (a phenomenon known as code switching) but also that this was relatively common for the relevant population.

4.1.4 Statistical Evaluation

Statistical evaluation computes LR as the ratio of evidence probabilities under H1 versus H2, using models like Gaussian Mixture Models (GMM) or Multivariate Kernel Density (MVKD) on acoustic features. Databases calibrate typicality, providing verbal scales (e.g., "strong support") for court, with validation ensuring error rates below admissibility thresholds.

4.1.5 Computer-Based Analysis

Computer-based analysis of speech employs specialized software to process forensic audio objectively, enhancing precision in speaker comparison amid inherent human variability. Software proves essential by automating feature extraction, reducing subjectivity, and handling noisy or degraded recordings beyond manual limits.

4.1.6 Why Essential

Software handles vast data volumes, applies signal processing for enhancement (e.g., denoising, normalization), and computes statistical likelihood ratios (LRs) reproducibly. It mitigates perceptual biases in experts, supports large reference databases for typicality assessment, and integrates automatic speaker recognition (ASR) for triage in high-volume cases.

1. **Acoustic Domain:** Acoustic analysis extracts parameters like fundamental frequency (F0), formants (F1-F3 via LPC), intensity, jitter, and shimmer using tools like Praat or Wavesurfer. Software models long-term distributions (e.g., GMM-UBM) for voice quality and prosody, yielding LRs from cepstral coefficients or MFCCs.
2. **Phonetic Domain:** Phonetic analysis automates forced alignment for segmental features, compares vowel spaces or consonant spectra, and profiles linguistic traits like accent via n-gram models. Tools like ELAN or custom scripts in Praat quantify idiosyncratic realizations resistant to disguise.
3. **Spectrographic Domain:** Spectrogram generation software (Praat, spectrographic displays in Audacity) produces narrow–/wide-band views for formant tracking, overlay comparisons, and anomaly detection. Advanced versions apply dynamic time warping (DTW) to align tracings temporally, visualizing mismatches in forensic overlays.
4. **Workflow Steps:** The workflow begins with audio acquisition and enhancement (filtering, equalization), followed by transcription and segmentation. Feature extraction across domains feeds multivariate analysis and LR computation, ending in expert validation and reporting with visualizations.

Praat, Wavesurfer, VoiceSauce, iZotope RX, Adobe Audition, BATVOX, and SAS-SPA represent core software in forensic speech analysis, each addressing enhancement, measurement, visualization, or automated comparison. These tools integrate into workflows from preprocessing to likelihood ratio reporting, balancing open-source flexibility with commercial automation.

4.2 Software Tools Used in Forensic Voice Analysis

4.2.1 Praat

Praat provides comprehensive acoustic analysis, including pitch tracking, formant extraction (F1-F3 via LPC), intensity, jitter/shimmer, and customizable spectrograms through scripting. The study of forensic investigation of the speeches with the help of Praat is highly significant because, with the help of Praat, each kind of sound produced by AI or any other source can be differentiated based on similarities and differences. PRAAT software is also useful for detecting voice changers in telephonic calls and for examining threatening or anonymous speech. These findings have direct applications in judicial proceedings and law-enforcement agencies.

Praat offers a wide range of features, including spectrogram, pitch, intensity, formant, and voice break analysis; speech synthesis from pitch, formant, and intensity parameters; manipulation of pitch, formant, and duration; annotation capabilities; and scripting support for automating complex analytical tasks. Tosi et al. describes Praat as a software tool capable of comprehensive speech analysis, allowing comparison of sounds using built-in analytical criteria (Tosi et al. 1972). Its functions include spectrogram analysis, formant analysis, pitch analysis, jitter, shimmer, intensity analysis, and voice break detection, enabling the generation of high-quality visual representations of acoustic features.

In real-life forensic situations, the natural state of restlessness and the voice of a suspected criminal are often recorded during police interrogation and subsequently analyzed using Praat. The most important parameters in Praat are fundamental frequency (F0) and formant frequencies F1 and F2, which help recognize suspects. Sondhi et al. point out that pitch contours often show a considerable rise when individuals answer crime-related questions, indicating that pitch and formant frequencies are closely linked with stress. Praat has therefore become a versatile and widely accepted standard software in the scientific community for linguistic and forensic speech analysis. Using the Easy Align function within Praat, automatic speech segmentation can be achieved when text-aligned sentences are provided (Pleva et al. 2015). Praat plays an important role across multiple fields, including speech-language pathology, medicine, engineering, and linguistics, supporting professionals in day-to-day life. Seong discusses that in-depth analysis can be conducted using the Advanced menu of the Object Window (Seong 2022). In this window, spectrum analysis, formant analysis, pitch analysis, pulse analysis, and intensity analysis are available. These parameters are particularly valuable in clinical contexts, as with the quality measurements, diagnosis of the patient can also be fulfilled. Ko et al. report that time-frequency analysis software such as TF32, MDVP, and Praat often yield difference in results due to variations in their underlying algorithms, so before using a particulars analyzer, an analyst must have to take the knowledge of the specific software working (Ko et al. 2020).

Sultana investigated pronunciation of the same words, phrases, and sentences produced by two non-native speakers using Praat (Sultana 2023). The study shows that there is a difference in the speaking of both the teachers' speakers. The same word has been produced by different pronunciation or sound by the creation of several phonemes in the speech which they produced. With the help of Praat, the study observed many differences while they were using the same words in their speech.

Benus says that the crucial part of the analysis in Praat speech analysis is the notion of prominence (Beňuš 2021). Different words in the phrases stay with the comparison to the other words in that phrase, and what are the communicative meanings of this pattern highlight? The fundamental frequency is marked as for, and it corresponds with the rate of the vocal cords vibration. By varying the tension of vocal cords and muscles, vibrations are controlled. Boersma advocated the role of technology in the field of phonetics and phonology to enahnce the clinical investigation and research perspective (Boersma 2002). But in phonetics, the emotional state of the persons such as mood, tempo etc. can influence the speech parameters which could be identified using Praat software.

Albin describes that many researchers use R programming language to visualize the statistical modelling of the data about acoustic phonetics however, R's digital processing has a lot of limitations (Albin 2014). Nowadays, Praat has been designed to overcome the inefficiency of the R functions. Spectrographic analysis consists of getting a narrow-hand spectrogram from a digitalized voice sample by two independent observers. The final result of the acoustic parameters like shimmer, jitter, and harmonic to the noise ratios with the fundamental frequency was obtained. Barreda came up with the idea of fast-tracking formant implemented in Praat and gave the explanations in this way: FastTrack is a formant tracker implemented in Praat that attempts to automatically select the best analysis from a set of candidates (Barreda 2021). The best track is selected by modelling smooth formant contours across the entirety of the sound, providing the researcher with rich information about static and dynamic formant. The strength of this software encompasses free availability, phonetic precision validated in forensic AI voice detection, and batch processing for long-term formant stats; limitations include manual segmentation errors, no native LR calculation, and steep scripting demands. It is usable by phoneticians via intuitive GUI plus scripts and ideal for detailed profiling but requires training for novices..

A study done by Krishna and Bansal on the forensic analysis of AI-modulated threatening using Praat provides insights into the differences between human and Ai-modulated robotic voices, revealing significant alterations in various acoustic parameters due to AI modulation, with implications for forensic voice identification and authentication (Krishna and Bansal 2024). The study found that median and mean pitch values are significantly higher in robotic voices, indicating a shift toward higher frequencies and affecting the natural pitch characteristics of the original speaker. The standard deviation of pitch is slightly higher in robotic voices, contributing to a more mechanical sound. The compression of pitch range reduces the dynamic range of the voice, resulting in less expressiveness. The reduction in the number of pulses and periods in robotic voices reflects a simplified speech pattern, and the slight increase in the standard deviation of period suggests more irregularity in speech timing. The reduction in voice breaks indicates a smoother but less naturally interrupted speech pattern, while the increase in locally unvoiced frames contributes to the mechanical nature of the voice. The substantial increase in jitter indicates greater frequency instability, making the voice sound less smooth and more artificial.

Another study done by Atif et al., *A Phonetic Forensic Analysis of Imran Khan's Speeches*, published in *Kurdish Studies* (Vol. 12, No. 4, pp. 720–732), presents an empirical investigation into the effectiveness of acoustic analysis for distinguishing AI-generated speech from authentic human speech (Atif 2024). Using Praat software, the authors analyzed selected lexical items from two speeches attributed to Imran Khan, one generated using artificial intelligence and another delivered at the United Nations. Acoustic parameters including pitch, intensity, pulse characteristics, spectrogram patterns, and formant frequencies were systematically examined. The findings revealed consistent phonetic differences between the two speech types, with AI-generated speech exhibiting lower values across most acoustic features except intensity, which showed higher values compared to human speech. The study highlights Praat's forensic utility in detecting synthetic speech and underscores its relevance for applications in forensic linguistics, judicial proceedings, and law enforcement, particularly in the context of rising audio-visual manipulation technologies.

4.2.2 VoiceSauce

VoiceSauce (VS) is an easy-to-use analytical tool designed for researchers interested in extracting multiple voice quality measures from running speech. It is implemented in MATLAB and can operate either within the MATLAB environment or as a stand-alone program for personal computers. VoiceSauce processes directories of.wav files and automatically generates acoustic measurements for each audio file, making it suitable for large-scale forensic voice analysis.

A study conducted by Jessen et al. found that VoiceSauce-derived voice quality measures demonstrated limited speaker-discriminatory power in forensic telephone recordings. Among the evaluated parameters, Cepstral Peak Prominence (CPP) emerged as the most distinguishing voice quality measure; however, its performance was inferior to that of formant frequencies. Furthermore, neither hand-corrected inputs nor multivariate fusion techniques improved speaker discrimination, as reflected in Equal Error Rate (EER) and log-likelihood ratio cost (Cllr) results. Similarly, Hughes et al. employed VoiceSauce to extract long-term laryngeal voice quality measures, including fundamental frequency (F0), CPP, Harmonic-to-Noise Ratio (HNR), and spectral tilt, from vowel-only speech under both studio and telephone recording conditions to evaluate their speaker-discriminatory value. Likelihood ratio testing revealed promising speaker discrimination in high-quality studio recordings but substantially reduced performance in telephone speech. Fusion of VoiceSauce measures with Mel-Frequency Cepstral Coefficients (MFCCs) produced inconsistent improvements, indicating that VoiceSauce-derived parameters contribute to speaker discrimination only under specific recording conditions. One of the critical measurements produced by VoiceSauce is the fundamental frequency (F0), which is used to estimate harmonic locations. VoiceSauce can extract F0 using three different algorithms, STRAIGHT, the Snack Sound Toolkit, or Praat, which offers both autocorrelation and cross-correlation methods. By default, VoiceSauce employs the STRAIGHT algorithm to estimate F0 at 1 ms intervals. All F0 detection methods require user-defined minimum and maximum F0 values to constrain estimation accuracy. Harmonic spectral magnitudes in VoiceSauce are computed pitch-synchronously, typically over a three-cycle window, although larger windows may be used in certain cases. This pitch-synchronous approach reduces variability compared to fixed-window spectral analysis. Harmonic magnitudes are identified using a maximum search algorithm centered around harmonic locations estimated from F0, with the total search range set to 10% of the estimated F0 value. This approach provides high spectral resolution without the need for large Fast Fourier Transform (FFT) calculations.

For formant estimation, VoiceSauce uses the Snack Sound Toolkit by default to extract the frequencies and bandwidths of the first four formants, employing the covariance method with a pre-emphasis value of 0.96, a window length of 25 ms, and a frame shift of 1 ms to match STRAIGHT processing. Alternatively, Praat's Burg algorithm can be used to estimate formants over entire files, with user-defined parameter settings. Previous work by Hanson and Iseli et al. introduced algorithms for estimating voice source parameters such as H1*–H2* and H1*–A3*, where the asterisk indicates correction for formant frequencies and bandwidths. In VoiceSauce, harmonic amplitudes for all spectral magnitude measures can be corrected on a frame-by-frame basis using measured formant frequencies and estimated bandwidths. Corrected measures are labeled with "c," while uncorrected measures are labeled with "u." For H1*–H2*, only F1 and F2 are used for correction, whereas F1 through F3 are used for H1*–A3*. These measures are further smoothed using a moving average filter with a default length of 20 samples.

VoiceSauce also computes the Subharmonic-to-Harmonic Ratio (SHR), a measure proposed by Sun that quantifies the amplitude ratio between subharmonics and harmonics. SHR is particularly useful for characterizing speech with alternating pulse cycles and is derived from the summed subharmonic and harmonic amplitudes calculated in the logarithmic domain using spectrum shifting techniques. Energy measurements in VoiceSauce are represented by Root Mean Square (RMS) energy, calculated at each frame over a variable window equal to five pitch periods. This adaptive window normalizes energy measurements with respect to F0, thereby reducing correlation between pitch and energy. Additionally, VoiceSauce computes cepstral measures such as Cepstral Peak Prominence (CPP), following the algorithm proposed by Hillenbrand et al. CPP is calculated using a window length equal to five pitch periods, followed by transformation into the real cepstral domain using a Hamming window. The cepstral peak corresponding to the pitch period is identified and normalized relative to a linear regression line computed across the cepstral range.

Harmonic-to-noise ratio (HNR) measures in VoiceSauce are derived using de Krom's algorithm. Using a variable window length equal to five pitch periods, HNR is computed by liftering the pitch-related component of the cepstrum and comparing harmonic energy with the noise floor. VoiceSauce reports HNR values across multiple frequency bands, including HNR05 (0–500 Hz), HNR15 (0–1500 Hz), and HNR25 (0–2500 Hz), whereas CPP reflects voice quality across the entire frequency spectrum. Refer to Fig. 4.1.

4.2.3 Wavesurfer

Wavesurfer is a sound analysis and visualization tool used for inspecting and manipulating speech and audio files. It is freeware software that can be freely modified and redistributed, making it accessible for research and forensic applications. One of the primary reasons for its selection in speech analysis research is that it supports most of the functional requirements needed by Interactive Speech Graphics (ISG). Additionally, the available documentation indicates that the program can be easily

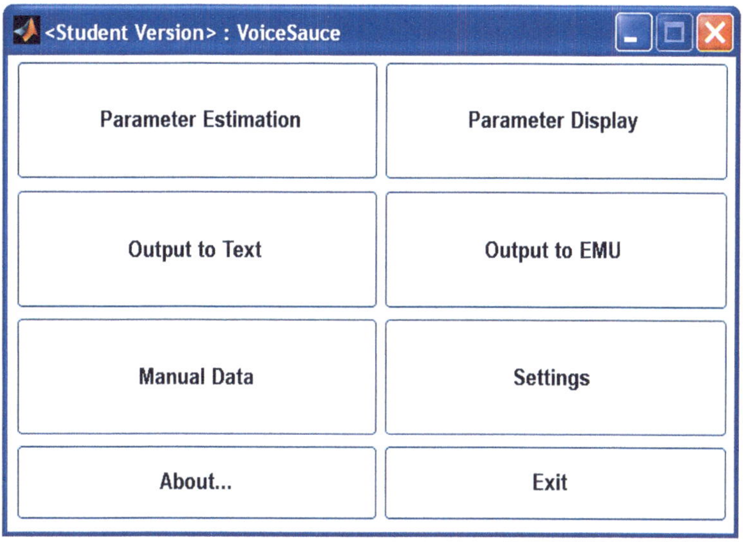

Fig. 4.1 VoiceSauce home screen

modified to suit specific analytical needs (Sjolander and Beskow 2006). Detailed information regarding the software and its documentation is available on the official Wavesurfer Web site (Sjolander and Beskow 2006).

Wavesurfer offers a variety of sound processing and visualization features. Among its most important capabilities is the graphical display of the speech waveform produced by a speaker's voice. Speech is generated through vibrations of the vocal folds, resulting in radiating waves of air pressure variation around an average resting value. As described by Carmell (1997), these radiating waves possess frequency characteristics that correspond to the number of wave repetitions over time (Carmell 1997). Microphones capture these pressure variations and convert them into electrical voltage signals, which are then displayed in Wavesurfer as a waveform. In the interface, the waveform is typically displayed at the top, with a central baseline representing the resting pressure value and shaded regions indicating the oscillatory nature of the speech signal. A time axis is provided to represent temporal progression. Another important feature of Wavesurfer is its support for auditory playback and manual transcription of selected speech segments. Researchers can listen to audio files and annotate specific portions by adding labels to mark silence, speech segments, or response signals. This functionality is particularly useful in forensic investigations and speech analysis tasks that require precise segmentation and annotation of speech events. In addition, Wavesurfer provides the capability to measure and plot pitch contours for speech signals. While waveforms represent the physical frequency of sound waves, pitch refers to the perceptual correlate of frequency, with higher frequencies perceived as higher pitch. Wavesurfer enables extraction and visualization of pitch values over time, allowing researchers to examine pitch variation and intonation patterns in speech. Similar to tools such as Didi,

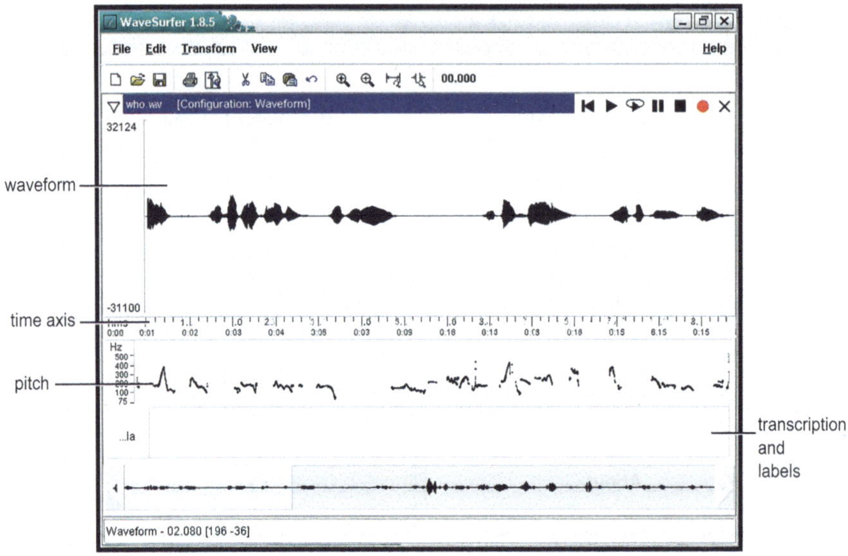

Fig. 4.2 Snapshot of Wavesurfer

Wavesurfer supports pitch contour plotting, which is valuable for qualitative and quantitative analysis of prosodic features in forensic and linguistic investigations. Refer to Fig. 4.2.

4.2.4 Audacity

Audacity software is used for the analysis of audio samples and edit the audio sample. It is free and open-source software that can help analyze frequency of voice samples. By using this software, we can analyze or differentiate two kinds of voice samples. This software provides both live recording and recorded sample analysis. Audacity is a free and open-source audio analysis and editing software widely used for the examination of speech samples in forensic investigations. The software enables both live recording and analysis of pre-recorded audio files, allowing investigators to examine and differentiate voice samples based on frequency characteristics. Audacity supports fundamental forensic tasks such as waveform visualization, frequency analysis, and spectral comparison, making it particularly suitable for preliminary forensic voice examination and speaker differentiation. In forensic applications, Audacity is commonly used to analyze voice samples through a systematic workflow. This process typically involves opening the audio file in Audacity, selecting a defined segment of speech (commonly a 10 s voice track), and analyzing the frequency content of the selected sample. The Plot Spectrum function is then employed to obtain spectral representations of the voice signal, from which peak frequency values and maximum peak values are extracted.

These peak values are subsequently compared across different voice samples, such as recordings obtained before and after physical exertion, to identify measurable acoustic differences.

Audacity is widely recognized as a practical and accessible tool for preliminary forensic audio analysis, particularly in cases involving speaker identification, authentication of recordings, and enhancement of low-quality audio evidence. As outlined in *Conducting Audio Forensics with Audacity*, the software supports a structured forensic workflow that emphasizes the preservation of evidentiary integrity through hash value generation, chain-of-custody documentation, and analysis performed on verified working copies rather than original recordings. Audacity allows forensic examiners to conduct waveform analysis to detect abrupt discontinuities, clipping, unnatural silences, and amplitude inconsistencies that may indicate audio tampering. Its spectrogram and logarithmic spectrogram views enable detailed examination of frequency distribution, background noise consistency, compression artifacts, and potential indicators of synthetic or edited speech.

Furthermore, Audacity provides controlled audio enhancement tools, including noise reduction, normalization, compression, and equalization, which improve speech intelligibility when applied with careful documentation to maintain forensic admissibility. The Plot Spectrum feature facilitates quantitative frequency analysis by displaying peak frequency values and amplitude distributions, allowing comparisons across speech segments to identify physiological variations, environmental changes, or possible splicing. Although Audacity does not replace specialized biometric speaker comparison systems, it plays a significant role in supporting forensic investigations, legal proceedings, and law enforcement work by enabling transparent, replicable, and well-documented acoustic analysis aligned with best practices in digital audio forensics.

A study conducted by Kamble and Hankare titled "Comparative Study of Vocal Frequencies Between Before Running and After Running" examined the application of Audacity in forensic speaker identification by analyzing acoustic variations in voice samples recorded before and after physical exertion in individuals aged 18–40 years (Kamble and Hankare 2023). The study revealed that peak frequency values in post-running voice samples were consistently lower than those recorded before running, demonstrating the physiological effects of exertion on vocal production. Plot spectrum analysis in Audacity enabled the calculation and comparison of peak frequency values, allowing clear differentiation between the two conditions. The findings indicate that factors such as fatigue, dry throat, or allergies can result in a raspy vocal quality after running, significantly altering vocal frequencies. This research highlights the forensic relevance of voice analysis in both criminal and civil cases and underscores Audacity's utility as a practical forensic tool for frequency-based voice comparison and the identification of unknown or anonymous speakers. Refer to Fig. 4.3.

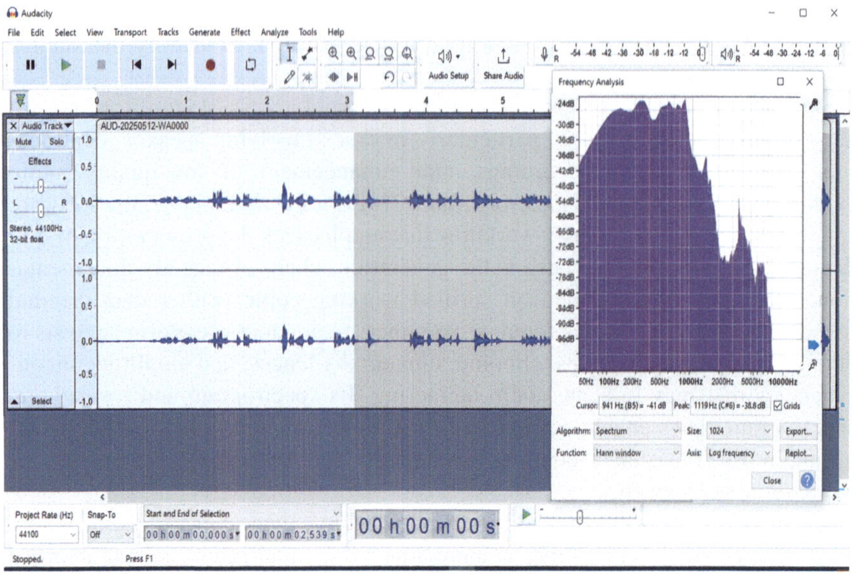

Fig. 4.3 Audacity Waveform Analysis

4.2.5 iZotope RX

iZotope RX is a specialized audio restoration and enhancement software extensively used in forensic investigations for the analysis of degraded or compromised audio evidence. The software is particularly effective in spectral repair, machine-learning-based denoising, de-clipping, and dialogue isolation, making it valuable for improving the intelligibility of undercover recordings, surveillance audio, and disputed speech samples. iZotope RX enables forensic examiners to eliminate ambient background noise, electrically generated interference, overload distortion, and low-frequency hums through dedicated processing modules, thereby restoring critical speech content without introducing perceptual artifacts. By progressively isolating speech components from complex acoustic environments, RX assists investigators in uncovering speaker characteristics embedded within noisy recordings.

iZotope RX 4 is designed as a comprehensive toolbox for cleaning and repairing damaged audio and supports forensic voice analysis, audio authentication, evidence enhancement, broadcasting, and archival preservation. The software incorporates an advanced spectrogram-waveform display that allows detailed visualization of both frequency content and amplitude variations. This high-resolution display enables forensic analysts to precisely identify clicks, noise bursts, clipping events, spectral inconsistencies, and other anomalies that may indicate recording defects, manipulation, or tampering. RX 4 is available in both 32-bit and 64-bit versions, with the 64-bit architecture offering enhanced memory access and improved performance for handling large forensic audio files and complex restoration tasks.

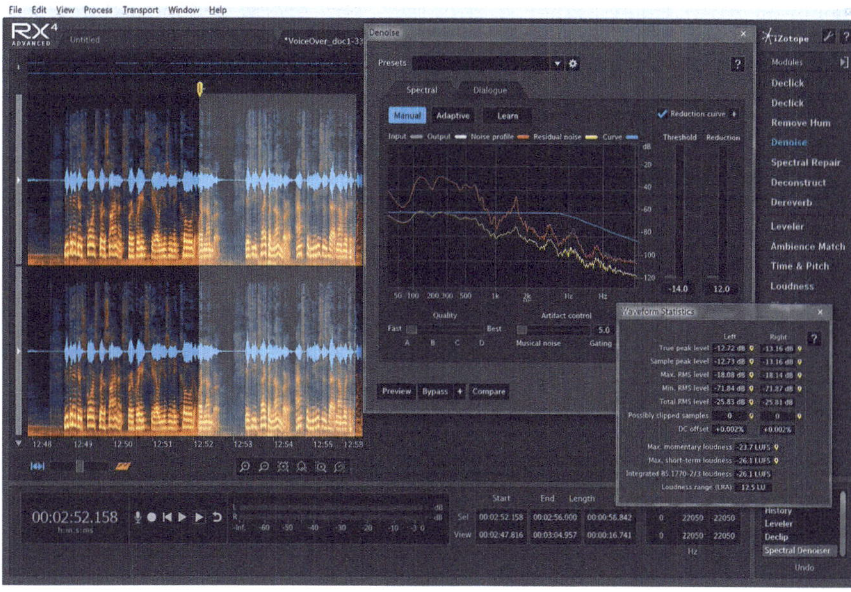

Fig. 4.4 iZotope RX

The Advanced version of iZotope RX 4 provides additional forensic-relevant tools, including adaptive noise reduction, dereverberation, de-clipping, advanced de-clicking, pitch and time manipulation detection, ambience matching, EQ matching, and detailed spectral selection controls. These features enhance the examiner's ability to isolate, repair, and analyze critical speech segments while maintaining evidential integrity. The software's visual, selection-based workflow, combined with undo history, batch processing, and customizable high-resolution spectrogram settings, supports transparent, repeatable, and well-documented forensic procedures, which are essential for legal admissibility in both criminal and civil cases.

Overall, iZotope RX 4 serves as a cornerstone in forensic speech analysis by preprocessing degraded audio evidence and preparing it for subsequent acoustic-phonetic and spectrographic evaluation using analytical tools such as Praat or BATVOX. Its spectral editing and restoration capabilities enable accurate isolation of speech from noise, assist in audio authentication, and facilitate tampering detection all while preserving the chain of custody and the forensic reliability of the evidence. Refer to Fig. 4.4.

4.2.6 Acceptance of Forensic Speech Analysis Software in Courtrooms

Forensic speech analysis software gains courtroom acceptance when meeting rigorous admissibility standards that ensure scientific reliability, often under Daubert (US) or equivalent frameworks emphasizing empirical validation (Morrison and

Thompson 2016). Courts scrutinize error rates, peer review, and method transparency to prevent junk science. The acceptance of forensic speech analysis software in judicial proceedings is contingent upon compliance with stringent admissibility, reliability, and validation standards. In the United States, courts apply the *Daubert* criteria, which require that forensic methods be testable, be subjected to peer review, possess known or quantifiable error rates, and be generally accepted within the relevant forensic and scientific community. Accordingly, forensic speech analysis tools must demonstrate case-relevant validation, often in alignment with NIST and OSAC guidelines, ensuring that performance testing reflects realistic recording conditions such as channel mismatch, noise, and speech duration (Van Leeuwen and Brümmer 2013). Likelihood ratios (LRs) generated by speaker recognition systems must be calibrated against appropriate population databases to support probabilistic interpretation of evidence (Van Leeuwen and Brümmer 2013). In the Indian legal context, admissibility of digital speech evidence is governed by Section 65B of the Indian Evidence Act, which mandates hash-verified chains of custody, preservation of original recordings, authenticated working copies, and expert certification to establish the integrity and authenticity of audio evidence (Geethapriya and Tvisha 2025).

Reliability and validity requirements further determine whether software-based speech evidence withstands judicial scrutiny. Validity depends on demonstrably low false-positive and false-negative rates, typically evaluated using receiver operating characteristic (ROC) curves (Kumar and Indrayan 2011). Advanced forensic speaker recognition systems, such as BATVOX, have demonstrated equal-error rates below 5% in controlled Bundeskriminalamt (BKA) validation tests, supporting their forensic applicability under defined conditions (Wagner 2019). Reliability additionally requires blind testing, inter-laboratory reproducibility, and rigorous bias-mitigation protocols that prevent contextual or case-related influence on examiners (Solewicz et al. 2012). Courts also expect explicit disclosure of methodological limitations, including the effects of disguise, emotional state, health conditions, and recording quality, to avoid overstated conclusions.

International guidelines play a critical role in standardizing forensic speech analysis practices and improving courtroom acceptance. The Scientific Working Group on Speech (SWG-SPEECH), a precursor to the OSAC Speaker Recognition Subcommittee, mandates likelihood-ratio-based reporting supported by verbal equivalence scales and recommends minimum speech durations of approximately 30 seconds for reliable comparison. Similarly, the ISCA Forensic Speech Science Special Interest Group and the European Network of Forensic Science Institutes (ENFSI) endorse the auditory-acoustic-phonetic (AAP) framework, hybrid human-machine analytical systems, and validation studies conducted under case-mimicking conditions to ensure scientific robustness and legal defensibility (Gold and Hughes 2014).

Practical implementation by law enforcement agencies further illustrates admissibility practices. The Federal Bureau of Investigation (FBI) employs tools such as Praat and Wavesurfer for detailed acoustic-phonetic analysis alongside proprietary automatic speaker recognition (ASR) systems validated in accordance with the

National Academy of Sciences (NAS) recommendations (Mnesota Law Review Editorial Board 1972; Ashar 1984). Emphasis is placed on expert manual verification rather than exclusive reliance on automated outputs. In India, the Central Bureau of Investigation (CBI) utilizes iZotope RX for forensic audio enhancement, custom Praat scripts for acoustic analysis, and BATVOX-like probabilistic speaker comparison systems for LR computation. Forensic reports generated by these agencies frequently cite ENFSI and international best-practice guidelines, particularly in cases involving threats, extortion calls, and bomb hoaxes. In both jurisdictions, software outputs are consistently paired with expert human interpretation to satisfy evidentiary standards.

Despite these advancements, forensic speech analysis software continues to face substantial challenges arising from data degradation, biological speaker variability, methodological limitations, and contextual mismatches (Rao et al. 2021). These issues are especially pronounced in multilingual legal environments such as India, where diverse languages, dialects, and code-switching practices complicate population modeling and likelihood-ratio calibration (Barreda 2021; Cao et al. 2024). Consequently, while forensic speech analysis software is increasingly accepted in courtrooms, its evidentiary value ultimately depends on scientifically validated methodologies, transparent reporting, expert interpretation, and strict adherence to legal admissibility frameworks.

4.2.7 Challenges in Using Software for Forensic Speech Evidence

Although forensic speech analysis software has substantially improved the objectivity and reproducibility of voice evidence examination, its application is constrained by several persistent challenges related to recording quality, environmental interference, speaker variability, methodological standardization, and linguistic diversity. These limitations directly influence the accuracy of acoustic measurements, likelihood ratio (LR) estimations, and ultimately the admissibility of forensic speech evidence in court.

4.2.7.1 Recording Quality Issues

Forensic speech evidence is frequently obtained from degraded sources such as mobile phones, VoIP calls, surveillance systems, or social media platforms. Low-bitrate codecs commonly used in mobile and Internet-based communication introduce compression artifacts that distort fundamental frequency (F0), formant structures, and spectral representations (Korycki 2016; Niebuhr and Siegert 2023). Short recording durations often under 30 seconds further reduce the reliability of acoustic measurements by limiting the amount of analyzable speech data (Nylén 2025; Awan et al. 2024). Empirical findings indicate that such degraded conditions can inflate equal-error rates (EERs) in automatic speaker recognition systems, including tools like BATVOX, by approximately 20–50%. Reverberation smears temporal and spectral features, obscuring formant transitions and consonantal boundaries, while clipping saturates intensity values, complicating enhancement procedures (Xia and Hansen 2018; Prieto et al. 2022). Although software such as iZotope RX provides advanced restoration tools, aggressive enhancement risks introducing artificial artifacts that may compromise forensic integrity.

4.2.7.2 Background Noise

Environmental noise poses a significant challenge in forensic speech analysis. Common noise sources such as conversational babble, traffic sounds, wind, or mechanical interference can mask critical speech components, particularly fricatives and harmonic structures (Fitzgerald et al. 2024). When signal-to-noise ratios fall below 10 dB, the reliability of acoustic feature extraction deteriorates, biasing likelihood ratios toward the defense hypothesis (H2: different speakers). While adaptive denoising techniques can effectively address stationary noise, they often fail to suppress transient or non-stationary noise events (Yong and Nordholm 2017) Such conditions degrade formant tracking accuracy in Praat and reduce the performance of automatic speaker recognition systems, leading to uncertain or unreliable forensic conclusions (Harrison et al. 2023).

4.2.7.3 Speaker Variability

Intra-speaker variability remains one of the most complex challenges in forensic speech analysis (Fitzgerald et al. 2024). Variations caused by emotional states, physical exertion, health conditions, or intentional disguise can significantly alter acoustic parameters. For instance, anger may elevate F0 by 20–40 Hz, while illnesses such as colds can cause vocal tract swelling, shifting formant frequencies (Kaur et al. 2023). Disguise strategies including falsetto phonation, whispering, or altered articulation often mimic inter-speaker differences, thereby confusing speaker comparison systems (Růžičková and Skarnitzl 2017; Vestman et al. 2018). Statistical models such as Gaussian Mixture Models (GMMs) and i-vector frameworks, which are typically trained on neutral speech, struggle to account for such variability (Al-Kaltakchi et al. 2017). These challenges are exacerbated in short-duration recordings, where limited speech material amplifies the loss of idiosyncratic speaker traits, resulting in unreliable likelihood ratios unless population-matched calibration data are available.

4.2.7.4 Lack of Standardization

A further obstacle lies in the absence of universally standardized methodologies for forensic speech analysis. Diverse analytical workflows ranging from manual Praat-based scripting to fully automated systems such as BATVOX limit inter-laboratory reproducibility. Differences in parameter settings, feature extraction algorithms, and reporting formats result in inconsistent outcomes across institutions (Morrison 2018). Moreover, no globally accepted verbal scales for likelihood ratio interpretation or validation protocols currently exist beyond draft recommendations by organizations such as ENFSI and OSAC (Humayun et al. 2024). Proprietary systems often lack algorithmic transparency, hindering peer review and increasing the risk of exclusion under Daubert standards (Harrington et al. 2021), while open-source tools such as Wavesurfer frequently lack forensic-specific error-rate documentation.

4.2.7.5 Cross-Linguistic Challenges: Indian Context

The linguistic diversity of India presents a particularly critical challenge for forensic speech analysis. With 22 officially recognized languages and over 1600 dialects, speech evidence often exhibits significant phonetic and prosodic variation that is not adequately represented in Western-centric forensic tools (Wagner et al. 2022). Acoustic norms derived from English-based datasets are frequently unsuitable, as Hindi and Dravidian languages display substantially different vowel systems and formant distributions, with reported F2 variances of up to ±300 Hz. Code-mixing practices such as Hinglish further disrupt phonetic alignment in tools like VoiceSauce, complicating segmental and suprasegmental comparisons (). Additionally, the absence of accent- or dialect-specific population databases for many Indian and tribal languages prevents accurate typicality assessment (), increasing the likelihood of false exclusions in forensic investigations conducted by agencies such as the Central Bureau of Investigation (CBI).

While forensic speech analysis software provides powerful analytical capabilities, its application is constrained by technical, biological, methodological, and linguistic challenges. Addressing these limitations requires cautious interpretation, rigorous validation under case-relevant conditions, development of language-specific databases, and greater standardization of forensic protocols to ensure scientifically reliable and legally admissible speech evidence.

4.2.8 Opportunities and Future Directions in Software Upgradation

The rapid evolution of digital audio technologies, artificial intelligence, and computational linguistics presents significant opportunities for advancing forensic speech analysis software. As the complexity of voice evidence increases through poor-quality recordings, multilingual speakers, and sophisticated voice manipulation techniques, future software upgrades must focus on automation, robustness, and legal defensibility. Emerging trends indicate that forensic speech analysis is moving toward data-driven, AI-assisted systems that complement expert judgement while adhering to strict scientific and legal standards.

4.2.8.1 Artificial Intelligence and Machine Learning in Voice Biometrics

Artificial intelligence (AI) and machine learning (ML) are transforming voice biometrics by enabling systems to learn complex, high-dimensional patterns in speech that are difficult to capture through traditional acoustic measures alone. Modern ML models, including deep neural networks (DNNs), convolutional neural networks (CNNs), and transformer-based architectures, can model speaker-specific traits across multiple acoustic domains such as spectral shape, prosody, and voice quality. In forensic contexts, these models offer improved discrimination between speakers, especially in challenging conditions involving noise, channel mismatch, or short-duration recordings. Future software upgrades are expected to integrate explainable

AI (XAI) frameworks that allow forensic experts and courts to understand which speech features contribute to system decisions, thereby increasing transparency and trust in AI-assisted voice evidence.

4.2.8.2 Advancements in Automatic Speaker Recognition (ASR)

Automatic speaker recognition systems have undergone substantial improvement with the introduction of i-vector, x-vector, and, more recently, embedding-based deep learning approaches. These systems can automatically extract speaker embeddings and compute similarity scores or likelihood ratios, enabling rapid screening and comparison of large volumes of audio data. In forensic applications, future ASR tools are likely to be more resilient to intra-speaker variability caused by emotion, health, or intentional disguise, as well as extrinsic factors such as recording devices and environments. Hybrid systems that combine ASR outputs with expert-driven acoustic-phonetic analysis are emerging as best practice, ensuring that automated results are interpreted within a scientifically informed and case-specific framework rather than being used as black-box solutions.

4.2.8.3 Need for Multilingual and Region-Specific Speech Datasets

One of the most pressing future requirements in forensic speech analysis is the development of large, validated multilingual datasets, particularly for underrepresented languages such as Hindi and other Indian languages. Most existing forensic voice databases are dominated by English or European languages, limiting their applicability in linguistically diverse regions. Indian languages exhibit wide variation in phoneme inventories, prosodic structures, vowel systems, and code-switching patterns, all of which significantly affect acoustic parameters such as formant distributions and pitch contours. Future software upgradation must therefore include language- and dialect-specific calibration datasets to ensure accurate typicality assessments and likelihood ratio computation. The creation of ethically sourced, legally compliant Indian speech corpora will be critical for improving the reliability and fairness of forensic voice comparisons in regional and national legal systems.

4.2.8.4 Greater Courtroom Acceptance Through Standardized Protocols

Forensic speech analysis software will achieve broader courtroom acceptance only when supported by standardized protocols governing data handling, analysis, validation, and reporting. Future directions emphasize harmonization with international guidelines such as those from OSAC, ENFSI, and ISCA, alongside compliance with national legal frameworks like India's Evidence Act and Section 65B requirements for digital evidence. Software upgrades should incorporate built-in documentation tools for chain of custody, parameter logging, version tracking, and audit trails, enabling full transparency and reproducibility. Additionally, standardized likelihood ratio reporting scales and clearly articulated limitations will help judges and legal practitioners interpret forensic speech evidence appropriately. As software becomes more sophisticated, its acceptance in courts will depend not on automation alone but on demonstrable scientific validity, peer-reviewed support, and responsible expert interpretation.

The future of forensic speech analysis software lies in the convergence of AI-driven innovation, robust automatic speaker recognition, multilingual resource development, and legally standardized workflows. By addressing current limitations and aligning technological advancements with forensic and judicial expectations, upgraded software systems can significantly enhance the accuracy, credibility, and societal value of forensic voice evidence. Forensic speech analysis software has become an indispensable component of modern forensic science, enabling the systematic, objective, and scientifically grounded examination of speech evidence in legal contexts. As demonstrated throughout this chapter, speech is inherently variable, shaped by physiological, linguistic, emotional, and environmental factors. The integration of computer-based analytical tools allows forensic practitioners to manage this variability by extracting, visualizing, and statistically evaluating acoustic-phonetic features such as fundamental frequency, formant structures, intensity, temporal patterns, and voice quality measures. Software-assisted analysis thus strengthens the evidential value of speech by complementing expert auditory judgement with reproducible, data-driven methods.

The chapter has highlighted the complementary roles of widely used forensic speech analysis tools, including Praat, VoiceSauce, Wavesurfer, Audacity, and iZotope RX. Open-source platforms such as Praat and Wavesurfer provide precise acoustic measurement and visualization capabilities essential for phonetic profiling, while VoiceSauce enables large-scale extraction of voice quality parameters under controlled conditions. Audacity serves as a practical and accessible tool for preliminary analysis, frequency comparison, and audio authentication, whereas iZotope RX plays a critical role in the enhancement and restoration of degraded forensic recordings. Together, these tools form an integrated workflow spanning evidence preprocessing, feature extraction, comparison, and interpretation.

Despite these advances, the chapter underscores that forensic speech analysis software is not a stand-alone solution. The reliability and admissibility of software-based findings depend on rigorous validation, transparency of methods, and adherence to international forensic standards such as those proposed by OSAC, ENFSI, and ISCA. Likelihood ratio–based statistical evaluation, when properly calibrated against relevant population data, offers a principled framework for expressing evidential strength, but it remains sensitive to recording quality, speaker variability, and cross-linguistic differences. These challenges are particularly pronounced in multilingual and dialectally diverse contexts such as India, where the lack of representative speech databases can limit the robustness of conclusions.

4.3 Conclusion

In conclusion, forensic speech analysis software enhances the scientific credibility of voice evidence when used within a holistic auditory-acoustic-phonetic framework and interpreted by trained experts. Future progress in the field depends on the development of language- and dialect-specific reference databases, standardized validation protocols, improved handling of degraded and short-duration recordings, and transparent reporting practices that clearly communicate limitations to the courts. As audio manipulation technologies and synthetic speech continue to evolve, the responsible and validated use of forensic speech analysis software will remain central to ensuring the fair, accurate, and ethical use of speech evidence in the justice system.

References

Albin A (2014) Praat R: an architecture for controlling the phonetics software "Praat" with the R programming language. J Acoust Soc Am 135:2198–2199

Al-Kaltakchi MT, Woo WL, Dlay SS, Chambers JA (2017) Comparison of I-vector and GMM-UBM approaches to speaker identification with TIMIT and NIST 2008 databases in challenging environments. In: 2017 25th European signal processing conference (EUSIPCO). IEEE, pp 533–537

Ashar LC (1984) Admissibility of scientific evidence: voice Spectrography. Akron Law Rev 17(4):12

Atif M, Rashid A, Arslan MF, Ullah F, Amjad M, Haroon H (2024) A phonetic forensic analysis of Imran Khan's speeches. Kurdish Studies 12(4):720–732. https://doi.org/10.53555/ks.v12i4.3050

Atkinson JE (1976) Inter-and intraspeaker variability in fundamental voice frequency. J Acoust Soc Am 60(2):440–445

Awan SN, Bahr R, Watts S, Boyer M, Budinsky R, Bridge2AI Voice Consortium, Bensoussan Y (2024) Validity of acoustic measures obtained using various recording methods including smartphones with and without headset microphones. J Speech Lang Hear Res 67(6):1712–1730

Barreda S (2021) Fast track: fast (nearly) automatic formant-tracking using Praat. Linguistics Vanguard 7(1):20200051

Beňuš Š (2021) Investigating spoken English: a practical guide to phonetics and phonology using Praat. Springer

Boersma P (2002) Speak and unSpeak with P RAATRAAT

Cao GW, Hughes V, Wang BX, Mok P (2024) Cross-language forensic voice comparison of Hong Kong trilingual speakers using filled pauses and an automatic speaker recognition system. In: 2024 IEEE 14th international symposium on Chinese spoken language processing (ISCSLP). IEEE, pp 279–283

Carmell T (1997) Spectrogram reading. http://cslu.cse.ogi.edu/tutordemos/SpectrogramReading/waveform.html

Cenceschi S, Meluzzi C, Trivilini A (2021) The variability of vowels' formants in forensic speech. IEEE Inst Measure Magaz 24(1):38–41

Drygajlo A, Jessen M, Gfroerer S, Wagner I, Vermeulen J, Niemi T (2015) Methodological guidelines for best practice in forensic semiautomatic and automatic speaker recognition. Verlag für Polizeiwissenschaft, Frankfurt

Eriksson A (2005) Tutorial on forensic speech science. In: Proceeding European conference speech communication and technology, pp 1–14

Fitzgerald LP, DeDe G, Shen J (2024) Effects of linguistic context and noise type on speech comprehension. Front Psychol 15:1345619

Geethapriya S, Tvisha G (2025, November) Challenges of electronic evidence and its admissibility in court. Int J Res Trend Innov (IJRTI)

Gold E, Hughes V (2014) Issues and opportunities: the application of the numerical likelihood ratio framework to forensic speaker comparison. Sci Justice 54(4):292–299

Harrington L, Rhodes R, Hughes V (2021) Style variability in disfluency analysis for forensic speaker comparison. Int J Speech Lang Law 28(1):31–58

Harrison O, Reed-Jones J, Morrison K, Robinson C, Jones K (2023) The effect of noise reduction upon voiceprint integrity. In: ICISNA 23 proceedings book, pp 211–213
Humayun MA, Shuja J, Abas PE (2024) A review of social background profiling of speakers from speech accents. PeerJ Comput Sci 10:e1984
Jain P, Chinmayee P, Kaur K, Chaudhary S, Kaur K, Karunya S (2024) Advancements in forensic voice analysis: legal frameworks and technology integration. Asian Journal of Advances in Research 7(1):369–384
Kamble AS, Hankare V (2023) Comparative study of vocal frequencies between before running and after running. Int J Res Analy Rev 10(2)
Kaur J, Juglan KC, Sharma K, Sharma V (2023) An acoustic analysis of fluctuations for inter-and intra-speaker variability in speech sounds. J Forensic Sci Med 9(1):38–43
Kersta LG (1962) Voiceprint Identification. Nature 196(7)
Ko H, Woo MR, Choi Y (2020) Comparisons of voice quality parameter values measured with MDVP, Praat, and TF32. Phonetics and speech sciences 12:73
Korycki R (2016) Methods of investigating the authenticity of recording of telephone conversations. Problems of Forensic Sciences 107:515–536
Krishna G, Bansal K (2024) Forensic analysis of AI-modulated threatening voices: a PRAAT-based study. Int J Innov Res Technol (IJIRT) 11(1):795–802
Kumar R, Indrayan A (2011) Receiver operating characteristic (ROC) curve for medical researchers. Indian Pediatr 48(4):277–287
Mnesota Law Review Editorial Board (1972) Evidence: admissibility of spectrographic voice identification. Minnesota Law Review 56:123–140
Morrison GS (2018) The impact in forensic voice comparison of lack of calibration and of mismatched conditions between the known-speaker recording and the relevant-population sample recordings. Forensic Sci Int 283:e1–e7
Morrison GS, Thompson WC (2016) Assessing the admissibility of a new generation of forensic voice comparison testimony. Colum Sci Tech L Rev 18:326
Niebuhr O, Siegert I (2023) A digital "flat affect"? Popular speech compression codecs and their effects on emotional prosody. Front Commun 8:972182
Nylén F (2025) On acoustic voice quality index measurement reliability in digital health applications: a narrative review and empirical evaluation of speech sample length requirements. Front Digital Health 7:1610353
Paver AEG (2020) Dynamic variability in speech: a forensic phonetic. Study of British English
Pergolizzi J, LeQuang JAK, Pergolizzi J Jr (2024) Black robes and white coats: Daubert standard and medical and legal considerations for medical expert witnesses. Cureus 16(9)
Pleva M, Juhár J, Thiessen AS (2015) Automatic acoustic speech segmentation in Praat using cloud based ASR. In: 2015 25th international conference Radioelektronika (RADIOELEKTRONIKA), pp 172–175
Prieto S, Ortega A, Lopez-Espejo I, Lleida E (2022) Shouted and whispered speech compensation for speaker verification systems. Digit Signal Process 127:103536
Rao S, Farhath H, Ekka P, Panchal V, Mia R, Sinha RK (2021) Forensic aspects of voice analysis in India. Int J Res Appl Sci Eng Technol 9(8):1990–1993
Růžičková A, Skarnitzl R (2017) Voice disguise strategies in Czech male speakers. AUC PHILOLOGICA 2017(3):19–34
Seong C (2022) Guidance to the Praat, a software for speech and acoustic analysis. Journal of The Korean Society of Laryngology, Phoniatrics and Logopedics 33:64
Sjolander K, Beskow J (2006) Wavesurfer documentation. Speech, Music and Hearing part of School of Computer Science and Communication. http://www.speech.kth.se/wavesurfer/documentation.html
Solewicz YA, Becker T, Jardine G, Gfrörer SG (2012) Comparison of speaker recognition systems on a real forensic benchmark. In: Odyssey, pp 86–91
Sultana R (2023) Are non-native speakers' English pronunciations similar?: evidence through PRAAT recording software. Qeios

Tiwari M (2012) Speech acoustics: how much science? J Nat Sci Biol Med 3(1):24–31. https://doi.org/10.4103/0976-9668.95942

Tosi O, Oyer HJ, Lashbrook W, Pedney C, Nichol J, Nash W (1972) Experiment on voice identification. J Acoust Soc Am 51:2030–2043

Van Leeuwen DA, Brümmer N (2013) The distribution of calibrated likelihood-ratios in speaker recognition. arXiv preprint arXiv:1304.1199

Vestman V, Gowda D, Sahidullah M, Alku P, Kinnunen T (2018) Speaker recognition from whispered speech: a tutorial survey and an application of time-varying linear prediction. Speech Comm 99:62–79

Wagner I (2019) Examples of casework in forensic speaker comparison. In: Calhoun S, Escudero P, Tabain M, Warren P (eds) Proceedings of the 19th international congress of phonetic sciences, Melbourne, Australia, pp 5–9

Wagner I, Boss D, Hughes V, Svirava T, Siparov I, Rolfes M (2022) Best practice manual for the methodology of forensic speaker comparison

Wang Z, Hansen JH (2022) Impact of naturalistic field acoustic environments on forensic text-independent speaker verification system. arXiv preprint arXiv:2201.13246

Xia W, Hansen JH (2018) Speaker recognition with nonlinear distortion: clipping analysis and impact. In: INTERSPEECH, pp 746–750

Yong PC, Nordholm S (2017) Real time noise suppression in social settings comprising a mixture of non-stationary and transient noise. In: 2017 25th European signal processing conference (EUSIPCO). IEEE, pp 588–592

Trajectory of Speech Change Across Age: Its Application in Forensic Investigation

5

Srirangam Vijayakumar Narasimhan
and Kashyap Sahana

Abstract

This chapter examines the complex relationship between speech aging and forensic phonetics, emphasizing the scientific and ethical challenges involved in speaker comparison and age estimation. As the human voice evolves across the lifespan due to physiological, emotional, and sociolinguistic factors, age-related acoustic variations—such as changes in fundamental frequency, formant patterns, and temporal measures—affect the reliability of forensic analysis. The chapter discusses interpersonal variability, health and emotion effects, and multilingual speech dynamics, highlighting their implications for forensic interpretation. It also critically explores the ethical dimensions of automated age profiling, including issues of bias, privacy, and transparency. Future directions emphasize the creation of longitudinal, multilingual databases, standardized protocols, and explainable AI models that integrate biological, linguistic, and ethical considerations. By treating aging not as forensic "noise" but as an informative dimension of human variability, the chapter redefines forensic voice analysis as a scientifically grounded and ethically responsible practice.

Keywords

Acoustic variations · Age estimation · Automated age profiling · Explainable AI (XAI) · Forensic phonetics · Speech aging

S. V. Narasimhan (✉) · K. Sahana
Department of Speech Language Pathology, JSS Institute of Speech and Hearing, Mysore, India

V. Kumar et al. (eds.), *Forensic Speech Sciences*, New Horizons in Forensic Science, https://doi.org/10.1007/978-981-92-1475-4_5

5.1 Introduction to Age-Related Speech Changes in Forensics

Speech is one of the most distinctive and dynamic human characteristics. In forensic science, it serves as an essential biometric—capable of linking individuals to criminal activity, verifying identity, or exonerating the innocent. Yet unlike fingerprints or DNA, speech is inherently variable. This variability stems from a combination of biological, physiological, psychological, and environmental factors that continuously shape a person's speech throughout their life. One of the most profound sources of this variation is aging. Understanding age-related changes in speech is therefore indispensable to forensic speech science. As investigations increasingly involve non-contemporaneous recordings—where a suspect's current voice must be compared to an older sample—the ability to model and interpret these natural transformations becomes critical. Without accounting for speech aging, forensic analyses risk misattributing natural variation to identity differences or, conversely, overlooking genuine distinctions between speakers.

5.1.1 Age-Related Speech Changes and Their Acoustic Manifestations

Speech evolves as the human body ages. These changes are not abrupt but gradual and cumulative, reflecting structural modifications in the vocal mechanism, neural control, and cognitive processing. Research has shown that laryngeal and respiratory alterations, such as muscle atrophy, ossification of laryngeal cartilages, and decreased tissue elasticity, lead to reduced breath support and a weaker, less stable voice (Linville 2001). These physiological changes produce measurable acoustic consequences. For example, the fundamental frequency (F0), commonly perceived as pitch, tends to decrease in men until middle age and rise again in later years as vocal fold tension diminishes. In women, hormonal changes associated with menopause often cause a lowering of F0 (Linville 2001; D'Haeseleer et al. 2011). These biological trajectories introduce temporal shifts in acoustic patterns that can complicate forensic speaker comparisons.

Additionally, formant frequencies—which correspond to the resonances of the vocal tract—show systematic variation with age. Reduced muscle tone and articulatory precision may cause formant bandwidths to broaden and centralize vowel space (Xue and Hao 2003). As speakers grow older, vowels may become less distinct, and their dynamic formant transitions slower and shallower. However, not all acoustic cues degrade with age. Schötz (2007) further explored the perceptual dimension, showing that listeners and computational models alike can often estimate a speaker's age range from acoustic cues. Using machine learning and regression-based approaches, Schötz (2007) demonstrated that certain features—such as spectral tilt, F0 range, and speech rate—correlate with chronological age. This has paved the way for emerging forensic applications of automatic age estimation and speaker

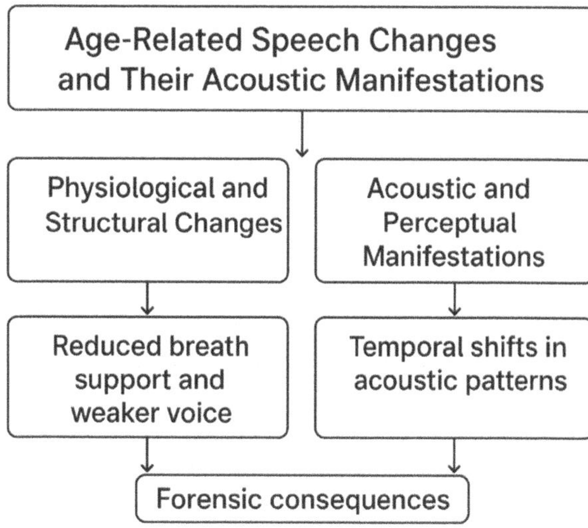

Fig. 5.1 The age-related speech changes and their acoustic and perceptual manifestations

profiling, which complement traditional auditory-phonetic analysis. Figure 5.1 summarizes the age-related speech changes and their acoustic manifestations.

5.1.2 Forensic Implications of Non-contemporaneous Recordings

The forensic consequences of speech aging are most pronounced in non-contemporaneous comparisons, where two speech samples are recorded years apart. These cases are increasingly common in criminal justice, particularly in cold case investigations, re-trials, and counterterrorism contexts, where archived recordings are revisited after long intervals. Rhodes (Department for International Development 2014) assessed the strength of non-contemporaneous forensic speech evidence and emphasized that analysts must interpret similarities and differences with extreme caution. Rhodes (Department for International Development 2014) also argued that many forensic comparisons neglect to account for expected within-speaker change over time, which can distort the likelihood that two samples originate from the same person. The analysis underscored a significant legal risk: courts, lacking a detailed understanding of speech physiology, might misinterpret natural acoustic drift as evidence of non-identity or deliberate disguise. Similarly, Hughes and Foulkes (2015) demonstrated that age-related variation influences the reliability of forensic voice comparisons. Their research found that when reference populations were age mismatched with the target speaker, error rates increased significantly. This indicates that forensic voice comparison systems must consider the speaker's age and the temporal distance between recordings when establishing relevant populations for likelihood ratio calculations. Enzinger and Morrison (2017) provided empirical validation of this principle by testing a forensic acoustic-phonetic method under real-world conditions. Their study revealed poor discriminative performance when comparing voices separated by time, particularly when relying on features such as F0 and the second formant (F2), which are sensitive to aging. These findings emphasize that forensic methodologies should be data driven, empirically tested, and statistically calibrated for time-dependent variation. Collectively, these studies reveal that speech aging is not merely a background factor—it is a central variable that can affect both the reliability and admissibility of forensic evidence. Without accounting for age-induced change, analysts risk producing conclusions that are scientifically unsound and legally vulnerable.

5.1.3 Toward a Data-Driven and Ethically Informed Framework

Modern forensic speech science increasingly advocates for integrating empirical modeling and statistical frameworks to manage the complexities of aging. By incorporating expected age-related variation into the likelihood-ratio framework, analysts can express evidential strength in a transparent, scientifically defensible way. For instance, computational approaches like those developed by Schötz (2007) demonstrate how machine learning models can be trained on age-labeled speech corpora to estimate or normalize for aging effects. When properly calibrated, these methods can significantly improve the fairness and reliability of forensic evaluations.

However, the adoption of such technology must be ethically grounded. As Linville (2001) and Hughes and Foulkes (2015) caution, the biological variability of aging is immense and is influenced by gender, health, lifestyle, and environmental exposure. Algorithms must therefore be transparent, population representative, and subjected to rigorous forensic validation before use in court. Equally, sociophonetic research has shown that speech change across the lifespan is not purely physiological. Deluce et al. (2019) highlighted that individuals also adapt their speech socially, aligning with or diverging from linguistic communities over time. Forensic practitioners must therefore view speech change as a multifactorial process, where biological aging, social factors, and recording context all intersect.

Therefore, age-related speech change represents both a scientific challenge and an opportunity for forensic advancement. On one hand, it introduces uncertainty into long-term comparisons; on the other, it offers measurable parameters that can enhance speaker profiling and temporal modeling. As forensic speech science continues to advance, integrating robust acoustic modeling, large-scale longitudinal data, and interdisciplinary collaboration will be essential to ensure that justice remains scientifically sound in the face of time.

5.2 Biological and Acoustic Foundations of Age-Related Speech Changes

Ageing is a common phenomenon in normal individuals; it affects speech at multiple levels in terms of the anatomical changes and physiological changes of the vocal mechanism and its structure, to the variations in acoustic and prosodic patterns that listeners perceive when they listen to the speech. This review of literature suggested that current empirical and theoretical work on how anatomical changes in the vocal tract and larynx alter acoustic features of the parameters, how prosodic features shift with advancing ageing in normal individuals, how patterns differ by gender across the lifespan, and how declines in muscle tone, tissue elasticity, and sensorimotor control mechanisms reduce articulatory precision in the speech productions. When we compare across the parameters of biological and acoustic foundations of age-related speech changes, it provides evidence to know about the variations in the following domains.

5.2.1 Anatomical and Physiological Changes That Alter the Speech Acoustics

Usually, normal ageing mechanism produces structural changes throughout the speech apparatus, starting from infancy to the geriatric population. In the laryngeal system, common changes include thinning of the vocal folds and atrophy of the thyroarytenoid cartilage and muscle, loss of tissue density in the vocal folds and their layers, bowing of the vocal-fold edges, and reduced mucosal changes (Eichhorn et al. 2018). These tissue-level density alterations change the mass of the vocal folds, stiffness in the vocal folds, and vibratory patterns of the vocal folds, which in turn change the parameters such as F0 variations, increase aperiodicity and breathiness in the components, and often reduce harmonic to noise energy (Taylor et al. 2020). At the level of the vocal tract, bone density was reduced, as well as dentition, and changes in the pharyngeal and oral cavity shapes (e.g., decreased muscle tone of the soft palate and tongue base) affect the resonant characteristics and formant frequencies, especially for the formants like F1, F2, and F3 that depend on the articulatory features. Together, these laryngeal, supraglottal, and subglottal changes in the larynx produce the spectral parameters commonly associated with the ageing voice, like increased noise-to-harmonic ratio, altered spectral slope, and shifts in F0 trajectory (Eichhorn et al. 2018; Cavallaro et al. 2024). Importantly, the acoustic consequences are not uniform across the individuals: some older individuals show prominent hoarseness and reduced harmonic structural changes, whereas others retain relatively preserved spectral patterns across ageing. Cross-sectional work finds group-level tendencies but substantial individual variability that reflects the health status of the individuals, history of vocal usage, and comorbidities associated with the individuals (Taylor et al. 2020).

5.2.2 Influence on Prosody: Intonation, Tempo, and Pauses

Prosody is one of the critical suprasegmental patterns of pitch, loudness, timing, and pausing that show consistent age-related shifts in geriatric populations. Longitudinal and cross-sectional studies conducted in the past frequently report several convergent changes in individuals, like reduced mean and maximum F0 parameters in some older speakers, which led to a flatter intonation contour, followed by slower articulation rate and speech rates, and increases in both the frequency and duration (Ivanova et al. 2024). These changes usually reflect a combination of peripheral and central factors that lead to the reduction of laryngeal power and respiratory capacity, which may produce lower intensity and reduced pitch range, slower neuromotor timing, and precision variations and also cause longer inter-word and intra-phrase pauses in the geriatric group, and strategic alterations like speaking more slowly to enhance intelligibility can magnify rate differences among the individuals (Taylor et al. 2020; Ivanova et al. 2024). Functionally, prosodic changes impact communicative effectiveness in individuals. Increased pausing and slower tempo can impair turn-taking and listener comprehension problems in rapid interactions but may also reflect adaptive strategies that older speakers use to maintain intelligibility under declining motor capacity.

5.2.3 Gender Differences Across the Lifespan

Gender difference exerts a complex influence on how speech changes with age across the lifespan. Developmental history establishes different baseline measurements of parameters for male and female voices. Many studies reported that age-related increases in male F0 are due to a partial feminization of pitch and decreases in female F0 are due to a partial masculinization of pitch, especially in the post-menopausal period when hormonal shifts affect vocal fold mass and mucosal properties as well as elastic and stiffness variations of the vocal folds (Taylor et al. 2020; Cavallaro et al. 2024). Conversely, measures of voice quality like harmonic-to-noise ratio, breathiness component, and roughness component sometimes worsen more in women than in men (Eichhorn et al. 2018). Gender differences are also evident in prosodic variations. Usually, older men may exhibit larger increases in pause usage compared to women, while women may show greater variability in intensity measures with age than compared to men (Ivanova et al. 2024). Social and behavioral factors, differences in vocal demands across various occupations, healthcare access of an individual, and the threshold for seeking voice care further modulate observed gender differences over the lifespan.

5.2.4 From Muscle Tone and Elasticity to Articulatory Precision

Ageing reduces the muscle strength of individuals, endurance, and fine motor control across the respiratory, laryngeal, resonatory, and articulatory subsystems of speech. At the tissue level, decreased muscle strength and elasticity, along with the reduced neuromuscular recruitment, lead to slower, lower-amplitude movements of the tongue, lips, palate, and jaw (Taylor et al. 2020; Dromey et al. 2014). Earlier Kinematic studies using electromagnetic articulography and other motion-tracking methods in speech assessment show age-related reductions in peak articulator velocities, increased movement variability, and, sometimes, prolonged movement durations. However, not all articulatory parameters decline uniformly across individuals. Usually, older speakers often adopt compensatory strategies such as larger articulatory excursions or slower timing to preserve segmental intelligibility (Dromey et al. 2014).

Articulatory imprecision characteristics mainly manifest acoustically as reduced spectral distinctiveness of vowels from smaller formant dispersion variations to increased co-articulation effects on the adjacent sounds, and occasional consonant undershoot for most of the consonants, which can decrease intelligibility (Kong et al. 2024). All these effects depend on the balance between neuromuscular decline in an individual and compensatory motor planning occurring at a brain level (Dromey et al. 2014).

Biological changes in tissue mechanics and neuromuscular control explain much of the acoustic and prosodic shifts observed with age. Still, the link is mediated between the characteristic exhibited at the behavioral level and the context level. Respiratory decline usually constrains subglottal pressure variations and thus intensity reductions, which in turn limit F0 modulation variations. Laryngeal atrophy alters vibratory patterns and harmonic structure of the speech segment, and reductions in articulatory speed and coordination change timing and spectral clarity (Cavallaro et al. 2024). These interacting effects produce a profile in older speech characterized by a slower rate, longer pauses, altered pitch range, increased spectral noise, and sometimes reduced vowel distinctiveness.

Clinically, distinguishing between normal age-related changes and pathological processes usually requires a multidimensional assessment of acoustic measures, perceptual ratings, aerodynamic/laryngeal imaging, and, when available, kinematic data. Interventions may be restorative, along with the compensatory and or medical/surgical procedure for a disordered voice. Moreover, because gender and individual history modulate trajectories, personalized assessment and intervention plans are essential (Taylor et al. 2020). Hence, age-related changes in speech emerge from biological processes like tissue atrophy, reduced elasticity, diminished respiratory and laryngeal capacity of an individual, and slower neuromotor control that vary the acoustic output and prosodic organization. Prosodic changes and articulatory consequences are empirically well documented in the literature, though individual and gender-based variability remains substantial.

5.3 Acoustic Markers of Age-Related Speech Change

The human voice is a dynamic acoustic system, continually shaped by biological maturation, sociolinguistic influences, and physiological aging. In forensic phonetics, recognizing age-related acoustic markers is crucial to understanding intra-speaker variability over time and enhancing the interpretability of voice evidence. Aging affects almost every measurable component of the speech signal—from F0 and formant frequencies to temporal measures, amplitude perturbations, and formant trajectories. These acoustic markers, when properly understood, can help differentiate between natural speech variation and identity differences across non-contemporaneous recordings.

5.3.1 Core Measurable Acoustic Features

F0, perceived as pitch, is among the most extensively studied correlates of vocal aging. It reflects the rate of vibration of the vocal folds and depends on their mass, tension, and elasticity (Titze 1989). Longitudinal and cross-sectional studies reveal consistent age-related trends. In men, F0 tends to decrease from adolescence to middle age, reflecting increased vocal fold mass and length, followed by a gradual increase in older age due to atrophy and loss of tension (Linville 2001; Hollien and Shipp 1972). Women, conversely, experience a postmenopausal decrease in F0 as hormonal changes induce thickening of the vocal folds (Eichhorn et al. 2018). Forensic implications arise when comparing speech samples separated by decades. An older male voice may sound perceptibly higher in pitch, potentially misleading auditory comparison. Therefore, analysts must rely on objective F0 distributions rather than perceptual judgments alone (Hughes and Foulkes 2015).

Formants (F_1, F_2, F_3) represent resonant frequencies of the vocal tract and are shaped by articulatory configuration. As speakers age, structural and neuromuscular changes in the vocal tract contribute to shifts in formant values and their bandwidths (Xue and Hao 2003). Aging typically leads to centralization of vowel space—a reduction in the acoustic distinctiveness between vowels (Reubold et al. 2010). This centralization is attributed to reduced tongue mobility, slower articulatory transitions, and diminished motor precision. Formant bandwidths tend to increase, reflecting greater acoustic damping due to tissue stiffening and changes in vocal tract shape (Eichhorn et al. 2018). For forensic phonetics, formant measures remain highly relevant. While mean formant frequencies may drift with age, their relative configuration patterns across vowels are often preserved, offering speaker-specific cues even in older voices (Eichhorn et al. 2018). On the other hand, the inclusion of formant frequency trajectories of diphthongs in forensic likelihood-ratio systems has been shown to improve the modeling of speaker variability (Morrison 2009).

Temporal aspects of speech also show clear age-related modulation. Older adults often exhibit a slower speech rate and longer segment durations (Yuan et al. 2006; Benjamin 1997). These temporal changes are linked to declines in cognitive-linguistic processing and reduced neuromotor efficiency. Forensic relevance lies in the fact that speech timing is both speaker specific and context dependent. When comparing non-contemporaneous samples, analysts must distinguish habitual speech rate changes due to aging from intentional variation or disguise.

Voice parameters such as jitter (cycle-to-cycle variation in F0) and shimmer (cycle-to-cycle variation in amplitude) reflect vocal stability and are highly sensitive to physiological aging (Linville 2001; Cavallaro et al. 2024; Gregory et al. 2012; Kost and Sataloff 2018; Ramig et al. 2001; Kosztyła-Hojna et al. 2023). With age, vocal fold elasticity and neuromuscular control diminish, which might lead to increased jitter and shimmer (Beton et al. 2022). In forensic applications, these parameters can indicate speaker health or temporal degradation but should be interpreted cautiously. Voice perturbation is also influenced by emotional state, recording conditions, and microphone quality. Nonetheless, sustained increases in perturbation measures across non-contemporaneous recordings can support an inference of natural aging rather than disguise.

5.3.2 Normative Data from Speech Aging Studies

Normative databases of acoustic aging are crucial for contextualizing forensic interpretations. Over the past three decades, several large-scale studies have established baseline expectations for how specific acoustic parameters evolve with age. For example, Linville (2001) compiled normative data indicating a mean increase in male F0 and a decrease in female F0 beyond age 60. Similarly, Xue and Hao (2003) found systematic formant lowering in both genders after 50, with F_2 showing greater variability due to articulatory factors. Yuan et al. (2006) provided extensive speech rate data across age groups, showing a decline in speech rate in speakers over 65. Such normative values enable forensic analysts to evaluate whether observed acoustic changes fall within the expected biological range or suggest other influences such as pathology or disguise. More recent reviews reaffirm that although there is broad inter-speaker variability, the overall direction of change—increased F0 for older men, decreased for women, lower formants, greater jitter and shimmer, and slower speech rate—is robust across studies and languages (Eichhorn et al. 2018).

5.3.3 Cultural and Linguistic Influences on Acoustic Aging Patterns

Speech aging does not occur in a vacuum. Linguistic and cultural environments significantly modulate the evolution of acoustic features across the lifespan. Cross-linguistic research reveals that the rate and degree of acoustic aging can vary across languages, depending on language-specific phonetic structures. Sociolinguistic factors also play a role. Older adults might often adjust their speech patterns to align with community norms. Such social adaptation may mask or exaggerate biological aging effects. Cultural attitudes toward speech and aging can further shape vocal behavior. From a forensic perspective, these findings stress the importance of language-specific reference data. Using acoustic norms from one language or dialect to evaluate another can lead to systematic bias in age estimation or speaker comparison. Therefore, forensic analysts must consider linguistic diversity, sociophonetic context, and dialectal influence when interpreting age-related voice change.

5.3.4 Forensic Application and Future Perspectives

The forensic application of acoustic aging research is twofold: to quantify expected intra-speaker variation due to aging and to model speech trajectories over time to enhance comparison accuracy. Modern approaches increasingly integrate statistical and machine learning models capable of accounting for temporal variability.

Techniques such as Gaussian mixture modeling (GMM) and i-vector systems, when trained on age-diverse datasets, have shown promise in adjusting similarity scores to reflect expected acoustic drift (Enzinger and Morrison 2017). Looking ahead, expanding longitudinal speech databases across languages, genders, and social contexts will be vital. Collaboration between forensic scientists, linguists, and clinicians can refine our understanding of the interplay between physiology, identity, and culture in the acoustic manifestation of age.

5.4 Forensic Applications—Speaker Comparison and Age Estimation

The forensic examination of speech has evolved from a primarily auditory practice to a sophisticated scientific discipline that integrates acoustic-phonetic, probabilistic, and computational methods. Among the many sources of variability that affect speaker comparison, biological aging stands out as a gradual, inevitable process that influences speech production mechanisms. Over time, physiological, hormonal, and anatomical changes in the vocal system lead to systematic acoustic drift in features such as F0, formant structure, temporal rate, and spectral balance (Linville 2001; Hollien and Shipp 1972; Reubold et al. 2010). In forensic contexts, such changes complicate both speaker comparison and age estimation. When recordings are made years apart, analysts ought to distinguish natural age-related differences from speaker identity differences. Similarly, estimating a speaker's chronological or apparent age from speech can guide investigations but must be approached cautiously, given wide inter-speaker variability.

5.4.1 Age-Related Speech Change and Its Impact on Forensic Voice Comparison

The speech signal is the acoustic result of several physiological subsystems— respiration, phonation, articulation, and resonance, all of which undergo age-related transformations. Vocal fold elasticity decreases with age due to changes in the collagen and elastin fiber composition, leading to alterations in vibration frequency and stability (Beton et al. 2022). Similarly, ossification of laryngeal cartilages and atrophy of intrinsic laryngeal muscles reduce phonatory efficiency, increasing breathiness and irregularity in voice production (Beton et al. 2022; Awan 2006; Lundy et al. 1998). Acoustically, these physiological changes are reflected in F0 drift: decreases in adulthood, increases in elderly males, and decreases in postmenopausal females (Xue and Hao 2003; Eichhorn et al. 2018; Hollien and Shipp 1972); formant centralization—vowels occupy a smaller acoustic space due to reduced articulatory precision (Narasimhan and Karunarathne 2021); temporal slowing or decreased speech rate; and increased pausing (Yuan et al. 2006; Benjamin 1997) and increased perturbation measures (Gregory et al. 2012).

When comparing voice samples separated by several years, forensic analysts must account for expected intra-speaker variability due to aging, as speech characteristics might change in predictable yet individual ways. If such changes are not considered, analysts risk false exclusions or false inclusions. Morrison (2009) proposed the likelihood ratio framework for forensic voice comparison, which evaluates the probability of observed acoustic similarities under two competing hypotheses—H_1, where both recordings come from the same speaker, allowing for aging effects, and H_2, where recordings come from different speakers. By including age as a covariate or by modeling expected within-speaker variation using population data, forensic systems can quantify the evidential value of observed differences. Such models might be crucial to the empirical validation approach.

5.4.2 Techniques for Estimating Speaker Age from Speech Samples

Age estimation relies on measurable acoustic correlates that reflect vocal tract aging. Numerous studies identify F0, formant dispersion, temporal measures, and perturbation indices as primary indicators (Linville 2001; Xue and Hao 2003). Perceptual experiments showed that listeners can estimate speaker age with moderate accuracy, especially when given long speech segments (Harnsberger et al. 2008). These perceptual judgments align with acoustic findings that higher jitter/shimmer and a slower rate correlate with older voices.

Age estimation can be particularly informative in criminal or asylum cases involving anonymous calls or disputed identities. However, results must always be contextualized within linguistic, cultural, and recording constraints. Early statistical approaches used multiple linear regression to relate acoustic features to age. More recently, machine learning models, including support vector regression (SVR) and convolutional neural networks (CNNs), have achieved improved performance in automatic age estimation. In forensic contexts, however, interpretability and robustness take precedence over accuracy. However, forensic experts should prefer hybrid models combining acoustic-phonetic validation with statistical inference to avoid black-box decision-making.

5.4.3 Challenges in Matching Speech Recorded at Different Life Stages

The first challenge is the temporal distance and non-contemporaneity. Non-contemporaneous comparisons—recordings separated by years or decades—pose one of the most complex problems in forensic phonetics. Rhodes (2012) systematically investigated non-contemporaneous samples and found that temporal distance increases acoustic divergence, particularly in F0 and formant distributions. Such findings have significant forensic implications; therefore, analysts must use reference data quantifying typical acoustic drift to accurately interpret differences. The second challenge is the variability in channel, style, and recording. Differences in microphone type, environment, compression, and speech style introduce further variability. However, channel mismatch can distort cepstral features more than natural aging itself (Univaso 2017). Modern systems therefore employ channel compensation techniques, such as within-class covariance normalization (WCCN), nuisance attribute projection (NAP), and i-vector frameworks, to minimize channel-related differences (Dehak et al. 2011). The next challenge is the sociophonetic and linguistic adaptation. The investigator must be aware that differences in vowel formants or speech rhythm between two recordings might also reflect sociolinguistic adaptation rather than solely biological aging. Additionally, speakers may modify their voices voluntarily in forensic contexts (e.g., disguise), complicating interpretation. Therefore, forensic analysts must contextualize observed changes within linguistic, social, and recording frameworks rather than attributing them solely to aging.

5.4.4 Bayesian and Likelihood Ratio Approaches to Forensic Inference

Bayesian inference provides a transparent probabilistic framework for evaluating forensic voice evidence. Rather than making categorical judgments, analysts can compute the likelihood ratio (LR) (Morrison 2009). This method quantifies how much more probable the observed data are under one hypothesis versus another, enabling graded expressions of evidential strength. Age can be modeled as a nuisance variable or covariate in the likelihood computation. By calibrating LRs using age-stratified population data, forensic systems can adjust for expected acoustic drift (Morrison 2009).

Therefore, age-related change in speech production poses both a scientific challenge and an analytical opportunity for forensic phonetics. While physiological aging alters the acoustic fabric of the voice, careful modeling and empirical calibration allow forensic analysts to distinguish natural variation from speaker identity differences. Accurate forensic practice now integrates biologically informed acoustic analysis, machine learning tools, and Bayesian inference to assess voice evidence probabilistically. The goal is not to eliminate uncertainty but to quantify it transparently. As forensic speech science advances, further longitudinal corpora and cross-linguistic data will be essential to refine age models and ensure that justice systems can rely on scientifically validated and explainable voice evidence.

5.5 Challenges, Ethical Considerations, and Future Directions

Forensic speech science stands at the intersection of linguistics, signal processing, and legal interpretation. While advances in acoustic modeling, machine learning, and probabilistic reasoning have increased objectivity, practical and ethical challenges persist. Voices are deeply personal, dynamic, and influenced by physiology, emotion, health, and social identity—characteristics that complicate forensic interpretation.

5.5.1 Interpersonal Variability and the Influence of Health and Emotion

The challenges of interpersonal variability, health-related voice change, and emotional modulation affect both the reliability of forensic voice comparison and the interpretability of automated systems. Similarly, globalization and linguistic diversity raise questions about how well current models handle multilingual or code-switching speakers. Finally, as speech technologies move toward automation and big-data modeling, there is a growing need for ethical frameworks, data standardization, and cross-linguistic databases that respect privacy, fairness, and scientific rigor.

Voice quality is sensitive to a range of health conditions affecting respiration, phonation, and articulation. Laryngeal diseases (e.g., presbyphonia, vocal fold paralysis), respiratory illnesses, and hormonal fluctuations can significantly alter spectral and temporal characteristics (Narasimhan 2020; Narasimhan and Dhanya 2020; Soumya and Narasimhan 2020). Aging and pathology might produce overlapping acoustic effects such as increased jitter, shimmer, and spectral noise. This complicates forensic evaluation, as analysts may misinterpret health-related deviations as evidence of speaker differences. To mitigate this misclassification, it is crucial to maintain comprehensive metadata on the health status, medication use, and vocal condition of speakers within forensic databases. Yet, such data are often unavailable in casework recordings, emphasizing the need for cautious interpretation.

Emotion also has a profound impact on acoustic patterns. Emotions such as fear, anger, or stress can alter acoustic parameters (Vroomen and Collier 1993), and forensic recordings often occur in high-stress environments where these effects may be prominent. Analysts are therefore encouraged to interpret acoustic evidence in light of emotional context rather than assuming neutral baseline conditions. Emerging approaches combining emotion normalization algorithms with Bayesian modeling might show promise for separating emotional variance from speaker identity.

5.5.2 Speech Changes in Multilingual and Multidialectal Speakers

In an increasingly globalized world, many speakers alternate between languages or dialects. Multilingual and multidialectal speech introduces an additional layer of acoustic-phonetic complexity. The phonological and prosodic system of each language can reshape the realization of vowels, consonants, and suprasegmental patterns (Foulkes and French 2012; Narasimhan et al. 2013). Code-switching—alternating between languages within a conversation—is common among bilingual speakers. Therefore, code-switched utterances reflect hybrid phonetic properties, influenced by both language systems (Bullock and Toribio 2009; Sahana et al. 2025). In forensic contexts, this means that cross-language comparisons may confound language-specific articulatory habits with identity-related differences. To mitigate such effects, forensic comparisons should, wherever possible, be language matched, using similar lexical and phonotactic contexts. Additionally, multilingual reference corpora might be essential for estimating expected variability across languages. Further, sociophonetic factors such as language dominance, education, and migration history might also influence how bilinguals produce speech sounds. Thus, forensic interpretation must consider not only physiological aging but also cultural-linguistic identity.

5.5.3 Ethical Implications of Automated Speech-Based Age Profiling

Machine learning and deep neural networks have transformed voice analysis, enabling systems to infer attributes such as age, sex, and emotional state from acoustic patterns. Automated age estimation systems are now applied in contexts ranging from security to online age verification. While promising, such systems raise serious ethical and legal concerns. Speech encodes sensitive biometric and behavioral data; using it for automated profiling risks privacy invasion, bias, and misuse if deployed without oversight (Whittaker et al. 2018). Collecting and using speech data engages legal frameworks that classify biometric voice data as "sensitive personal information." Furthermore, automated inference of age, gender, or emotion may cross ethical boundaries if used for surveillance or profiling without consent. Ethical guidelines require informed consent, anonymization, and purpose limitation in the development of speech corpora.

Bias is also an essential factor in speech-based models and can arise from unbalanced training data—particularly when datasets overrepresent specific accents, age groups, or genders. In forensic age estimation, similar biases could disproportionately affect speakers from underrepresented linguistic or ethnic backgrounds. Ethical practice, therefore, demands that models undergo bias auditing and performance reporting across subgroups.

5.5.4 Future Directions: Databases, Modeling, and Standardization

A persistent limitation in forensic speech science is the lack of comprehensive longitudinal and multilingual datasets. Existing corpora databases are valuable but restricted mainly to English and short-term recordings. Longitudinal datasets capturing speech change over decades are rare. Establishing internationally shared databases encompassing multiple languages, dialects, and age ranges would enable robust modeling of age-related drift, multilingual variability, and channel diversity. Developing cross-linguistic acoustic normalization is another key goal. Techniques such as voice conversion, bottleneck feature mapping, and transfer learning can adapt models trained on one language to another. In forensic contexts, this enables language-agnostic speaker comparison, reducing the bias inherent in English-centric models. However, this requires rigorous validation and transparency to ensure admissibility in court. Future databases must also integrate metadata beyond demographics—including health status, emotional context, and sociolinguistic background. Such metadata would allow analysts to separate physiological from situational effects, improving forensic interpretability. Cross-disciplinary collaboration between phoniatrics and psychology is crucial for building multimodal datasets that link acoustic, perceptual, and physiological dimensions. Further, international standards and open protocols remain fragmented. An integrated governance model could unify forensic speech data collection, validation, and reporting. Transparency in algorithms, validation metrics, and bias audits will be essential for maintaining trust in automated systems.

The future of forensic speech science depends on balancing technical innovation with ethical responsibility. The challenges posed by biological variability, emotional and health influences, and linguistic diversity underscore that the human voice cannot be reduced to a static biometric template. Ethical frameworks must evolve alongside technology, ensuring that automated age and identity profiling respects privacy, avoids bias, and remains explainable. Meanwhile, scientific progress requires building inclusive, longitudinal, and multilingual databases and developing standardized cross-linguistic models that accurately represent human diversity. Only through collaboration between linguists, phoneticians, computer scientists, ethicists, and legal experts can forensic speech science fulfill its potential as a fair and transparent instrument of justice.

5.6 Summary and Conclusion

Speech, unlike static biometric markers such as fingerprints or DNA, is a dynamic and multifactorial phenomenon. Across the lifespan, it reflects the interaction of biological aging, health, sociolinguistic context, and emotional states. This book explored how the natural trajectory of speech change across age influences forensic investigation—especially in speaker comparison, age estimation, and the evaluation of non-contemporaneous recordings. The synthesis of current research presented here establishes that understanding age-related transformations in the human voice is indispensable to the scientific and ethical advancement of forensic speech science.

5.6.1 Biological and Acoustic Foundations of Speech Aging

The biological process of aging induces a range of structural and functional transformations within the vocal apparatus. The vocal folds undergo atrophy, thinning, and bowing; cartilage ossifies; and respiratory efficiency diminishes. These anatomical shifts reduce vocal fold tension and stability, producing measurable acoustic effects, including changes in F0, altered formant structure, and increased jitter and shimmer. In men, F0 generally declines through middle age and then rises in later years, whereas in women, postmenopausal hormonal changes lower F0. Articulatory and resonatory adjustments, including reduced tongue mobility and weakened palatal control, lead to vowel centralization and broader formant bandwidths. Consequently, the acoustic distinctiveness of vowels narrows, and temporal features such as speech rate and pausing patterns change. These biological and acoustic patterns form the empirical basis for differentiating normal aging from pathological conditions such as presbyphonia or voice disorders secondary to systemic disease. Further, individual trajectories are highly variable, reflecting differences in health, lifestyle, and gender. Recognizing this variability is critical for forensic contexts where misinterpretation of natural acoustic drift could result in evidential error.

5.6.2 Acoustic Markers and Quantitative Modelling

Age affects multiple measurable dimensions of speech. The six most salient acoustic markers—fundamental frequency, formant frequencies, formant bandwidths, speech rate, jitter, and shimmer—have all been studied longitudinally. Formant trajectory analysis enhances forensic speaker comparison by modelling diphthongal transitions rather than relying solely on static measurements. This technique accommodates intra-speaker temporal variation, making it especially useful in non-contemporaneous forensic cases. Normative datasets provide expected reference ranges for age-dependent acoustic change, allowing practitioners to distinguish normal aging from anomalous deviations. Cultural and linguistic factors further modulate these markers. Studies across languages show that vowel reduction, timing, and formant shifts vary with phonological systems and sociolinguistic norms. Thus, cross-language modelling must integrate both physiological and cultural diversity to ensure fair forensic interpretation.

5.6.3 Forensic Applications: Speaker Comparison and Age Estimation

The forensic application of these findings centers on two domains: speaker comparison and age estimation. Over time, physiological and acoustic drift complicate the task of matching speech samples recorded at different life stages. Modern forensic systems adopt Bayesian inference and likelihood-ratio frameworks that explicitly incorporate age as a covariate. These methods quantify evidential strength by calculating how much more probable observed similarities are under the same-speaker versus different-speaker hypotheses, adjusting for expected aging. When supported by normative databases, such models enhance transparency and reproducibility. For age estimation, acoustic correlates such as F0, formant dispersion, and perturbation indices can predict chronological or apparent age with moderate accuracy. Although deep learning models show improved performance, interpretability remains paramount in forensic settings. Experts advocate hybrid approaches that combine statistical learning with acoustic-phonetic rationale to avoid "black-box" judgments.

5.6.4 Interpersonal Variability, Health, and Emotion

Voice variability arising from health conditions and emotional states remains a major source of forensic uncertainty. Laryngeal disorders, respiratory diseases, or hormonal imbalances can mimic or obscure the effects of natural aging. Similarly, emotional stress alters F0, tempo, and spectral features, and forensic recordings often capture speakers under duress. Without contextual data, analysts may mistakenly attribute emotion-driven deviations to identity differences. Future databases should therefore integrate metadata on health, medication, and affective state to guide interpretation.

5.6.5 Speech Change in Multilingual and Multidialectal Contexts

Globalization has rendered monolingual assumptions obsolete. Multilingual and code-switching speakers exhibit language-specific acoustic patterns influenced by phonological transfer and sociolinguistic context. Forensic voice comparison must be language matched and dialect sensitive to prevent systematic bias. For instance, vowel centralization or rhythm differences may stem from language structure rather than speaker identity. Cross-linguistic modelling using multilingual corpora and adaptation algorithms such as transfer learning or bottleneck mapping offers a promising way forward.

5.6.6 Ethical and Legal Considerations in Automated Profiling

The expansion of automated age and identity estimation raises profound ethical questions. Voice contains intimate biometric and behavioral data; using it for surveillance or profiling without consent risks violating privacy and human rights. Bias in training data can lead to discriminatory outcomes, particularly when certain dialects or age groups are underrepresented. Ethical forensic practice, therefore, demands transparency, informed consent, and bias auditing. Data must be anonymized, models must publish subgroup performance metrics, and forensic deployment should remain explainable to legal stakeholders. Furthermore, as AI-driven models increasingly enter forensic practice, legal frameworks must evolve to regulate the admissibility of algorithmic evidence. Courts require interpretability, reproducibility, and validated methodology—criteria that "black-box" neural systems often fail to meet. Hence, forensic phonetics should prioritize explainable AI, incorporating human oversight and clearly documented uncertainty estimates.

5.6.7 Future Directions: Databases, Modelling, and Standardization

Progress in forensic speech science hinges on developing longitudinal, multilingual, and metadata-rich databases. Existing corpora are often short term, monolingual, and demographically narrow. Expanding datasets across languages and age ranges would enable more accurate modelling of intra-speaker variability, health effects, and sociophonetic adaptation. Collaborative projects integrating speech science, medicine, and computational linguistics are needed to create standardized protocols for recording, annotation, and acoustic feature extraction. Another critical frontier lies in cross-language normalization. Algorithms capable of mapping acoustic parameters across phonological systems would allow language-agnostic speaker comparison, minimizing the dominance of English-centric data. Equally important are open standards for validation and reporting. Adopting unified frameworks for likelihood-ratio calibration, metadata documentation, and bias evaluation will strengthen scientific credibility and judicial acceptance.

5.6.8 Conclusion

The trajectory of speech change across age reflects a lifelong interplay between biology, behavior, and society. Forensic science, tasked with interpreting this complex signal, must move beyond simplistic notions of "voice prints" toward a probabilistic understanding of speech as a dynamic biometric. Accurate forensic evaluation requires integrating normative aging data, linguistic diversity, and ethical safeguards into every stage of analysis. This chapter collectively demonstrates that age-related variation is not noise—it is meaningful evidence. When properly modelled, it enhances the precision of speaker comparison and the fairness of forensic inference. Conversely, neglecting it risks scientific and legal error. Future research must continue to bridge empirical phonetics with computational modelling, grounded in transparent, multilingual, and ethically governed data infrastructures. Ultimately, the future of forensic speech science lies in embracing human variability—not eliminating it. By respecting the biological, social, and ethical dimensions of voice, practitioners can ensure that speech evidence remains a tool for truth rather than prejudice—serving justice with both scientific rigor and humanity.

References

Awan SN (2006) The aging female voice: acoustic and respiratory data. Clin Linguist Phonetics 20(2–3):171–180. https://doi.org/10.1080/02699200400026918

Benjamin BJ (1997) Speech production of normally aging adults. Semin Speech Lang 18(2):135–141. https://doi.org/10.1055/s-2008-1064068

Beton S, Yücel L, Başak H, Çiler Büyükatalay Z (2022) The Elderly Voice: Mechanisms, Disorders and Treatment Methods. Turkish Arch Otorhinolaryngol 60(4):220–226. https://doi.org/10.4274/tao.2022.2022-8-1

Bullock BE, Toribio AJ (2009) The Cambridge handbook of linguistic code-switching. Cambridge University Press, Cambridge. https://doi.org/10.1017/CBO9780511576331

Cavallaro G, Fiorella ML, Barbara F, Quaranta N, Di Nicola V (2024) Exploring age-related changes in acoustic voice analysis parameters: insights from a study on older people. J Gerontol Geriatr 72(2):51–59. https://doi.org/10.36150/2499-6564-N612

D'Haeseleer E, Depypere H, Claeys S, Wuyts FL, De Ley S, Van Lierde KM (2011) The impact of menopause on vocal quality. Menopause 18(3):267–272. https://doi.org/10.1097/gme.0b013e3181f3ee36

Dehak N, Kenny PJ, Dehak R, Dumouchel P, Ouellet P (2011) Front-end factor analysis for speaker verification. IEEE Trans Acoust 19(4):788–798. https://doi.org/10.1109/iccomm.2018.8453731

Deluca V, Rothman J, Pliatsikas C (2019) Linguistic immersion and structural effects on the bilingual brain: a longitudinal study. Bilingualism 22(5):1160–1175. https://doi.org/10.1017/S1366728918000883

Department for International Development (2014) Assessing the strength of evidence. The University of York. [Online]. Available: https://www.gov.uk/government/uploads/system/uploads/attachment_data/file/291982/HTN-strength-evidence-march2014.pdf

Dromey C, Boyce K, Channell R (2014) Effects of age and syntactic complexity on speech motor performance. 57(6). https://doi.org/10.1044/2014_JSLHR-S-13-0327

Eichhorn JT, Kent RD, Austin D, Vorperian HK (2018) Effects of aging on vocal fundamental frequency and vowel formants in men and women. https://doi.org/10.1016/j.jvoice.2017.08.003

Enzinger E, Morrison GS (2017) Empirical test of the performance of an acoustic-phonetic approach to forensic voice comparison under conditions similar to those of a real case. Forensic Sci Int 277:30–40. https://doi.org/10.1016/j.forsciint.2017.05.007

Foulkes P, French P (2012) Forensic Speaker Comparison: A Linguistic–Acoustic Perspective. Oxford University Press. https://doi.org/10.1093/oxfordhb/9780199572120.013.0041

Gregory ND, Chandran S, Lurie D, Sataloff RT (2012) Voice disorders in the elderly. J Voice 26(2):254–258. https://doi.org/10.1016/j.jvoice.2010.10.024

Harnsberger JD, Shrivastav R, Brown WS, Rothman H, Hollien H (2008) Speaking rate and fundamental frequency as speech cues to perceived age. J Voice 22(1):58–69. https://doi.org/10.1016/j.jvoice.2006.07.004

Hollien H, Shipp T (1972) Speaking fundamental frequency and chronologic age in males. J Speech Hear Res 15(1):155–159. https://doi.org/10.1044/jshr.1501.155

Hughes V, Foulkes P (2015) The relevant population in forensic voice comparison: effects of varying delimitations of social class and age. Speech Comm 66:218–230. https://doi.org/10.1016/j.specom.2014.10.006

Ivanova O, Martínez-Nicolás I, Meilán JJG (2024) Speech changes in old age: methodological considerations for speech-based discrimination of healthy ageing and Alzheimer's disease. Int J Lang Commun Disord 59(1):13–37. https://doi.org/10.1111/1460-6984.12888

Kong C, Long X, Liu J (2024) An acoustic study on age-related changes in vowel production of Chinese. J Phon 104. https://doi.org/10.1016/j.wocn.2024.101324

Kost KM, Sataloff RT (2018) Voice disorders in the elderly. https://doi.org/10.1016/j.cger.2018.01.010

Kosztyła-Hojna B, Zdrojkowski M, Duchnowska E (2023) Presbyphonia as an individual process of voice change. J Voice 37(2):303.e1–303.e14. https://doi.org/10.1016/j.jvoice.2020.12.046

Linville S (2001) Vocal aging. Singular Thomson Learning, San Diego

Lundy DS, Silva C, Casiano RR, Lu FL, Xue JW (1998) Cause of hoarseness in elderly patients. Otolaryngol-HeadNeckSurg118(4):481–485.https://doi.org/10.1016/S0194-5998(98)70205-0

Morrison GS (2009) Likelihood-ratio forensic voice comparison using parametric representations of the formant trajectories of diphthongs. J Acoust Soc Am 125(4):2387–2397. https://doi.org/10.1121/1.3081384

Narasimhan SV (2020) Cepstral analysis of voice in dysphonic subjects. J. Hear. Lang. Speech 1(1)

Narasimhan SV, Dhanya S (2020) Cepstral measures of voice in women with polycystic ovarian syndrome. Asia Pacific J Multidiscip Res 8(1):81–85

Narasimhan SV, Karunarathne WGSS (2021) Effect of age and gender on voice onset time: data from Sinhalese. Vidyodaya J Sci 24(02):65–74. https://doi.org/10.31357/vjs.v24i02.5416

S. V Narasimhan, M. Thingom, and R. Kiran, "Influence of stress pattern of native language on non-native language: a comparative study between tone and non-tone language speakers," 2013. [Online]. Available: www.languageinindia.com

Ramig LO et al (2001) The aging voice: a review, treatment data and familial and genetic perspectives. https://doi.org/10.1159/000052680

Reubold U, Harrington J, Kleber F (2010) Vocal aging effects on F0 and the first formant: a longitudinal analysis in adult speakers. Speech Comm 52(7–8):638–651. https://doi.org/10.1016/j.specom.2010.02.012

Rhodes RW (2012) Assessing the strength of non-contemporaneous forensic speech evidence. The University of York

Sahana K, Narasimhan SV, Yashaswini G (2025) Adaptation and Validation of the Bilingual Code-Switching Profile Into Kannada. J. Speech, Lang. Hear Res:1–13. https://doi.org/10.1044/2025_JSLHR-24-00214

Schötz S (2007) Acoustic analysis of adult speaker age. In: Müller C (ed) Speaker Classification I. Lecture Notes in Computer Science, vol 4343. Springer, Berlin Heidelberg, pp 88–107. https://doi.org/10.1007/978-3-540-74200-5_5

Soumya M, Narasimhan SV (2020) Correlation between subjective and objective parameters of voice in elderly male speakers. J Voice 36(6):823–831. https://doi.org/10.1016/j.jvoice.2020.10.006

Taylor S, Dromey C, Nissen SL, Tanner K, Eggett D, Corbin-Lewis K (2020) Age-related changes in speech and voice: spectral and cepstral measures. J Speech Lang Hear Res 63(3):647–660. https://doi.org/10.1044/2019_JSLHR-19-00028

Titze IR (1989) Physiologic and acoustic differences between male and female voices. J Acoust Soc Am 85(4):1699–1707

Univaso P (2017) Forensic speaker recognition. IEEE Lat Am Trans 15(9):1754–1770. https://doi.org/10.1007/978-1-4614-0263-3

Vroomen J, Collier R, Mozziconacci S (1993) Duration and intonation in emotional speech. Third Eur Conf Speech Commun Technol 1p:577–580. [Online]. Available: http://arno.uvt.nl/show.cgi?fid=14382

Whittaker M et al (2018) AI now report 2018. AI Now:1–62

Xue SA, Hao GJ (2003) Changes in the human vocal tract due to aging and the acoustic correlates of speech production: A pilot study. J. Speech, Lang. Hear Res 46(3):689–701. https://doi.org/10.1044/1092-4388(2003/054)

Yuan J, Liberman M, Cieri C (2006) Towards an integrated understanding of speech timing and aging: evidence from large corpora. In: Interspeech, Pittsburgh

Voice Matching Strategies and Algorithms

6

Himanshu Singh, Gaurav Saxena, and Yogendra Kumar Awasthi

Abstract

Voice matching is a crucial technology in the domains of speaker verification, forensic analysis, human-computer interaction, and personalized services. Over the years, various strategies and algorithms have evolved to improve the accuracy, robustness, and real-time capabilities of voice matching systems. Traditional techniques such as Mel-Frequency Cepstral Coefficients (MFCC) and Dynamic Time Warping (DTW) laid the foundation for acoustic feature extraction and temporal alignment. Modern algorithms incorporate advanced machine learning models, including deep neural networks and attention-based architectures, to capture speaker-specific nuances from speech signals. Techniques such as the Iterative Nearest Conversion and Alignment (INCA), multi-dimensional perception flow matching, and spectral envelope mapping with residual prediction have significantly enhanced the performance in noisy and cross-domain environments. Recent advancements also emphasize few-shot and self-supervised learning approaches to address limited data scenarios. Additionally, multi-modal fusion strategies that integrate facial cues or textual inputs are being explored for improved reliability. The field is increasingly focused on adversarial robustness, explainability, and privacy-preserving mechanisms to build trustworthy systems. This abstract outlines the historical evolution, core methodologies, and emerging directions in voice matching algorithms, offering insights into their applications

H. Singh
Department of Physics, Hindu College, University of Delhi, New Delhi, India

G. Saxena
Electronics and Communication Engineering, Ajay Kumar Garg Engineering College, Ghaziabad, UP, India

Y. K. Awasthi (✉)
Electronics and Communication Engineering, Galgotias University, Greater Noida, UP, India

V. Kumar et al. (eds.), *Forensic Speech Sciences*, New Horizons in Forensic Science, https://doi.org/10.1007/978-981-92-1475-4_6

and potential for future development in real-world voice recognition and authentication systems.

Keywords

Acoustic feature extraction · Deep neural networks (DNN) · Dynamic time warping (DTW) · Mel-Frequency Cepstral Coefficients (MFCC) · Voice matching · Speaker verification

6.1 Introduction

Voice matching refers to the identification or verification of a speaker's identity through the analysis and comparison of vocal characteristics. It plays an essential role in a wide range of domains, from biometric security systems and forensic investigations to the personalization of AI-driven virtual assistants and the increasingly sophisticated realm of voice cloning technologies (Zhang et al. 2024; Alzain and Wang 2023a; Xie et al. 2023). As the demand for natural, secure, and intuitive human–machine interaction grows, so does the importance of accurate and efficient voice matching systems. At its core, voice matching is grounded in the unique physiological and behavioral features of a person's voice—such as pitch, timbre, formant structure, and speaking style—which serve as distinctive identifiers much like fingerprints or facial patterns (Heo et al. 2023a). These features are extracted from voice recordings using various signal processing techniques and are then analyzed using machine learning or statistical models to determine whether two voice samples belong to the same individual (Johri et al. 2021).

The development of voice matching strategies has seen significant evolution over the past few decades. Early techniques were based on simple spectral comparisons and template matching, while later advancements introduced sophisticated algorithms such as Mel-Frequency Cepstral Coefficients (MFCC) and Dynamic Time Warping (DTW). With the rise of deep learning and artificial intelligence, contemporary systems now leverage complex neural architectures capable of learning high-dimensional speaker embeddings, enabling more robust performance even in noisy or cross-channel environments (Thienpondt et al. 2024).

This chapter delves into both classical and modern voice matching methodologies. It begins with a brief historical overview of speaker recognition systems and outlines the core principles behind feature extraction and pattern matching. Key algorithms—such as MFCC and DTW, Iterative Nearest Neighbor and Conversion Alignment (INCA), Multi-Dimensional Perception Flow Matching, and spectral envelope mapping strategies—are discussed in detail, highlighting their operational mechanisms and comparative effectiveness. Additionally, the chapter explores current limitations, such as susceptibility to spoofing, variability in recording conditions, and challenges in multilingual and cross-age matching scenarios (Kinnunen and Sahidullah 2024). Finally, the chapter outlines promising directions for future research, emphasizing the need for adaptive, explainable, and privacy-preserving voice matching algorithms. As voice-based technologies continue to proliferate across sectors, the development of innovative, resilient voice matching strategies will be crucial in ensuring their ethical and effective deployment (Kraetzer et al. 2023).

6.2 Historical Background of Voice Matching Strategies

The evolution of voice matching strategies is closely tied to the broader developments in signal processing, pattern recognition, and artificial intelligence. The origins of this field trace back to the mid-20th century, when the primary methods for analyzing and comparing voices were rooted in analog spectrographic techniques. During this period, trained forensic experts would visually inspect spectrograms—visual representations of the speech signal's frequency content over time—to manually compare voice samples. These early systems, while groundbreaking at the time, were limited by subjective interpretation, lack of automation, and restricted applicability to real-world scenarios (Nagrani et al. 2023a).

1970–1980s: The Digital Signal Processing Era

A significant leap occurred in the 1970s and 1980s with the advent of digital signal processing (DSP). Researchers began developing mathematical models to analyze speech signals numerically, leading to the first generation of automated voice matching systems. Linear predictive coding (LPC) emerged as a prominent technique during this time, enabling the estimation of the vocal tract parameters by minimizing the prediction error in speech frames. LPC helped compress speech data efficiently and also laid the groundwork for speaker-specific feature extraction (Desplanques et al. 2023a). Parallelly, template matching methods were introduced. These techniques relied on storing prototypical voice patterns and comparing incoming voice samples directly against these templates. Although simple and computationally feasible, these early systems struggled with variations in speaking style, recording conditions, and environmental noise (Nolan et al. 2023).

1990s: Rise of Statistical Modeling

The 1990s marked a major shift with the integration of statistical pattern recognition techniques into speaker recognition. Hidden Markov Models (HMM)—already well established in automatic speech recognition—were adapted to model the sequential nature of speech for speaker verification tasks. These models captured temporal dynamics more effectively than static templates and showed improved performance in real-world conditions (Jhaveri et al. 2022). Additionally, Gaussian Mixture Models (GMM) gained popularity as robust speaker modeling tools. GMMs represented the distribution of acoustic features across a speaker's voice sample, offering a probabilistic framework that could model intra-speaker variability. The combination of GMMs with universal background models (UBMs) and maximum a posteriori (MAP) adaptation strategies significantly boosted the performance of speaker verification systems and became a standard approach in the field for over a decade (Rose 2023).

2000s: Feature Engineering and Distance-Based Matching

During the early 2000s, feature engineering became a central focus of voice matching research. Mel-frequency Cepstral Coefficients (MFCC)—which mimics the human auditory perception of sound—was widely adopted as the de facto standard for representing speech signals. MFCCs effectively captured the spectral envelope of speech and demonstrated high discriminability across speakers (Desplanques et al. 2023b). To compare MFCC sequences between different voice samples, techniques such as Dynamic Time Warping (DTW) were employed. DTW enabled alignment of speech frames that may vary in length or speaking speed, allowing for more flexible and accurate comparisons. These techniques marked a shift toward distance-based approaches, where the similarity between two voice samples could be computed using dynamic alignment algorithms (Heo et al. 2023b).

2010s to Present: The Deep Learning Revolution

The 2010s ushered in a paradigm shift with the rise of deep learning, dramatically transforming the landscape of voice matching. Convolutional neural networks (CNNs) were employed to process spectrograms and learn hierarchical representations of speech features directly from raw data, bypassing the need for handcrafted features like MFCCs. Simultaneously, recurrent neural networks (RNNs) and their variants such as long short-term memory (LSTM) networks gained traction due to their ability to model temporal dependencies and sequential structure in speech signals (Alzain and Wang 2023b). These architectures provided significant improvements in speaker embedding quality and verification accuracy. More recently, transformer-based models—originally introduced in the field of natural language processing—have been adapted for speaker recognition tasks. Models such as ECAPA-TDNN and variants of self-attention networks now achieve state-of-the-art results, benefiting from large-scale training, self-supervised learning, and the use of speaker embeddings such as x-vectors and d-vectors (Rajasekar et al. 2023).

Summary of Milestones

- 1970–1980s: analog spectrogram inspection, LPC for feature extraction, and early template matching
- 1990s: introduction of HMM and GMM for probabilistic speaker modeling
- 2000s: MFCCs and DTW popularized for robust, data-driven voice comparison
- 2010s–present: emergence of deep learning, CNNs, RNNs, and transformer-based models revolutionizing accuracy and scalability

These advancements have progressively addressed key challenges in voice matching, such as robustness to noise, channel variability, and speaker adaptation (Todisco et al. 2024). Yet, the field continues to evolve, with current efforts focusing on few-shot learning, zero-shot speaker verification, privacy-preserving models, and real-time voice authentication in dynamic environments.

6.3 Key Techniques in Voice Matching Algorithms

Modern voice matching systems rely on a combination of acoustic feature extraction, statistical modeling, temporal alignment, and machine learning strategies. This section explores the foundational and advanced techniques that underpin voice matching algorithms, elaborating on their operational principles, advantages, and application contexts (Todisco et al. 2024).

6.3.1 Mel-Frequency Cepstral Coefficient (MFCC) and Dynamic Time Warping (DTW): Mel-Frequency Cepstral Coefficient (MFCC)

MFCC is one of the most widely used feature extraction techniques in the field of speech and speaker recognition. It is based on the human auditory perception, which perceives sound frequencies on a nonlinear scale known as the Mel scale. The algorithm aims to capture the spectral envelope of speech, which encodes speaker-specific vocal tract characteristics (Yamagishi et al. 2023).

Key Steps

- Framing and Windowing: The audio signal is divided into overlapping frames (typically 20–40 ms) to capture short-term spectral properties. A windowing function (e.g., Hamming window) is applied to reduce spectral leakage.
- Fast Fourier Transform (FFT): Converts the time-domain signal into the frequency domain.
- Mel Filter Bank Processing: Applies a triangular filter bank spaced along the Mel scale to simulate the human ear's frequency response.
- Logarithmic Compression: Applies a logarithmic function to simulate the ear's sensitivity to loudness variations.
- Discrete Cosine Transform (DCT): Compacts the signal energy into the first few coefficients (usually 12–13), known as MFCCs.

Advantages

- Effective in capturing speaker-dependent features such as the shape of the vocal tract
- Compact representation of speech suitable for downstream processing
- Relatively robust to background noise and channel variation with proper preprocessing

Dynamic Time Warping (DTW) DTW is a sequence alignment algorithm originally developed for speech recognition and widely used in time-series analysis. It measures similarity between two temporal sequences that may vary in length and speaking speed (Nagrani et al. 2023b).

Working Principle

- Computes a distance matrix between two feature sequences.
- Uses dynamic programming to find an optimal warping path that minimizes the cumulative distance.
- The warping path aligns the time axes of the sequences non-linearly, accommodating variations in speech tempo or duration.

Applications in Voice Matching

- Effective in text-independent speaker recognition where the speaker may utter different content across sessions
- Useful in systems requiring lightweight computation and template-based matching

MFCC-DTW Pipeline Combining MFCC and DTW allows for a powerful speaker verification pipeline. MFCC extracts speaker-relevant features, and DTW aligns them temporally, enabling comparison of speech samples recorded under different conditions.

6.3.2 Iterative Combination of a Nearest Neighbor Search Step and a Conversion Step Alignment (INCA)

The INCA algorithm introduces an iterative optimization framework tailored for complex voice matching tasks, particularly when dealing with speaker adaptation, cross-lingual data, or mismatched recording conditions (Namasudra and Roy 2018).

Algorithm Overview

- Step 1: Nearest Neighbor Search—identifies the closest matches to the input voice sample in a reference dataset based on an initial similarity metric or embedding space
- Step 2: Conversion Step Alignment—refines the alignment by transforming the target voice features to better match the source voice in terms of prosodic and spectral characteristics.

Iterative Refinement The algorithm repeats these two steps, updating the similarity measurement each time, thereby converging to a more accurate match. The iterative nature allows for dynamic adaptation to inter-speaker variability and mismatches in pronunciation, pitch, and accent.

Advantages

- Particularly suited for low-resource speaker identification or cross-domain verification
- Performs well under non-parallel training data and non-native speaker scenarios
- Enhanced robustness to linguistic content mismatch

6.3.3 Algorithm Based on Multi-dimensional Perception Flow Matching

This advanced approach treats voice features as multi-dimensional flow fields that represent the perceptual evolution of speech attributes over time. Instead of comparing static features or embeddings, this method captures temporal dynamics across multiple acoustic dimensions (Prasad et al. 2019).

Key Dimensions in Perception Flow

- Pitch contour
- Timbre spectral trajectory
- Rhythmic structure
- Amplitude dynamics (intensity)

Methodology

- Utilizes tensor decomposition techniques to represent these dynamic flows
- Applies flow alignment algorithms to match the perceptual trajectories between source and target voice samples
- Computes similarity as a function of flow congruence across perceptual axes

Strengths

- Handles emotional and prosodic variations effectively
- Better captures speaker identity embedded in expressive cues
- Suitable for emotion-aware voice authentication and speaker recognition in expressive speech domains

6.3.4 Algorithm Based on Spectral Envelope Mapping and Residual Prediction

This technique decomposes a speech signal into two components

1. Spectral Envelope—represents the vocal tract shape (slow-varying frequency response)
2. Residual Signal—represents the excitation source (e.g., glottal pulse train, voicing)

Processing Steps

- Apply linear predictive analysis or cepstral analysis to extract the spectral envelope.
- Use mapping functions (e.g., regression or neural networks) to align envelopes between voices.
- Predict and adjust the residual signal for better source-to-target transformation.

Applications

- High-fidelity voice conversion and speaker morphing, where the identity of one speaker is mapped onto another while preserving linguistic content.
- Voice synthesis systems, where naturalness and identity preservation are paramount.

Benefits

- Facilitates fine-grained control over voice timbre and texture
- Improves intelligibility and naturalness in matched or converted speech
- Essential for voice anonymization and identity obfuscation technologies

6.3.5 Deep Semantic Matching Network-Based Algorithms

Deep learning has revolutionized voice matching by enabling end-to-end learning of semantic-level speaker representations. These models transcend traditional acoustic feature matching by capturing high-level abstract features learned from vast speech datasets (Mittal et al. 2022).

Key Architectures

- Siamese Networks: Learn to compare two voice samples directly by minimizing a contrastive or triplet loss.
- Transformer Networks: Leverage self-attention mechanisms to model long-range dependencies and variable-length inputs.
- Speaker Embedding Networks: Such as SpeakerNet, x-vector, and d-vector architectures.

Core Concepts

- Speaker Embeddings: Voices are embedded into a fixed-dimensional vector space where similarity is measured using metrics like cosine similarity or Euclidean distance.
- Intra- and Inter-Speaker Variability Modeling: Networks are trained to minimize within-speaker variation and maximize between-speaker separation.

Notable Examples

- x-vectors: DNN-based embeddings trained with speaker labels, widely used in speaker diarization and verification.
- Wav2Vec 2.0: Self-supervised pretraining that captures contextual acoustic representations, further fine-tuned for speaker-related tasks.
- SpeakerNet: End-to-end deep speaker verification system using metric learning.

Advantages

- Superior performance in real-time, large-scale speaker verification
- Can generalize to unseen speakers with minimal additional training

- Amenable to domain adaptation, multilingual training, and emotion-aware speaker verification

The landscape of voice matching algorithms has evolved from signal processing techniques to deep learning-powered architectures. Each method—whether based on statistical modeling, perceptual alignment, or semantic embeddings—offers unique strengths tailored to specific challenges in speaker verification, identification, and transformation. The integration and hybridization of these approaches continue to push the boundaries of voice-based authentication and personalization technologies (Kraetzer et al. 2023; Rose 2023).

6.4 Need for Voice Matching Algorithms

The rapid integration of voice as a natural interface for human–machine interaction has made voice matching algorithms a critical component across a wide array of industries. These algorithms are not merely tools for identity verification—they also enable personalization, enhance system intelligence, and improve user experience. The rising demand for secure, scalable, and user-friendly voice-based solutions has further accelerated the development and deployment of advanced voice matching systems. Below, we explore the multifaceted need for such algorithms in greater detail.

6.4.1 Biometric Security

In the era of contactless interaction and rising concerns about digital identity theft, voice biometrics offers a secure and user-friendly alternative to traditional authentication mechanisms such as passwords or PINs (Prasad et al. 2019).

Applications

- Mobile banking apps and financial institutions increasingly deploy voice authentication as a secondary or even primary mode of user verification.
- Smartphone unlocking and secure device access using voice as a biometric identifier.
- Multi-factor authentication (MFA) in combination with facial recognition or fingerprint scanning for heightened security.

Challenges Addressed

- Resistance to spoofing and replay attacks through liveness detection and anti-spoofing measures.
- Ability to function in hands-free environments, supporting accessibility and convenience.

6.4.2 Forensics and Criminal Investigations

In the domain of forensic phonetics and law enforcement, voice matching plays a crucial role in identifying suspects, verifying claims, and presenting evidence in legal proceedings.

Applications

- Speaker verification in recorded phone calls, emergency call centers, ransom cases, or covert surveillance recordings
- Voiceprint databases maintained by government agencies for tracking criminal activity
- Courtroom admissibility of voice evidence, requiring high reliability and interpretability

Benefits

- Can assist investigations even when visual evidence is unavailable
- Enables cross-validation with other biometric traits such as fingerprints or DNA
- Facilitates speaker profiling, including language, accent, age, and emotional state

6.4.3 Healthcare and Assistive Technologies

Voice matching algorithms have transformative potential in healthcare diagnostics, particularly for detecting and monitoring neurological, psychological, and speech disorders.

Applications

- Early diagnosis of diseases such as Parkinson's, Alzheimer's, or ALS by analyzing voice irregularities and articulatory deficits
- Speech therapy and rehabilitation, where patient progress is monitored via automated voice pattern analysis
- Mental health screening, identifying stress, depression, or anxiety through vocal biomarkers

Innovations

- Integration with telemedicine platforms to provide non-invasive, continuous health monitoring
- Support for assistive voice technologies that adapt to users with dysarthria or stuttering, enabling clearer communication

6.4.4 Intelligent Virtual Assistants and Human–Computer Interaction

With the widespread adoption of AI-powered virtual assistants like Amazon's Alexa, Google Assistant, and Apple's Siri, the need for personalized and context-aware voice interfaces is greater than ever.

Applications
- Personalized user experiences, where the assistant tailors responses and content based on the recognized voice
- Multi-user environments, where the system distinguishes between household members to provide customized calendars, reminders, or media content
- Voice-controlled smart home devices, enabling seamless interaction with connected appliances (Rajasekar et al. 2023)

User Benefits
- Enhanced user satisfaction and system responsiveness
- Privacy and security, as only registered voices can access sensitive information or perform critical tasks

6.4.5 Telecommunication and Customer Experience

Voice matching techniques are increasingly used in telecommunications to enhance both network performance and customer service personalization.

Applications
- Adaptive noise suppression and voice enhancement in VoIP and mobile calls, improving clarity in real time
- Personalized call routing in call centers, where the system identifies frequent callers and connects them with preferred agents or services
- Speaker-aware speech enhancement, where background noise suppression adapts to the speaker's vocal characteristics (Mittal et al. 2022)

Operational Gains
- Improved call quality and user satisfaction
- Reduction in call handling time and customer churn in service-based industries

6.4.6 Broader Societal and Technological Implications

The growing reliance on voice as an interface is driving a paradigm shift toward voice-first ecosystems in both consumer and enterprise technologies. As devices become more embedded, context aware, and intelligent, robust voice matching algorithms are needed to address:

- Multilingual and multicultural user bases across global platforms
- Cross-device authentication, where a user's voice must be recognized consistently on phones, cars, wearables, and IoT devices
- Ethical and legal considerations, including voice data privacy, consent, and regulation compliance (e.g., GDPR, HIPAA)

Table 6.1 Summary of across domain application of voice matching tools

Domain	Use case	Impact
Biometric security	Banking apps, device unlocking, MFA	Enhanced security, seamless user experience
Forensics	Criminal investigations, legal voice evidence	Reliable speaker identification, judicial admissibility
Healthcare	Diagnosis of speech and cognitive disorders	Non-invasive, early detection, improved patient care
Virtual assistants	User personalization, multi-user identification	Context-aware, adaptive AI interaction
Telecommunications	Call enhancement, agent routing, speaker-aware processing	Better audio quality, efficient service delivery
Cross-domain	Multi-device voice interfaces, multilingual systems	Consistent and scalable voice authentication

The need for voice matching algorithms is not confined to security or convenience—it is fundamental to the next generation of human–machine interaction. As these systems become more pervasive, the demand for voice matching solutions that are accurate, resilient, explainable, and ethically sound will continue to grow (Thienpondt et al. 2024). Refer to Table 6.1.

6.5 Challenges and Limitations of Existing Algorithms

While voice matching technologies have made remarkable progress—especially with the advent of deep learning and large-scale speech datasets—they are still far from perfect. Real-world deployment scenarios introduce a range of challenges that limit their accuracy, robustness, scalability, generalizability, and ethical applicability. Understanding these limitations is crucial to guide future research, ensure reliable deployments, and maintain public trust in voice-enabled systems.

6.5.1 Variability in Speech Signal

Speaker-Intrinsic Variability

- A speaker's voice is not constant—it changes due to mood, health conditions, fatigue, stress, aging, and even time of day.
- These natural fluctuations cause a single person's voiceprint to span a wide acoustic space, reducing intra-speaker consistency.

Speaker-Extrinsic Variability

- Channel effects, such as differences in microphones, transmission media, codecs, and ambient noise, significantly alter the signal characteristics.

- Language and accent diversity pose challenges for models trained on monolingual or narrow-accent datasets.

Impact Models often misclassify intra-speaker variation as inter-speaker differences, leading to false rejections or mismatches.

6.5.2 Environmental and Contextual Noise

- Real-world deployments expose voice systems to background noises—from traffic and crowd chatter to echo and reverberation.
- Algorithms trained on clean or studio-recorded data often perform poorly in noisy, reverberant, or overlapping speech environments.
- Far-field recordings (from a distance) degrade the signal-to-noise ratio (SNR), impacting feature quality.

Impact Decreased recognition accuracy and increased false positives or negatives, especially in mobile or public settings

6.5.3 Cross-Domain and Cross-Condition Generalization

- Many models overfit to training conditions and fail to generalize to unseen domains.
- Cross-lingual voice matching—matching voices across different languages or dialects—remains an open research problem due to variations in phoneme inventories and speech patterns.
- Domain mismatch between training and test datasets (e.g., adult vs. child voices, studio vs. field recordings) causes significant performance drops (Desplanques et al. 2023a).

Impact Need for domain adaptation, transfer learning, and large annotated datasets from diverse user populations

6.5.4 Spoofing and Presentation Attacks

- Voice spoofing attacks use recorded, synthesized, or converted voices to impersonate a speaker and bypass authentication.
- Techniques like voice replay, text-to-speech (TTS), voice conversion (VC), and deep fake audio have become increasingly sophisticated and difficult to detect.
- Existing anti-spoofing techniques (ASVspoof) still face difficulty distinguishing between real and synthetic voices, particularly in low-resource environments.

Impact Serious security vulnerabilities in voice biometric systems; undermines trust in voice-based identity verification

6.5.5 Data Scarcity and Annotation Bottlenecks

- High-quality labeled datasets for speaker recognition, especially in low-resource languages or under-represented demo-graphics, are limited.
- Gathering long-duration, multi-session, cross-device voice samples for each user is resource intensive and raises privacy issues.
- Speaker labels may be ambiguous in multi-speaker recordings, overlapping speech, or anonymized data.

Impact Limits scalability and inclusivity of voice matching systems; biases result toward over-represented groups or accents.

6.5.6 Model Interpretability and Explainability

- Most modern systems, particularly those based on deep learning architectures, operate as black boxes.
- They lack transparency regarding which voice features contribute to a match or rejection, which is problematic in:
  - Forensic scenarios, where evidence must be legally explainable
    Healthcare or HR applications, where fairness and transparency are critical

Impact Hinders legal admissibility, user trust, and accountability in sensitive applications

6.5.7 Scalability and Real-Time Processing

- Real-time speaker verification in large-scale systems (e.g., telecom networks, smart homes with multiple users) requires:
  - Low-latency processing
  - Efficient memory usage
    Robustness to speaker overlap
- Computational demands of models like transformers and CNNs can be prohibitive for edge devices or low-power systems.

Impact Necessitates trade-offs between model complexity and deployment feasibility

6.5.8 Privacy, Ethics, and Legal Constraints

- Voice is personally identifiable biometric data and is increasingly covered under regulations like GDPR (EU), HIPAA (US), and DPDP Act (India).
- Concerns include:
  - Consent management for voice data collection and usage
  - Voice cloning risks, where one's voice is used maliciously without authorization
  - Data retention policies, which are not standardized across jurisdictions

Impact Limits the ways voice data can be collected, stored, and used; necessitates strong safeguards, anonymization, and ethical frameworks (Rajasekar et al. 2023)

6.5.9 Handling Emotional and Expressive Speech

- Voice matching algorithms often perform well in neutral or read speech but struggle when the speaker exhibits:
  - Emotional intensity (anger, excitement)
  - Expressive modulation (laughter, whispering, sarcasm)
  - Prosodic shifts (intonation, pitch variation)
- These expressive traits can mask or distort the acoustic features used for identity recognition.

Impact Decreases reliability in human-facing applications like virtual assistants, customer support bots, or emotional AI interfaces

6.5.10 Lack of Standardization and Benchmarks

While there are community efforts like VoxCeleb, CommonVoice, and ASVspoof, there remains a lack of:

- Uniform benchmarking criteria across tasks (verification, identification, diarization)
- Standardized protocols for testing in multilingual, noisy, or adversarial scenarios
- Public datasets for specific applications like healthcare or forensic voice matching

Impact Makes it difficult to compare results, generalize research, or ensure reproducibility across deployments

Despite significant progress, voice matching systems are still evolving toward being universally robust, secure, interpretable, and inclusive. Refer to Table 6.2. Addressing these limitations requires interdisciplinary collaboration across machine learning, linguistics, signal processing, cyber security, ethics, and law. Future research must focus on:

Table 6.2 Summary of limitations

Challenge area	Key issues
Speaker and channel variability	Intra-speaker variation, recording inconsistencies
Environmental noise	Poor performance in real-world, noisy, or far-field conditions
Cross-domain generalization	Mismatch between training and testing domains
Spoofing and deepfakes	Voice replay, synthetic speech, lack of robust anti-spoofing
Data and annotation constraints	Scarcity of labeled data, especially in underrepresented languages
Black-box models	Lack of interpretability and legal transparency
Scalability	High latency and compute requirements on edge or real-time systems
Privacy and ethics	Biometric data concerns, consent, misuse of voice data
Expressive speech handling	Struggles with emotion, laughter, whisper, etc
Benchmarking and evaluation	Inconsistent testing protocols and limited domain-specific datasets

Table 6.3 Overall challenges

Challenge	Description
Environmental noise	Most algorithms degrade in noisy or reverberant conditions
Cross-lingual variability	Performance drops when language, accent, or dialect varies
Temporal variations	Speaking rate and emotional state introduce variability
Scalability	Large-scale matching requires optimized search and storage strategies
Data scarcity	Supervised deep models require massive labeled datasets
Privacy concerns	Sensitive voice data storage and processing raises ethical issues
Spoofing and adversarial attacks	Synthetic voices and replay attacks can fool systems

- Multimodal fusion (voice + face, voice + text)
- Few-shot and zero-shot learning for speaker generalization
- Explainable AI (XAI) in speaker verification
- Federated learning and privacy-preserving computation
- Bias mitigation and fairness auditing in voice biometrics

Overall challenges are summarized in Table 6.3.

6.6 Scope for Development of Novel Algorithms

As voice-based technologies become integral to security, healthcare, communication, and human–AI interaction, there is a growing demand for next-generation voice matching algorithms that are more adaptive, efficient, ethical, secure, and explainable. Existing algorithms, while effective under controlled conditions, often falter in real-world applications due to limitations in robustness, generalization, interpretability, and data dependency (Yamagishi et al. 2023).

This section highlights the key research avenues and technological innovations that define the scope for the development of novel voice matching algorithms.

6.6.1 Self-Supervised Learning (SSL)

Motivation One of the critical bottlenecks in advancing voice matching technology is the lack of large-scale labeled datasets, especially in underrepresented languages, dialects, and age groups. Self-supervised learning (SSL) offers a promising solution by leveraging unlabeled audio data to learn meaningful speech representations (Thienpondt et al. 2024).

Research Directions

- **Contrastive Learning**: Learn representations by maximizing agreement between different augmented views of the same audio (e.g., SimCLR, CPC).
- **Masked Prediction Models**: Inspired by BERT-style pretraining, frameworks like Wav2Vec 2.0, HuBERT, and TERA mask portions of the input and train the model to predict the missing parts.
- **Pretext Tasks**: Develop pretext objectives like frame reordering, segment classification, or audio jigsaw puzzles to learn structure-aware embeddings.

Benefits

- Reduces reliance on human-annotated data
- Facilitates pretraining on massive multilingual corpora
- Boosts performance in low-resource and zero-shot scenarios

6.6.2 Few-Shot and Zero-Shot Learning

Motivation Traditional voice matching algorithms require multiple samples per speaker for enrollment and training. However, in practical deployments (e.g., emergency calls, forensic scenarios, or one-time authentication), only one or two utterances may be available.

Research Directions

- Prototypical networks and meta-learning frameworks that can generalize to new speakers with minimal data
- Embedding-based Siamese and triplet networks that focus on learning similarity rather than classification
- Zero-shot speaker recognition models trained to infer unseen identities from contextual or auxiliary data (e.g., demographic cues, known speaker traits)

Benefits

- Empowers personalized user experience with minimal training
- Critical for real-time speaker enrollment, emergency response systems, and scalable voice authentication

6.6.3 Robustness Against Adversarial Attacks and Spoofing

Motivation The increasing sophistication of voice cloning, deepfake audio, and adversarial inputs poses a serious threat to the security of voice-based systems.

Research Directions

- Adversarial Training: Incorporates adversarial examples during training to improve model resilience
- Spoofing Detection Systems: Builds binary classifiers to distinguish genuine from replayed, synthesized, or converted speech
- Multi-task Learning: Combine speaker verification and spoofing detection tasks in a unified framework
- Generative Adversarial Networks (GANs): Used not just for attacks but to simulate and defend against audio manipulation

Benefits

- Essential for high-stakes applications in banking, surveillance, and military communication
- Promotes secure biometric deployment in IoT and embedded systems

6.6.4 Multi-modal and Cross-modal Fusion

Motivation Human identity is multifaceted, and relying solely on voice may be insufficient in noisy, ambiguous, or spoof-prone environments. Multi-modal fusion strengthens identity verification by combining complementary signals.

Research Directions

- Audio-Visual Fusion: Combines voice with facial expressions, lip movement, or gaze direction to improve verification in video calls, surveillance footage, or smart kiosks
- Voice-Text Fusion: Uses speaker-specific linguistic patterns or phrasing style in combination with acoustic features
- Physiological Signals: Explores fusion with heart rate, respiratory sounds, or EEG for identity verification in clinical settings

Techniques

- Fusion strategies at feature level, score level, or decision level

- Cross-modal embeddings that learn a shared latent space for audio and visual/text features

Benefits
- Enhances accuracy and robustness, especially in multi-user environments
- Enables emotion-aware and context-sensitive authentication

6.6.5 Explainability and Interpretable AI in Voice Matching

Motivation Most deep learning models used in voice matching are opaque black boxes, which pose challenges in forensics, legal validation, and ethical AI deployment.

Research Directions
- Saliency Mapping: Identifies which features or time frames contribute most to a verification decision
- Attention Mechanisms: Leverage interpretable attention scores to visualize decision focus in speaker embeddings
- Rule-Based Hybrid Systems: Combine statistical models with interpretable rules for partially transparent systems
- Post hoc Analysis: Uses techniques like LIME, SHAP, or Layer-wise Relevance Propagation (LRP) to explain model outputs

Benefits
- Builds user trust and enables human-in-the-loop auditing
- Required for courtroom admissibility and compliance with AI ethics standards

6.6.6 Ethical, Secure, and Energy-Efficient Algorithm Design

Motivation As voice matching systems are deployed on billions of devices, the ethical implications, environmental cost, and user privacy concerns become increasingly relevant.

Research Directions
- Privacy-Preserving Learning: Uses federated learning, differential privacy, and homomorphic encryption to train models without exposing raw voice data
- Bias Auditing: Develops metrics and debiasing techniques to correct for gender, accent, age, and ethnicity-related disparities
- Green AI: Optimizes model architectures for low-power consumption, especially in mobile and embedded systems

Table 6.4 Future research scope in voice matching

Focus area	Core goal	Key approaches
Self-supervised learning	Learn from unlabeled data	Wav2Vec 2.0, HuBERT, masked prediction, contrastive
Few-/zero-shot learning	Match voices with minimal samples	Siamese, Prototypical Nets, meta-learning
Spoofing robustness	Detect adversarial or synthetic voices	Adversarial training, GANs, spoof classifiers
Multi-modal fusion	Combine audio with visual/ textual inputs	Audio-visual embeddings, cross-modal networks
Explainability	Make models interpretable	Attention maps, LIME/SHAP, saliency-based methods
Ethical and secure AI	Ensure privacy, fairness, and sustainability	Federated learning, bias mitigation, green modeling

Benefits
- Aligns voice technology with global data protection laws (e.g., GDPR, DPDP Act)
- Reduces carbon footprint of training and inference
- Ensures fair, inclusive, and socially responsible AI deployment

The next wave of voice matching innovation will be driven by data-efficient learning paradigms, adversarial robustness, multi-modal reasoning, interpretability, and ethical compliance. Researchers and developers must address the complex trade-offs between accuracy, security, transparency, and energy use to design algorithms that are not just powerful but trustworthy, scalable, and human centric. These goals are essential for enabling voice biometrics and speaker recognition to serve as reliable foundations for future communication systems and personalized AI and secures digital identity (Rose 2023). Refer to Table 6.4.

6.7 Evaluation Metrics and Accuracy

Valuating voice matching algorithms involves assessing both the correctness and reliability of the system under various conditions such as noise, variability in speech, speaker emotion, and recording quality. To ensure a comprehensive evaluation, a combination of quantitative metrics and qualitative assessments is used.

1. **Accuracy-Related Metrics**
   These metrics reflect how well the system can correctly match or distinguish between voices:

- **Accuracy (%):** Indicates the percentage of correct identifications or matches made by the system.

$$Accuracy = \frac{TP + TN}{TP + TN + FP + FN} \tag{6.1}$$

where:
TP = True Positives, *TN* = True Negatives, *FP* = False Positives, *FN* = False Negatives

- False Acceptance Rate (FAR): The probability that an unauthorized voice is incorrectly accepted as a match. Lower FAR is crucial for security-sensitive applications.
- False Rejection Rate (FRR): The probability that a legitimate match is incorrectly rejected.
  Balancing FAR and FRR is critical.
- Equal Error Rate (EER): The point at which FAR equals FRR. A lower EER implies better system performance and is commonly used for benchmark comparisons.
- Detection Error Tradeoff (DET) Curve: A plot of FRR vs. FAR on a log-log scale. Helps visualize tradeoffs and compare systems.
- Receiver Operating Characteristic (ROC) Curve and Area under Curve (AUC): ROC plots True-Positive Rate (TPR) against False-Positive Rate (FPR). AUC provides a scalar value summarizing overall performance.

2. **Verification vs. Identification Metrics**
   Voice matching tasks are typically divided into:
   - Speaker Verification (1:1 matching): Metrics: EER, FAR, FRR, ROC Curve
   - Speaker Identification (1:N matching): Metrics: Top-1 Accuracy, Top-K Accuracy, Confusion Matrix, Precision, Recall, and F1-Score
3. **Robustness and Consistency Metrics**
   - Signal-to-Noise Ratio (SNR) Impact: Evaluates algorithm performance at different SNR levels to ensure robustness in real-world environments.
   - Cross-Session Consistency: Tests the ability to match the same speaker across different sessions, devices, or background noise.
   - Latency and Computational Efficiency: Especially relevant for real-time or embedded systems. Metrics include response time, memory usage, and CPU/GPU load.
4. **Statistical Significance Testing**
   - t-tests or ANOVA may be used to validate whether differences in accuracy between competing models are statistically significant.
   - Confidence intervals (e.g., 95%) are used to express certainty in evaluation scores.
5. **Subjective Evaluation**
   - MOS (Mean Opinion Score): In some applications, especially with synthesized or converted speech, human listeners are asked to rate the naturalness or similarity of voice on a scale (typically 1 to 5). Refer to Tables 6.5 and 6.6.

Table 6.5 Voice matching evaluation metrics

Metric	Purpose	Typical Use Case
Accuracy	Overall correctness	General performance
FAR/FRR	Security evaluation	Verification systems
EER	Balanced performance indicator	Benchmarking
ROC/AUC	Classification performance	Threshold tuning
Top-1/Top-K Accuracy	Rank-based evaluation	Speaker identification
SNR impact	Noise robustness	Real-world testing
Latency	Real-time performance	Embedded/edge deployment
MOS	Perceptual evaluation	Voice synthesis/conversion

Table 6.6 Evaluating voice matching algorithms requires robust performance metrics

Metric	Description
Reliability	Consistency in performance across sessions, devices, and environments
Validity	Correct identification of speaker-specific characteristics
Sensitivity	Ability to detect true matches (true positives)
Specificity	Ability to reject imposters (true negatives)
Equal Error Rate (EER)	The point at which false acceptance rate equals false rejection rate; lower is better
Detection Cost Function (DCF)	Weighted cost of errors under specific conditions

High-performing systems like deep neural networks and hybrid algorithms (e.g., MFCC + CNN) have achieved EERs below 2% in controlled environments but may falter under real-world variability.

6.8 Conclusion

Voice matching is a dynamic and rapidly advancing field that incorporates classical signal processing, statistical modeling, and deep learning. While foundational techniques like MFCC and DTW laid the groundwork, modern approaches like semantic embedding and deep perception matching promise unprecedented accuracy and adaptability. However, challenges such as environmental variability, spoofing, and ethical concerns must be addressed. The future of voice matching lies in developing intelligent, secure, and explainable systems capable of functioning across diverse contexts and platforms.

References

Alzain MA, Wang X (2023a) Voiceprint authentication: a survey on models, attacks, and countermeasures. ACM Comput Surv 56(4):67. https://doi.org/10.1145/3574567

Alzain MA, Wang X (2023b) Voiceprint authentication: models, attacks, and countermeasures. ACM Comput Surv 56(4):67

Desplanques B, Thienpondt J, Demuynck K (2023a) SpeechBrain: an open-source toolkit for advanced speaker recognition. IEEE Open J Signal Process

Desplanques B, Thienpondt J, Demuynck K (2023b) ECAPA-TDNN: strong speaker embeddings for voice matching. Comput Speech Lang 84:101458

Heo HS et al (2023a) ClovaBaseeline: a robust speaker embedding system for the VoxSRC challenge. In: ICASSP 2023

Heo HS et al (2023b) ClovaBaseline: deep speaker embedding system. In: ICASSP 2023

Jhaveri RH, Revathi A, Ramana K, Raut R, Dhanaraj RK (2022) A review on machine learning strategies for real-world engineering applications. Mobile Inf Syst 2022., 1833507:26. https://doi.org/10.1155/2022/1833507

Johri P, Khatri SK, Al-Taani AT, Sabharwal M, Suvanov S, Kumar A (2021) Natural language processing: history, evolution, application, and future work, lecture notes in networks and systems, vol 167. Springer, Singapore. https://doi.org/10.1007/978-981-15-9712-1_31

Kinnunen T, Sahidullah M (2024) Speaker verification: advances and challenges in forensic applications. IEEE Signal Process Mag 41(2):44–57

Kraetzer C et al (2023) Deepfake detection and voice matching: a synergistic approach. Forensic Sci Int: Digit Investig 45:301256

Mittal A, Roy I, Gandhi S (2022) Magnetic nanoparticles: an overview for biomedical applications. Magnetochemistry 8(9) Multidisciplinary Digital Publishing Institute:107

Nagrani A, Chung JS, Zisserman A (2023a) VoxCeleb: large-scale speaker identification dataset. Comput Vis Image Underst 230:103689

Nagrani A, Chung JS, Zisserman A (2023b) VoxCeleb 1 & 2: large-scale speaker datasets. Comput Vis Image Underst 230:103689

Namasudra S, Roy P (2018) PpBAC: popularity based access control model for cloud computing. J Organ End User Comput 30(4):14–31

Nolan F et al (2023) Forensic speaker comparison and the likelihood ratio. Forensic Linguist J 30(1):65–92

Prasad S, Purwar S, Kishor N (2019) Load frequency regulation using observer based non-linear sliding mode control. Int J Electr Power Energy Syst 104(2):178–193

Rajasekar V, Vaishnnave MP, Premkumar S, Sarveshwaran V, Rangaraaj V (2023) Lung cancer disease prediction with CT scan and histopathological images feature analysis using deep learning techniques. Results Eng 18:101111

Rose P (2023) Technical and legal aspects of voice comparison in forensic phonetics. Int J Speech, Lang Law 30(2)

Thienpondt J et al (2024) ECAPA-TDNN: emphasized channel attention, propagation and aggregation for speaker verification. Comput Speech Lang 84. https://doi.org/10.1016/j.csl.2024.101458

Todisco M, Delgado H, Evans NWD (2024) ASVspoof: benchmarking spoofing countermeasures in speaker verification. In: IEEE transactions on biometrics, behavior, and identity science

Xie W, Nagrani A, Zisserman A (2023) Self-supervised learning for speaker representation and matching. NeurIPS 2023 Proc. [arXiv:2303.14225]

Yamagishi J et al (2023) Synthetic speech detection using audio and spectral features. Speech Commun 149:31–45

Zhang C, Wang X, Li Z (2024) A comprehensive survey on voice biometrics and speaker matching algorithms. IEEE Trans Artificial Intell 5(1):12–29. https://doi.org/10.1109/TAI.2024.1234567

Speaker Profiling for Forensic Investigations

7

Bhavya Sharma, Bhuvnesh Yadav, and Aman Sharma

Abstract

Speaker profiling constitutes a crucial element in forensic inspection and is an essential part of criminal investigations, threat assessments, and legal proceedings. This chapter discusses speaker profiling; scientific, technical, and legal frameworks; as well as the judicial implications and case studies. Speaker profiling involves the extraction and analysis of voice parameters. It involves examination of the acoustic, spectrographic, and linguistic features of voice that ultimately help establish the identity of the speaker. The last decade has witnessed the traditional techniques of speaker profiling to highly advanced computational tools that enhanced the quality of speaker identification and profiling. Specifically in the cases related to voice disguise, cross-language, and dialect transformation, computational methods turned out to be highly helpful. However, speech variability due to emotions, health, recording conditions, and the rise in artificial intelligence has led to several challenges and limitations of speaker profiling.

Keywords

Speaker profiling · Linguistic Variability · Acoustic parameters · Spectrographic analysis

B. Sharma · B. Yadav (✉) · A. Sharma
Department of Chemistry, Biochemistry and Forensic Science, ASAS, Amity University Haryana, Gurugram, Haryana, India

V. Kumar et al. (eds.), *Forensic Speech Sciences*, New Horizons in Forensic Science, https://doi.org/10.1007/978-981-92-1475-4_7

7.1 Introduction

Speaker profiling has emerged as the most important tool in forensic investigations, providing a scientific means for the identification of an individual by law enforcement and other legal entities based on the attributes extracted from the voice (Gold and French 2011). In this era, when the use of digital communication through mobile phones, social media, voice messaging apps, and online calls is increasing rapidly, voice has now become the most common medium in legitimate as well as illicit interactions. It drastically increases the forensic value of voice evidence (Chien et al. 2016). Speaker profiling is a central component of the forensic phonetics and linguistics domain, which focuses on obtaining personal information about a speaker from the recordings of his/her voice. It not only includes the factors of identity but also covers such indicators as age, gender, emotion, accents, regional dialect, socioeconomic status, or even region of origin. Unlike other biometric identifiers such as fingerprints or DNA, voice is a dynamic characteristic, which changes due to both physiological and psychological conditions of the speaker (Gonzalez-Rodriguez et al. 2007). Although the vocal apparatus consisting of vocal cords, oral and nasal cavities, and the numerous articulatory organs provides the fundamental anatomy of voice characteristics, many factors may stress its distinctiveness, from expression and stress to health state and deliberate coverup. However complex, voice profiling rapidly develops further, and forensic professionals continue to work on improving the acoustic and linguistic evidence-based methods to increase the reliability of voice evidence.

Speaker profiling is indispensable when there is no suspect as such, and all that is available for one to investigate is a sample of the voice. This consequently implies that we must not identify the speaker but outline specific traits that allow us to describe the range of likely suspects as such. This profile is based on linguistic, para- and acoustic symptoms and draws the most probable demographic and sociolinguistic sketch and outlines certain directions to work on. This is especially true of the anonymous threat, ransom demand, prank call, terrorist communication, and cyber-crime cases (Rose 2002). Even in countries where speaker profiling scope is limited by laws and regulations that view it as intelligence and not the conclusive evidence, it may get a transnational approach for the sake of narrowing the circle of the investigations. A relatively narrow field of speaker profiling becomes a comprehensive forensic process when integrated with audio enhancement, speaker diarization, forensic transcription, and multilingual analysis. The development of this field requires the collaboration between linguists, phoneticians, programmers, and police officers. Training programs and forensic certification will also be important components to standardization and scientific rigor for speaker profiling (Nair and Savithri 2021). Applications in the solving and exclusion of suspects in high-profile criminal cases have proven the utility of speaker profiling.

Some of the most impactful examples include voice samples obtained from ransom calls, tips from unidentified informants, and recordings of tapped phone calls. Moreover, as the applications of voice-activated virtual assistants and transcription and audio recordings features within messengers continue to gain popularity and wide-scale acceptance, the ability of forensic scientists to emerge in forensic voice analysis is only going to become more feasible. It is likely that as audio evidence becomes more frequently utilized in the courtroom settings, the need for accurate speaker profiling is set to rise as well.

7.2 Foundation and Linguistic Description

From a foundational perspective, speaker profiling is founded on solid ground due to the effective combination of acoustic-phonetic theory and sociolinguistics its fundamental provision. Speech is a complex signal that does not only convey a message but also provides information about the speaker.

7.2.1 Acoustic-Phonetic Principles

Fundamentally, the source-filter model of speech production is at the core of forensic phonetics. Indeed, the voice source is generated by the vocal cords' vibration, after which it is transferred by the vocal tract cavities' resonance process into formants F1, F2, and F3, which contains key identity information about a speaker. As a result, F0 is the first harmonic. F1 and F3 frequencies correlate with vowel quality and back/release types of consonants. F2, in turn, gives orientation concerning place of articulation and fricatives release. In addition to these three aspects of voiced speech signal, the jitter-shimmer ratio also acts as an indicator of voice stability (Fant 1971). Each speaker maintains a unique acoustic pattern due to vocal tract length, oral cavity shape, and habitual ways of speaking. These patterns get recorded using tools like spectrograms and pitch tracings, which further identify consistent traits across samples.

The acoustic-phonetic theory of speech perception assumes that listeners unfold the speech signal merely by associating the acoustic signal with its corresponding spatial and dynamic properties. Developed in the middle of the twentieth century, this theory postulates that speech sounds are acoustic spectral phenomena and that they carry invariant physical properties, formant frequencies, voice-onset time, pitch, and intensity, which associate with specific articulatory information. The listener thus discerns the invariant patterns, specifically, the formant and dynamic characteristics of the speech signal; hence, this theory is alternatively known as dynamic invariance theory of speech perception. In other words, people discern these properties using the physical attributes of the speech waveform and do not initially use language or other contextual details. According to the assumptions of this theory, the human auditory system has sufficient sensitivity and capacity to detect and analyze a set of acoustic distinctive features that pertain across all languages (Fant 1971). Individual vowels are discriminated by the first and second formant frequencies that also determine the vowel space. In consonant distinctions, the rate tau is termed a temporal cue, and the formant transition, beta, is a spectral shape cue. The center of gravity of the spectrum is a cue that depends upon the distribution of energy. The primary tenet of the dynamic invariance is that speech cue pattern matching is a bottom-up process; thus, it begins by recognizing phonetic changes in acoustic signals sent to the brain before recognizing the phonemes by examining them against linguistic knowledge.

In forensic applications, the acoustic-phonetic theory provides a basis on which speaker-specific features can be analyzed. The forensic phonetician, by measuring acoustic parameters, can compare and identify voice samples under conditions of disguise or noise. One point of weakness in the theory, however, is its assumption of invariance that each phoneme would have a stable acoustic signature while coarticulation, speaking style, and various environmental factors may change acoustic patterns substantially. Despite these challenges, the acoustic-phonetic theory remains very important to speech science and forensic profiling of speakers alike, offering a systematic frame based on linking the physical properties of speech to human perception and identity recognition.

7.2.2 Linguistic Features in Profiling

A second approach to profiling that can be used in conjunction with linguistic analysis is the analysis of speech production in various dimensions. The phonological patterns, including the peculiarities of pronunciation, like regional accents, vowel shifts, consonant degeneration, and rhythmic features, may reveal the geographical or social origin and may remain even when a speaker tries to disguise his/her voice (Ladefoged 2015). The lexical options are additional clues; vocabulary and language containing the slang, jargon, expressions, and technical terms can show the level of education of the speaker, his or her professional identity, age group, or cultural group (Ladefoged 2015). Syntactic structures and word order of choice, syntactic complexity, and grammatical construction are linguistic fingerprints that are hard to change intentionally (Ahmed 2018). Discourse aspects, including turn-taking, sequencing of narrative, and shifts of topic of discussion, enlighten on personality traits, communicative style, and the level of familiarity with the interlocutors (Ahmed 2018). Pragmatic cues such as politeness strategies, fillers such as "um" or "you know," hedging, and indirectness are expressions of how a speaker uses language in context providing information about social norms, emotional states, and also intentions.

These linguistic aspects enhance the forensic profiling process through the identity markers that go beyond the acoustic salience. Linguistic analysis is complementary to acoustic evidence and spectrographic evidence, and when combined with either, it can help improve the accuracy of the speaker identification process, especially when it pertains to disguised speech, multiple languages, or damaged recordings. A multidimensional method, thus, enhances the evidences of voice samples in criminal cases, which carries indications of age, gender, geographical and social origin, level of education, and state of mind.

7.2.3 Speaker-Specific vs. Speaker-State Features

It is essential to separate speaker-specific traits, relatively stable, from speaker-state characteristics, variable. For example, pitch and formants are relatively stable, whereas the speech rate and intensity might vary with emotional state or health (Morrison et al. 2021). Such variations must be taken into consideration for forensic analysts to avoid arriving at wrong conclusions. Combined, the acoustic and linguistic features create a multidimensional profile of the speaker that can be extremely useful in narrowing down pools of suspects or in the evaluation of voice evidence in a legal context.

By contrast, speaker-state features are temporary and dependent upon context like the speaker's physical, emotional, or situational state at the time of speaking including changes in pitch or speech rate due to stress, fatigue, illness, or intoxication; altered articulation caused by background noise; or emotional expressions such as anger or nervousness. Such features may vary considerably among recordings of the same individual and are therefore not as reliable for identification over longer periods (Tomić and Milenković 2021).

7.3 Methodologies in Speaker Profiling

A variety of methods have been used for extracting, analyzing, and interpreting voice data in forensic speaker profiling. These methods can be further divided into two categories: manual techniques (human based) and automatic techniques (computer based).

7.3.1 Voice Sample Collection

Effective voice profiling starts with the collection of high-quality voice recordings. Forensic experts have to ensure that the recording environment minimizes noise and distortion. There should be sufficient speech duration for analysis, and the speaker is not coerced, unless the context of the analysis includes coercion.

The chain of custody is maintained to ensure admissibility in court. The voice samples can be a recording of a telephone conversation, a video of a surveillance or a video of a conversation on the Internet, or a digital storage retrieval. The problems with each source are particular, e.g., artifacts of compression or a speech overlap. Effective profiling of speakers requires the careful and systematic purchase of good-quality voice recordings; the accuracy of any further analysis requires a fundamental basis of the quality of the original sample. Forensic specialists have the responsibility of ensuring that recordings are scientifically viable and admissible in court by following the standardized procedures.

The recording setting must be very restricted to reduce the background noise, reverberation, and electronic interference as these may reduce some important acoustic or language cues. As much as possible, high-fidelity equipment should be used to record, and the settings should be adjusted to the maximum frequency range of the human voice without distortion (Gold and French 2011). The speech sample should last long enough to achieve a complete set of acoustic characteristics: the pitch and formants, the spectro-temporal patterns, and the linguistic characteristics, i.e., the syntax, vocabulary, and the style of the speech. Short or fragmented recordings can limit the scope and reliability of analysis; for example, see challenges with short-utterance speaker recognition (Fant 1971). This also includes considering the condition of the speaker at the time of recording.

If the speaker is under duress, fatigued, ill, or emotionally agitated, the resultant sample will include changed characteristics of voice. These may well be relevant to the case context, but with the proviso that such temporary, speaker-state features are not mistakenly attributed as permanent features. Maintaining a chain of custody is essential to preserve the evidential value of the recording; it needs to document how, when, and by whom the sample was collected, stored, and transferred, making sure that it is unaltered and free from tampering. Sources for voice samples may originate from a variety of channels, such as telephone conversations, covert surveillance devices, Internet-based communications, or digital storage media.

Each origin has its own problems: telephone calls have artifacts of compression, surveillance recordings may have overlapped speech or environmental noise, and online audio recordings can be of variable quality depending on encoding by the particular platform. Such difficulties must be reduced by the wise use of filtering, improvement, and validation methods by forensic specialists. A voice sample is an effective tool in the profiling of speakers and, when gathered and properly recorded, provides sufficient means of deriving credible, reliable, and legally defensible results.

7.3.2 Acoustic Analysis

The basic component of the forensic speaker profiling process is the acoustic analysis, which provides objective and measurable indicators of vocal features against which the samples can be compared. Forensic phoneticians are able to use specialized software to extract a variety of parameters that define the stability and variability of speech in an individual. These parameters play a crucial role in determining speaker-specific characteristics, possibly ignoring the possible differences that appear as a result of environmental or contextual influences.

F0 defines what the voice sounds like and the rate of vibration of the voice folds. It is based on the anatomical variables including the length and tension of the vocal folds and the physiological and emotional states. An example is that F0 could temporarily increase due to stress (or excitement), but fatigue could decrease it (Fant 1971). Resonance frequencies depend on the length and the structure of the vocal tract, which are called formants (F1–F4). The morphology of formants contains the valuable information that could be utilized during the vowel and consonant identification and speaker recognition. Minor shifts in the patterns of formants can be used as a sort of acoustic fingerprint of the voice of a certain person (Fant 1971; Johnson

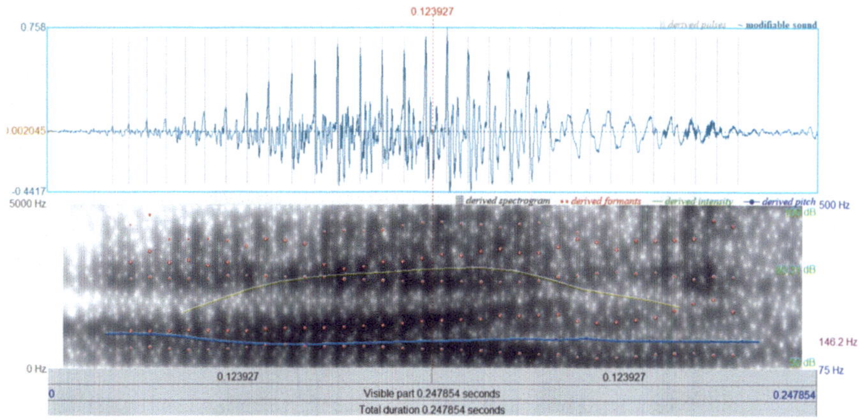

Fig. 7.1 Visualization of pitch, formants, and intensity using Praat software

and Sjerps 2021; Ahmed 2018). Jitter is a measure of minute, cycle-to-cycle deviation of frequency, while shimmer is the analogous measure of the amplitude deviation. Both the parameters provide data about voice stability and quality, and their change can be indicative of strain, pathology, or intentional disguise (Teixeira et al. 2013).

The speech rate and intensity are dynamic features that may express the speaker's emotional state, urgency, or cultural background and even physical condition; they can reflect habitual speaking patterns that persist over time (Brockmann et al. 2011). HNR expresses the proportion of periodic, harmonic energy to aperiodic, noise energy in a signal and gives information about breathiness, hoarseness, or vocal effort (Teixeira et al. 2013).

Praat, ESECTION, and Wavesurfer are some of the software tools available to assist in displaying and measuring these parameters by producing outputs such as pitch contours, spectrograms, and formant tracking graphs. Refer to Fig. 7.1. These graphical representations allow close comparisons of the recordings for correct forensic conclusions and increase the value of voice analysis evidence in court.

7.3.3 Spectrographic Analysis

Spectrograms are visual representations of frequency over time. These help identify patterns in formant transitions, voicing and articulation, and pauses and hesitations.

Spectrographic analysis is a cornerstone of forensic voice examination, offering a visual representation of the speech signal that reveals patterns often imperceptible to the human ear alone. A spectrogram is a graph of frequency versus the vertical axis, time versus the horizontal axis, and amplitude versus the degree of shading or coloration (Islam and Tarique 2024). This three-dimensional view enables the

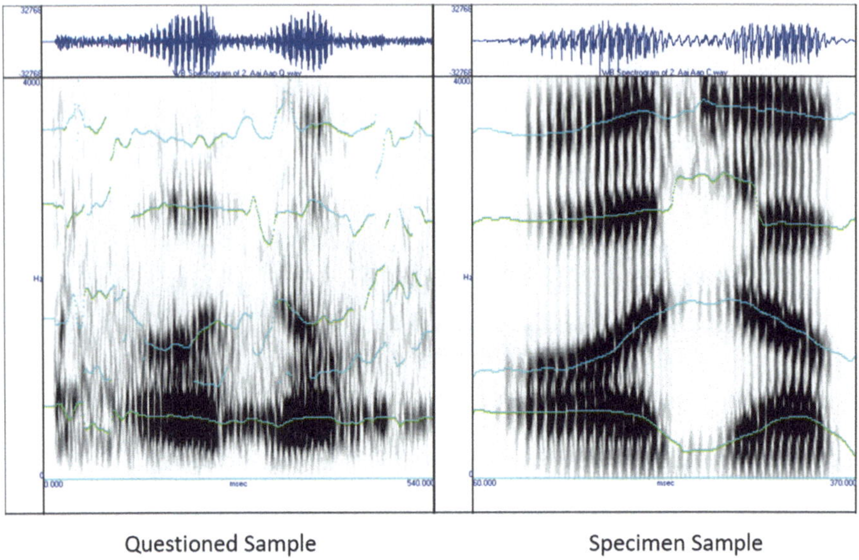

Fig. 7.2 Comparison of questioned and specimen voice sample spectrograph

forensic investigators to analyze very minute acoustic features and track the progression of speech parameters.

Formant transition is one of the most crucial parameters that are shown on spectrograms, the dynamic change of resonance frequencies when the speaker switches between two different vowels or consonants. These transitions are very individualized, depending on the various dimensions as well as the articulatory habits of the vocal tract of a speaker (Howard et al. 1995). Voice patterns and articulation patterns (are voiced sounds (vibrated by the vocal-fold) or voiceless sounds (vibrated by vocal-folds) and the exact point and method of consonant production are also recorded on spectrograms. This describes such information to determine phonetic peculiarities that are present in recordings. Further, pauses and hesitations, in terms of the length, time, and rate, are graphically outlined. These prosodic clues help the speaker produce his or her rhythmic and time mark (Islam and Tarique 2024). Refer to Fig. 7.2.

Spectrographic comparisons have been traditionally used in forensic work, as a visual corroboration of unique vocal qualities, to supplement auditory examination. Formant shape, separation, and proportionality may serve similarly to a voiceprint, helping differentiate speakers. Even though the usage of voiceprint is figurative, meaning that voices do not have fixed prints like fingerprints, the patterns that are always found in spectrograms may be used as convincing evidence, which would be admissible before courts as long as the methodology and interpretation of the patterns are solid (Reich et al. 1976). Spectrographic analysis also helps make speaker profiling more reliable and increases the value of voice recordings as a type of evidence in legal cases by combining visual examination with quantitative analysis.

7.3.4 Automatic Speaker Recognition (ASR)

Automatic Speaker Recognition (ASR) is utilized in order to recognize or control the identity of a speaker using a computer-based analysis to statistically assess the vocal characteristic. Unlike manual auditory or phonetic analysis, ASR makes use of sophisticated signal-processing and machine-learning algorithms to model and compare speaker-specific features in a high-precision and high-efficiency manner. The most common method is Mel-frequency Cepstral Coefficients (MFCCs) that summarizes the short-term spectral contour of human speech in relation to the human auditory perception. MFCCs are appropriate representations of the timbral properties of voice, which is why they have become a fundamental part of most ASR systems (Harshitha et al. 2024). i-Vectors are compact representations of speakers as fixed-length vectors summarizing the distinctive features that are present in variable-length recordings, and x-Vectors are built on top of deep neural-network embeddings to offer greater robustness to noisy and varied recordings (Perrot et al. 2007).

Neural network embeddings, especially those obtained from deep learning architectures such as convolutional and recurrent neural networks, directly learn high-dimensional representations of speaker identity from raw or processed audio. These techniques do exceptionally well in learning subtle and complex patterns of voice that may not be well modeled by more traditional statistical methods. As ASR systems have matured, they are also being used to flag anomalies that may indicate possible tampering or disguise. ASR tools have become essential in large-scale investigations, border security, counterterrorism, and intelligence operations due to their scalability and automation, enabling the rapid and accurate screening of enormous quantities of voice data. When combined with human expert analyses, ASR significantly enhances the efficiency and reliability of forensic speaker profiling. Speaker profiling, in criminal investigations, seldom operates solo; it operates best in concert with other forms of forensic evidence such as fingerprints, DNA analysis, digital forensics, and behavioral profiling. The multidisciplinary nature then reinforces the reliability of the conclusions and the acceptance thereof in judicial procedures.

7.3.5 Cross-Verification with Other Evidence

Cross-validation means a comparison of the results of the speaker's profile, whether acoustic, spectrographic, or linguistic, with other independent forensic evidence. For example, a voice recording may link a suspect to a threatening telephone call, while fingerprint and DNA evidence places them at the crime scene. Such convergence of evidence not only corroborates the results but also minimizes the occurrence of false positives or mistaken attribution (Rose 2002; Ladefoged 2015). Courts may view scientific results more favorably if independent methods provide corroborative results. This synergy is essential in complicated cases where a voice recording has a poor signal-to-noise ratio, a low speech duration, or background noise that prohibits reliance on voice evidence alone (Nair and Savithri 2021; Ahmed 2018). Speaker profiling can provide both investigative leads, helping identify suspects, and courtroom testimony that will be considered more convincing, scientifically sound, and resistant to cross-examination. Speaker profiling can be integrated into other forensic disciplines to ensure an evidence-based approach that ensures the overall strength and credibility of the case (Ladefoged 2015; Tomić and Milenković 2021).

7.4 Applications in Forensic Casework

The concept of speaker profiling is a key component in many of the forensic applications, both in the initial investigation and in the proceedings in court, and often serves as direct evidence as well as corroborative evidence.

7.4.1 Criminal Investigations

Among the most prominent uses of speech analysis is identification or elimination of suspects of crimes where voice tape records can provide conclusive evidence. In this case, speech may provide valuable leads in the situation where other physical evidence, including fingerprints or DNA, are limited or unproductive (Gonzalez-Rodriguez et al. 2007). Taped phone conversation or audio messages sent over the air usually become the key players in a scandal of ransom demands or even a kidnapping. The examination of such recordings allows law enforcement officers to decide whether multiple messages were sent by the same speaker, to evaluate the possibility of voice disguise, and obtain some information about the background of the caller.

Profiling is also helpful in highlighting any changes in speaker behaviors, which are signs of stress, coercion, or deception. The changes in pitch, speech rate, or language feature can be an indicator of whether a speaker is saying words under pressure or trying to hide his or her identity, thus, providing some information about the psycho-emotional status of a speaker (Ahmed 2018). Moreover, speaker profiling can be used to build a network based on the similarity of language or acoustic features found in that of the dissimilar voice samples. These analogies can reveal connections between the individuals of terrorist cells or criminal organizations and allow mapping the communications chain or hierarchy of operations in a more systematic way (Morrison et al. 2021). Voice-based profiling, when used together with metadata related to the time of the call, geolocation, and communication behavior, as well as other behavioral markers, would be used to build a complete intelligence picture. This multilayer approach allows a more accurate targeting, greater threat analysis, and a more effective interference with criminal or terrorist action and thus brings out the strategic worth of speaker profiling beyond traditional forensic uses.

7.4.2 Legal Admissibility

Forensic speaker profiling has become a part of the necessary components in legal proceedings in which voice evidence is a part. Its inclusion in the judicial system of most countries all over the world can be viewed as an important development in forensic science; however, the use of such evidence is strictly scrutinized and differs depending on the jurisdiction. Before accepting it as a scientifically validated and methodologically rigorous and reliable speaker profiling tool, courts carefully consider these factors. Such issues as the scientific soundness and peer-reviewed character of the applied methodology are regarded as the key determinants of admissibility. The judges insist that the methods applied in profiling of the speaker be based on established scientific material and supported by empirical data and whose results are published in academic journals that are recognized as reputable (Teixeira et al. 2013). This is necessary so that the techniques are highly scrutinized by the scientific community and are not grounded in untested hypotheses or anecdotal data.

Moreover, it must be ensured that there is reliability in the tools and procedures used. The validated software and standardized protocols used by the forensic analysts to extract features and compare voices should be used to minimize chances of errors or subjective opinions in making decisions (Brockmann et al. 2011). Regularity in the application of the procedures makes findings presented in court have a stronger evidentiary weight. Furthermore, it is the qualification and expertise of a forensic analyst, which is a crucial part of the chain of evidence. Courts thus require the testimony of specialists who have been highly trained in acoustic phonetics, forensic linguistics, or other relevant fields besides having a vast experience in voice comparison and interpretation. This is necessary so as to make the evidence sufficiently understood and interpreted by the judge and the jury. The admissibility standards that are used in the international arena vary.

Furthermore, there is a need to ensure reliability in the tools and procedures applied. Forensic analysts have to employ only validated software and standardized protocols in feature extraction and voice comparison to minimize the chances of errors or subjective bias in decision-making (Brockmann et al. 2011). Consistency in procedural application enhances the strength of findings presented in court. Moreover, qualifications and expertise are an important component of a forensic analyst. In this respect, courts require testimony from professionals with advanced training in acoustic phonetics, forensic linguistics, or related fields, as well as extensive experience in comparing and interpreting voices. This ensures that the evidence is interpreted correctly and understood by the judge and jury. On the international scene, standards adopted for admissibility vary.

With the ever-changing technologies and techniques of profiling speakers as forensic evidence, the generality of the legal community acceptance in India and other parts of the world is growing, but it is only on the basis of strict scientific and procedural approaches toward admissions. This development makes voice examination a tool of justice administration and would prevent false conviction based on false voice evidence.

7.4.3 Courtroom Testimony and Case Outcomes

Speaker profiling can:

- Support other classes of forensic evidence.
- Determine uniformity or lack of uniformity of the statements of the suspects.
- Reject or substantiate voice disguise assertions.

The presentation of visual spectrograms, formant plots, or statistical likelihood ratios are commonly used by analysts but not limited to prove a certain conclusion. Examples of visual and quantitative devices of this type make it easier to communicate complex acoustic comparisons in a manner more easily comprehensible to the judge or jury.

7.5 Challenges and Limitations

Speaker profiling has several issues despite its increasing significance and technological progress. These include technical, biological, linguistic, and legal challenges that cannot be overlooked to prevent overdependence or misinterpretation of results of the system.

7.5.1 Intra-speaker Variability

One of the most basic issues in the profiling of speakers is that the voice of an individual is not always the same. This variation is caused by the following factors:

- State of mind (e.g., anger, fear, happiness).
- Fatigue or illness.
- Aging and hormonal changes.
- Medication or intoxication.

All these lead to major differences in vocal production. Analysts are required to identify whether the variations in recordings are caused by variations among speakers or reflect different persons.

7.5.2 Inter-speaker Similarity

On the other hand, there can be astounding similarities between two distinct speakers especially in dialectically homogeneous areas. There is a threat of the convergence of speakers, particularly in the case of the use of acoustic parameters only.

7.5.3 Voices Disguise and Impression

Voice change with intent is a significant issue. The possible strategies of disguise are:

- Alterations in pitch, including falsetto.
- Dialect/accent impersonation.
- Mechanical filters or computer software.

Such strategies may blur personal features of speakers and lead to diminishing profiling. Some masks can be recognized by an efficient criminal investigator, but computer programs are easily deceived.

7.5.4 Recording Quality and Channel Effects

Audio-tape recordings will have channel effects that can distort voice parameters due to recording in different environments and by use of different recording devices. Issues include:

- Background noise.
- Echo or reverberation.
- Sensitivity and distance of microphones.

Digital artifacts and compression may hamper the extraction of acoustic and spectrographic features.

7.5.5 Limited and Non-standardized Databases

Forensic voice databases are usually small in scale and are not usually diverse in terms of age, gender, dialect, or emotional condition. There are no standardized procedures that are used in the collection, storage, or comparison of forensic voice samples that significantly affect the reproducibility and reliability of any speaker profiling system.

7.5.6 Ethical and Legal Issues

Speaker profiling also brings up a number of ethical concerns such as:

- Invasion of privacy because of voice surveillance.
- Dialect, accent or language profiling.
- The possible abuse of voice data by the law enforcement agencies.

The legal issues also include the admissibility and perceived objectivity of voice evidence in court. In particular, the courts can cast doubt on the scientific validity or transparency of complex machine learning models.

7.5.7 Risk of Overinterpretation

Considering that the stakes in forensic investigations are exceptionally high, there exist the propensity of overinterpreting speaker profiling results. Analysts are advised not to draw absolute conclusions, but they are expected to report probability with clear statements of limitations.

7.6 Conclusion

Identification is one of the most crucial aspects of forensic investigations. DNA, fingerprints, and handwriting are examples of scientifically and legally acceptable identification methods. Speaker profiling is a technique that is used by investigative agencies around the world to ensure that justice was served in the most accurate manner possible. Forensic speaker profiling has evolved to become one of the most important tactics that aid identification in today's investigative and legal systems. The science has been critical in enhancing criminal investigations, particularly in solving criminal acts such as injury commission, extortion, threats issuance, rape, killings, and terrorism. Speaker state features and speaker-specific characteristics are analyzed using acoustic analysis, the spectrographic method, and linguistic technology. Even in difficult conditions such as voice disguise, background distortion from other sounds, low-quality recording, emotion masking, and voice disguise, acoustic analysis ensures that facts result in speaker identification. The computational aspect has been made simple, reliable, and effective by improved statistical methods. Nevertheless, the credibility of the method is likely to be eroded by artificial intelligence and its development, and consequently, the methodology must always be upgraded. Speaker profiling in forensics maintains the highest degree of fairness and accuracy in the court while serving as an aid in suspect identification.

Speaker profiling is a forensic subdiscipline that investigates unique forensic features of unidentified speaker's characteristics and individuality. The field of speaker profiling is extremely multifaceted, and its practice is primarily based at the crossroads of speech, science, and law. The quality of application depends on harmonizing the interpretive assessment and supported review of the information. Research, ethics, and technology keep improving the accuracy and provides a legal opportunity to use the method in practice. Given the growing complexity and growing numbers of various digital crimes, speaker profiling is likely to remain a relevant and vital discipline in the quest to catch criminals and discover the truth.

References

Ahmed H (2018) The role of linguistic feature categories in authorship verification. Procedia Comput Sci 142:214–221. https://doi.org/10.1016/j.procs.2018.10.478

Brockmann M, Drinnan MJ, Storck C, Carding PN (2011) Reliable jitter and shimmer measurements in voice clinics: the relevance of vowel, gender, vocal intensity, and fundamental frequency effects in a typical clinical task. J Voice 25(1):44–53. https://doi.org/10.1016/j.jvoice.2009.07.002

Chien Y-F, Fiorentino R, Yang X, Sereno JA (2016) Surface phonetic or underlying phonological representations: a mismatch negativity study of mandarin tone assimilation. J Acoust Soc Am 140(4_Supplement):3224–3225. https://doi.org/10.1121/1.4970182

Fant G (1971) Acoustic theory of speech production: with calculations based on X-ray studies of Russian articulations. De Gruyter Mouton

Gold E, French P (2011) International practices in forensic speaker comparison. Int J Speech Lang Law 18(2):293–307. https://doi.org/10.1558/ijsll.v18i2.293

Gonzalez-Rodriguez J, Rose P, Ramos D, Toledano DT, Ortega-Garcia J (2007) Emulating DNA: rigorous quantification of evidential weight in transparent and testable forensic speaker recognition. IEEE Trans Audio Speech Lang Process 15(7):2104–2115. https://doi.org/10.1109/TASL.2007.902747

Harshitha TLP, Nair LM, Mary L (2024) Forensic automatic speaker recognition: coping with impersonated speech. In: 2024 IEEE international conference on signal processing, informatics, communication and energy systems (SPICES), pp 1–6. https://doi.org/10.1109/SPICES62143.2024.10779874

Howard DM, Hirson A, Brookes T, Tyrrell AM (1995) Spectrography of disputed speech samples by peripheral human hearing modelling. Int J Speech Lang Law 2(1):28–38. https://doi.org/10.1558/ijsll.v2i1.28

Islam R, Tarique M (2024) Spectrogram and Mel-spectrogram based dysphonic voice detection using convolutional neural network. In: 2024 International conference on electrical, computer and energy technologies (ICECET), pp 1–5. https://doi.org/10.1109/ICECET61485.2024.10698112

Jamwal A, Sehrawat SS, Kaur G, Verma R (2023) Likelihood ratio estimation and validation for discrimination of ten Hindi vowels in forensic speaker identification. Int J Med Toxicol Legal Med 26(3and4):179–181. https://doi.org/10.5958/0974-4614.2023.00068.2

Johnson K, Sjerps MJ (2021) Speaker normalization in speech perception. In: The handbook of speech perception. Wiley, pp 145–176. https://doi.org/10.1002/9781119184096.ch6

Ladefoged P (2015) A course in phonetics. Cengage Learning

Morrison GS, Enzinger E, Hughes V, Jessen M, Meuwly D, Neumann C, Planting S, Thompson WC, van der Vloed D, Ypma RJF, Zhang C, Anonymous A, Anonymous B (2021) Consensus on validation of forensic voice comparison. Sci Justice 61(3):299–309. https://doi.org/10.1016/j.scijus.2021.02.002

Nair AMSU, Savithri SP (2021) Classification of pitch and gender of speakers for forensic speaker recognition from disguised voices using novel features learned by deep convolutional neural networks. Traitement Du Signal 38(1):221–230. https://doi.org/10.18280/ts.380124

Perrot P, Aversano G, Chollet G (2007) Voice disguise and automatic detection: review and perspectives, pp 101–117. https://doi.org/10.1007/978-3-540-71505-4_7

Reich AR, Moll KL, Curtis JF (1976) Effects of selected vocal disguises upon spectrographic speaker identification. J Acoust Soc Am 60(4):919–925. https://doi.org/10.1121/1.381173

Rose P (2002) Forensic speaker identification. CRC Press. https://doi.org/10.1201/9780203166369

Tan T (2010) The effect of voice disguise on automatic speaker recognition. In: 2010 3rd International congress on image and signal processing, pp 3538–3541. https://doi.org/10.1109/CISP.2010.5647131

Teixeira JP, Oliveira C, Lopes C (2013) Vocal acoustic analysis—jitter, shimmer and HNR parameters. Procedia Technol 9:1112–1122. https://doi.org/10.1016/j.protcy.2013.12.124

Tomić K, Milenković K (2021) Forensic speaker profiling from the sample in ENGLISH as a foreign language—vowel duration analysis. Nasledje Kragujevac 18(49):29–46. https://doi.org/10.46793/NasKg2149.029T

Forensic Speech Evidence in Judicial Proceedings: Emerging Challenges and Evolving Jurisprudence

8

Manoj Kumar Sinha, Swaril Dania, and Priyatam Bhardwaj

Abstract

Forensic evidence has always remained critical in the legal system, providing scientific, objective, and verifiable links that can significantly aid the investigation process. Further, with an increase in digital communication in the present day and wide access and use of recording devices, forensic speech evidence has also emerged as a potent evidentiary tool. With several technologies enabling speaker identification with greater accuracy, it has a transformative potential in facilitating modern-day investigations. This has led to wide acceptance of forensic speech evidence in most legal systems. However, given the risks posed by the advent of new technologies and challenges such as deep fakes and AI-assisted voice conversion tools, the issue presents both ethical and procedural challenges. Thus, the judicial approach toward reliance on forensic speech evidence in court rooms requires to be tempered with caution, keeping in mind the concerns of ensuring constitutionally guaranteed safeguards for privacy and protection against self-incrimination as well as the valid investigative needs for accurate detection and protection against tampering. The present chapter attempts a critical assessment of the evolving intersection of law, technology, and evidentiary standards in courtroom proceedings in the context of forensic speech evidence with a view toward shaping coherent legislative and institutional responses for the future of forensic speech analysis in the Indian judiciary.

M. K. Sinha
Dharmashastra National Law University, Jabalpur, Madhya Pradesh, India

S. Dania (✉)
University School of Law and Legal Studies, Guru Gobind Singh Indraprastha University, Delhi, India

P. Bhardwaj
Indian Law Institute, Delhi, India

V. Kumar et al. (eds.), *Forensic Speech Sciences*, New Horizons in Forensic Science, https://doi.org/10.1007/978-981-92-1475-4_8

The Bharatiya Sakshya Adhiniyam ("BSA") has now preserved and clarified already established admissibility principles. Section 2(1)(d) of the statute explicitly defines "electronic records" to include digital sound recordings, while Sections 61 to 65 continue the framework for proving electronic documents through technical certification akin to the erstwhile Section 65B. Thus, the evidentiary basis for admitting an audio file, whether stored locally or transmitted through an electronic medium, remains intact but is now textually harmonized with contemporary digital realities.

Further, the BSA's version of Section 45 (now Section 39 of the new statute) continues to recognize expert opinion as admissible where scientific, technical, or specialized knowledge is required. The Supreme Court has repeatedly emphasized the probative importance of expert testimony in cases involving forensic reports, medical evaluations, ballistic analysis, and digital forensics.[5] In the context of voice identification and authentication, the expertise of forensic phoneticians or digital speech analysts is, therefore, received as opinion evidence, assisting the court in interpreting complex acoustic or spectral data.[6] Indian courts, in practice, treat such analytical findings not as primary proof of fact but as expert assistance whose credibility depends on methodological soundness and corroborative material.[7]

The combined effect of the BSA, BNSS, and the evolving judicial jurisprudence is the formal integration of forensic speech evidence into the mainstream evidentiary process. Voice samples are now explicitly contemplated as permissible investigative materials, and their admissibility, authentication, and probative value are grounded in statute as interpreted by judiciary, and their evaluation is guided by expert interpretation under judicial supervision. Yet, questions remain regarding standardization of laboratory methodologies, the regulation of AI-based speaker recognition tools, and the procedural safeguards necessary to balance forensic utility with the concerns relating to right to privacy and protection from coercion—issues that subsequent sections of this chapter will examine in detail.

---

[5] Section 45A of the Indian Evidence Act (inserted by the Information Technology Act, 2008), Now Section 39(2) BSA explicitly designates the Examiner of Electronic Evidence as an expert, making their opinion on any matter relating to digital information (e.g., computer resources, cell phones) a relevant fact. Under Section 45 (Now Section 39(1)), expert opinions on "science or art" cover areas like medical evaluations and ballistic analysis. The Court relies on the expert to introduce scientific findings (such as in a postmortem report or a ballistic report) to aid in the determination of guilt or innocence. Forensic phoneticians and digital speech analysts examine these spectral features (formants, spectral tilt, pitch (fundamental frequency or F0), and their dynamics) in the questioned voice sample and compare them to a known reference sample.

[6] Spectral data refers to the visual and measurable representation of the frequency content (energy distribution) of a speech sound over time, typically displayed as a spectrogram. This data reveals the unique acoustic features of a speaker's vocal tract (such as formants), providing the objective basis for forensic phoneticians to compare and authenticate voices.

[7] State (through CBI/New Delhi) v. S.J. Choudhary, 1996 SCC (2) 428. In *Malay Kumar Ganguly v. Dr. Sukumar Mukherjee & Ors.*, (AIR 2010 SC 1162) the Court held that an expert is not a witness of fact; their evidence is advisory. Their duty is to furnish the judge with the necessary scientific criteria for testing the accuracy of the conclusions, enabling the judge to form an independent judgment.

8.2.2 Admissibility of Voice Recordings

Voice samples, although classified as *identification data* under contemporary evidentiary frameworks, must be distinguished from recorded conversations, which constitute *electronic records* within the meaning of Section 65B of the Indian Evidence Act, 1872, and its successor, the Bharatiya Sakshya Adhiniyam, 2023. Under both statutes, any electronic record sought to be admitted in evidence must be accompanied by a certificate attesting to its authenticity and integrity. If a recorded conversation such as a telephonic exchange is sought to be relied upon by the prosecution, a certificate has to be produced by the person in charge of the recording device, which confirms that the process of recording was free from tampering; thus, the recording must have been continuous and accurate, and no subsequent tampering must have been done.[8] Recognizing how alteration and manipulation of data is easily possible in the present-day world, these procedural safeguards are of utmost necessity to protect the evidentiary sanctity of digital materials.

The Supreme Court's judgment in *R.M. Malkani v. State of Maharashtra* (AIR 1973 SC 157) remains the foundational authority governing the admissibility of clandestine audio recordings. The Court held that such recordings, even if made surreptitiously, are not per se inadmissible, provided that certain conditions ensuring reliability are met. The court declared that for the admissibility of tape-recorded conversations as evidence, it is necessary that the following three conditions are fulfilled: firstly, the conversation must be relevant to the matter in issue; secondly, there must be identification of the voice; and thirdly, the accuracy of the tape-recorded conversation must have been proved through elimination of the possibility of erasure of the tape-record. The safeguards laid down in the judgment were further reaffirmed in the case of *Yusufalli Esmail Nagree v. State of Maharashtra*[9] The court directed:

1. **Identification of the Speaker:** A competent witness who is personally familiar with the voice of the speaker must identify the voice in the audio recording, for the identification of the speaker.[10]
2. **Proof of Accuracy:** The individual operating the recording device must testify or certify that the record faithfully reproduces the conversation as heard.[11]
3. **Exclusion of Tampering:** The proponent must establish that the recording is free from editing, interpolation, or fabrication.[12]
4. **Relevance:** The recorded content must bear direct relevance to the issues in dispute.
5. **Proper Custody:** The recording must have been duly sealed and preserved to maintain a verifiable chain of custody.

---

[8] Section 63, Bhartiya Sakshya Adhiniyam, 2023.

[9] *Yusufalli Esmail Nagree* v. *The State of Maharastra* MANU/SC/0092/1967.

[10] Id. at para 5, 6, and 7.

[11] Ibid.

[12] Ibid.

6. **Audibility:** The speech on the recording must be sufficiently clear and intelligible for forensic and judicial evaluation.[13]

These safeguards are essential to ensure the probative value of audio evidence. The technical integrity and procedural propriety have to be maintained at all stages, for which compliance with the above criteria is indispensable. Apart from this, the requirement of certification mentioned under Section 65B of the erstwhile Evidence Act further substantiates the credibility of the evidence. The person responsible for the recording process or an authorized officer must furnish a written certificate specifying the particulars of the device, the manner of production, and the continuity of custody. In the absence of such certification, courts retain discretion to summon the relevant custodian or technical officer to issue or verify the requisite document, thereby preserving the evidentiary chain consistent with the principle of procedural fairness.[14]

8.2.3 Voice Sampling and the Question of Self-Incrimination

Whether compelling an individual to provide their voice sample is violative of the protection against self-incrimination under Article 20(3) or the fundamental right to privacy under Article 21 is another issue that has been a matter of much academic discussion. Quelling all doubts, the Supreme Court has addressed this progressively and established that a voice sample is identification data, not testimonial evidence, thus distinguishing the two. In *Sudhir Chaudhary v. State (NCT of Delhi)*,[15] the Court held that a voice sample "is not a testimony in itself since it only constitutes what was described as 'identification data,'" likening it to a fingerprint or handwriting specimen and therefore outside the scope of Article 20(3).

The Court in *Sudhir Chaudhary* also prescribed procedural safeguards to protect the fairness and reliability of the process. A standardized text should be prepared and read by the suspect in a controlled setting, and the recorded exemplar should be used for spectrographic comparison with the disputed recording.

Matters appear to become more complex when the recordings in question are covertly obtained. Sometimes referred to as "tainted" evidence, their admissibility has been called into question on the basis of the averment that the evidence has been

[13] Ibid.

[14] *Arjun Panditrao Khotkar* v. *Kailash Kushanrao Gorantyal and Ors.* (2020) 7 SCC 1. Court clarified that if a party could not procure the certificate (e.g., due to refusal by the custodian), the trial judge must invoke their powers to summon the person/persons referred to in Section 65B(4) to produce the certificate. The judgment stated that if a party has done all that is possible to obtain the certificate and the custodian refuses to grant it, the court can use its powers under the Code of Civil Procedure, 1908 (CPC); the Code of Criminal Procedure, 1973 (CrPC); and Section 165 of the Evidence Act to direct the production of the certificate by the relevant person in possession of the device/data. This action serves to preserve the evidentiary chain and ensure procedural fairness by preventing crucial evidence from being shut out due to a technical, procedural roadblock caused by a non-cooperating third party.

[15] *Sudhir Chaudhary* v *State (NCT of Delhi)* AIR 2016 SC 3772.

gained through illegal means. However, the matter has been settled by the Supreme Court through its judgment in *R.M. Malkani v. State of Maharashtra*. The foundational position that surreptitious recordings may be admissible if relevant and genuine, predates *Sudhir Chaudhary* case.[16] As discussed in the preceding section, *R.M. Malkani v. State of Maharashtra*,[17] remains the leading authority recognizing the admissibility of tape-recorded conversations subject to probative value and absence of tampering. Courts continue to rely on *Malkani* when assessing covert recordings.

Subsequent rulings have reinforced the non-testimonial character of voice samples and the magistrate's power to direct their collection for investigative purposes. Recent Supreme Court decisions have reiterated that voice sampling is a form of neutral physical evidence and does not, per se, amount to compelled testimony under Article 20(3)[18]; courts have also confirmed that magistrates may order the collection of voice samples where necessary for inquiry.[19]

At the same time, privacy remains a salient constraint on admissibility. The Supreme Court's recognition of privacy as a fundamental right in *K.S. Puttaswamy v. Union of India*[20] requires courts to scrutinize the context and manner in which recordings are obtained. While earlier High Court rulings had sometimes excluded secretly recorded spousal conversations on privacy grounds, the Supreme Court in 2025 clarified the law in the matrimonial context by holding that secretly recorded spousal calls may be admissible in matrimonial disputes, subject to judicial scrutiny of relevance and authenticity.[21] This development illustrates the nuanced approach courts now take, balancing investigatory needs and evidentiary utility against legitimate expectations of privacy.

Taken together, these authorities establish a balanced framework, viz., compelled voice sampling is constitutionally permissible as non-testimonial identification data, when obtained and used in accordance with procedural safeguards, but unauthorized or intrusive recordings that violate a reasonable expectation of privacy may be excluded depending on context and judicial scrutiny. Practitioners must therefore ensure strict adherence to due process, documented chain of custody, transparent sampling procedures, and judicial oversight so that voice evidence withstands challenges on both constitutional and evidentiary grounds.

---

[16] *Supra.*

[17] *R.M. Malkani* v *State of Maharashtra* AIR 1973 SC 157; 1973 SCR (2) 417.

[18] *Ritesh Sinha* v *State of Uttar Pradesh* 2019 SCC OnLine SC 855.

[19] *Rahul Agarwal* v *State of West Bengal & Anr.* 2025 INSC 1223.

[20] AIR 2017 SC 4161.

[21] Apoorva, "Privacy v Evidence: Supreme Court allows secretly recorded spousal conversations as admissible evidence in matrimonial disputes" *SCC OnLine Times* (July 15, 2025), available at: https://www.scconline.com/blog/post/2025/07/15/secretly-recorded-spousal-conversations-admissible-evidence-supreme-court/ (last visited on Oct 15, 2025).

8.2.4 Modernization Through the Bharatiya Sakshya Adhiniyam 2023: Implications for Forensic Speech Evidence

The Bharatiya Sakshya Adhiniyam 2023 (BSA) represents a significant modernization of India's evidentiary framework, particularly in recognizing digital and audio-visual records as primary evidence. Under Section 2(d) and 2(e), the Act expands the definition of "document" and "evidence" to include data recorded or transmitted by electronic means, thereby granting statutory recognition to audio and voice recordings used in forensic contexts.

Section 61 explicitly ensures that electronic or digital records are not denied admissibility solely because of their format and places them at par with traditional documentary evidence, subject to the conditions prescribed in Sections 62 and 63. These provisions, largely analogous to the earlier Section 65B of the Evidence Act, require certification of the device, chain of custody, and the process by which the record was produced. This framework simplifies the use of forensic voice samples, intercepted calls, and spectrographic reports by treating them as documents rather than ancillary exhibits, even when the original recording device is unavailable.[22]

However, arguably, while the BSA advances procedural clarity, it still lacks explicit standards for scientific reliability, for instance, in the admissibility of AI-driven speaker recognition, biometric voiceprints, or deepfake detection technologies. Consequently, questions of methodological validity, error rates, and accreditation of forensic labs are still governed by expert testimony and judicial scrutiny rather than statutory regulation.[23]

In practical terms, the BSA enhances the evidentiary value of forensic speech evidence by streamlining its admissibility but leaves open the challenge of ensuring scientific rigor and authenticity. The future task lies in harmonizing procedural compliance under the BSA with robust forensic standards so that voice evidence is not only admissible but also demonstrably reliable in India's courts.[24]

8.2.5 Key Judicial Developments on the Admissibility of Voice Evidence

Several landmark decisions have shaped the legal treatment of forensic voice evidence in India, illustrating the judiciary's evolving balance between technological realities and procedural safeguards.

---

[22] Decoding Bharatiya Sakshya Adhiniyam, 2023: Comparative Insights & Study with Indian Evidence Act, 1872, Lexis Nexis, Blog (March 24, 2025), available at: https://www.lexisnexis.in/blogs/decoding-bharatiya-sakshya-adhiniyam-2023-comparative-insights-study-with-indian-evidence-act-1872/ (last visited on Oct 15, 2025).

[23] Rahul Kailas Bharati and Sandeep Nagarale, "Digital Forensic Science and Evidentiary Standards in the Bharatiya Sakshya Adhiniyam 2023: A Legal Examination of Admissibility" Vol 15 (88) *Indian Journal of Natural Science* 53 (2025).

[24] John Varghese, "Evidentiary value of Electronic form evidence, Electronic and digital records under Bharatiya Sakshya Adhiniyam 2023, Part VII", *Judicial Vision* (2024).

In *Shafhi Mohammad v. State of Himachal Pradesh*,[25] the Supreme Court clarified that non-compliance with the certification requirement under Section 65B of the Evidence Act should not, by itself, render electronic evidence inadmissible. The Court emphasized that procedural formalities must yield to the objective of achieving "complete justice," allowing electronic records to be admitted when their exclusion would defeat substantive justice. Although the case arose in a different factual context, its reasoning extends to all forms of electronic evidence, including audio and voice recordings, thereby softening the earlier rigidity surrounding certification. Rapid technological advancement means no exhaustive rule can rigidly govern all audio/visual evidence. This case reflects the willingness of Indian Courts to admit recordings (including voice tapes) even where certification formalities are not strictly met *qua* authenticity, relevance, and absence of tampering are satisfied.[26]

Subsequently, in *Arjun Panditrao Khotkar v. Kailash Kushanrao Gorantyal*,[27] a Constitution Bench revisited Section 65B and clarified that while certification remains mandatory for electronic records, courts may relax the requirement if the producing party does not have possession or control of the device from which the data originated.[28] This ruling was an attempt to harmonize the judgments in *Anvar P.V. v. P.K. Basheer*,[29]which had strictly mandated the production of the certificate for the admissibility of electronic evidence as provided by Section 65B and *Shafhi Mohammad (Supra)*, providing a pragmatic framework for admitting electronic evidence in modern trials, including digital voice recordings. However, Arjun Panditrao case (supra) has been criticized on the premise that court has merely accepted the position in Anvar case (*Supra*) that the certificate requirement under section 65B is mandatory, without assigning adequate reasons of its own for why it should be so. Court failed to examine the text or its underlying policy imperatives, which in fact indicate that the certificate requirement is only a sufficient and not a necessary condition. Also, the court, while discussing historical trends in the interpretation of Section 65B, recognized it being borrowed from Section 69 of Police and Criminal Evidence Act, (1984) [PACE] of the United Kingdom and also noted that the United Kingdom does not draw a distinction between electronic evidence and other evidence in terms of admissibility and reliability any longer[30]; however, it did not take stock of how section 69 of PACE has been interpreted previously by the House of Lords. For instance, in *Reg v Shepherd*,[31] the House of Lords was required to examine the admissibility of certain computer-generated till rolls relied upon by the prosecution as evidence of theft from a departmental store. The defendant contended

[25] 2018 INSC 75.

[26] *Shafhi Mohammad* v *The State of Himachal Pradesh*, (2018) 5 SCC 311. (Special Leave Petition (Crl) 2302 of 2017, Supreme Court of India.)

[27] 2020 INSC 453.

[28] Id at Para 9.

[29] (2014) 10 SCC 473.

[30] Police and Criminal Evidence Act 1984, available at: https://www.legislation.gov.uk/ukpga/1984/60/contents.

[31] 1993 AC 380: (1993)2 WLR 102.

that such till rolls could only be admitted if accompanied by a certificate signed by a person holding a responsible position in relation to the computer. The House of Lords rejected this argument, holding that while a certificate could indeed be issued only by someone in a responsible position concerning the computer, oral testimony could equally be adduced in the absence of such a certificate. The Court further observed that the nature of evidence regarding the functioning of a computer would necessarily differ from case to case. It noted that expert testimony would seldom be required, and in most instances, the requisite proof could be provided through a witness acquainted with the computer's operation.

In *Ram Singh v. Col. Ram Singh*,[32] the Supreme Court reiterated the requirements laid down in *R.M. Malkani* case,[33] which remains a foundational precedent for tape-recorded evidence declaring that audio recordings are admissible if they are relevant, properly identified, and free from tampering. Essential safeguards were outlined by the Court, and the court emphasized that the identity of the speaker must be clearly established in such cases, the voice should have been clearly audible without any disturbances, and competent testimony must prove the accuracy of the recording. Further, the tape must be preserved with a verified chain of custody, and any possibility of alteration must be excluded. The Court also recommended that recorders announce the date, time, and identity of participants before taping begins, a practice which was later reaffirmed in subsequent judgments to ensure the reliability of voice identification in criminal investigations.

Together with later rulings such as *Ram Singh case (Supra)* and *Sudhir Chaudhary case*, *RM Malkani case (supra)* underscores the principle that forensic voice evidence is admissible when obtained and analyzed under fair, transparent, and scientifically sound conditions.

In a recent case,[34]the Gujarat High Court addressed the issue of admissibility of voice recordings in domestic violence proceedings. The Court held that a CD containing secretly recorded phone conversations supported by a Section 65B certificate and a verified hash value was admissible as electronic evidence. Importantly, it ruled that a magistrate may direct a party to provide a voice sample for spectrographic comparison when necessary for truth finding. While the trial court had initially refused such direction citing Article 20(3), the High Court clarified that voice sampling, when ordered by the court or given with consent, does not violate the privilege against self-incrimination. This decision reaffirms judicial willingness to facilitate scientific speaker identification where it advances justice. This case illustrates how courts are adapting forensic voice-science practices (hash values, voice-printing, spectrographic comparison) in civil proceedings beyond traditional

---

[32] 1985 SCC (Supp) 611.

[33] *RM Malkani* v *State of Maharashtra* (1973) 1 SCC 471.

[34] Bhavya Singh, "Family Conversation secretly recorded by wife to prove domestic violence and Cruelty admissible in Evidence: Gujarat High Court," Live Law, August 6, 2024, available at: https://www.livelaw.in/high-court/gujarat-high-court/gujarat-high-court-family-conversations-wife-recorded-prove-domestic-violence-cruelty-admissible-evidence-family-matters-265833 (last visited on Oct 15, 2025).

criminal trials. In *Vibhor Garg* v *Neha*,[35] the Supreme Court upheld the decision of trial court where the trial court had held that recorded telephone conversations are relevant and admissible under sect. 14 and 20 of the Family Courts Act, 1984.

Finally, a perusal of the judicial rulings on the matter indicates that the courts have adopted a pragmatic stand as to the issue; while they are increasingly recognizing the evidentiary value of electronic voice evidence, they have also been cautious as to demanding adherence to procedural safeguards that uphold authenticity and reliability of the evidence and constitutional rights of the accused.

8.3 Technological Advances in Forensic Speech Science

Forensic speech analysis is no longer just about listening to tapes and comparing voices by ear. With the rapid progress in artificial intelligence, signal processing, and voice-cloning technologies, the field of forensic speech science is undergoing a profound transformation. These changes open new possibilities for identifying speakers, authenticating recordings, and guarding against manipulated voices. However, simultaneously, they also present new vulnerabilities that courts must understand as they are susceptible to being misused.

8.3.1 AI-Driven Speaker Recognition and Voice Biometrics

Voice biometrics refers to the process of identifying or verifying a speaker based on the unique characteristics of their voice. It is particularly valuable in situations where voice is the only available means of identification, such as telephonic bomb threats, ransom demands in kidnapping cases, or other instances involving voice-based communication.

In the past, forensic voice comparison largely required an expert to visually inspect spectrograms and listen carefully to suspect and target recordings. Today, however, voice-biometric systems powered by machine learning can automate much of this work. These systems extract acoustic features such as pitch contours, formant frequencies, and timbre and use them to build a unique "voiceprint" for each speaker, much like a fingerprint.[36] Voice biometrics operates through two primary approaches[37]:

- **Text dependent**: The speaker is asked to recite a specific phrase, enabling comparison of known and questioned recordings of exactly the same phrase.

[35] 2025 SCC OnLine SC 1421.

[36] R. Sharma, D. Govind, J. Mishra et al. "Milestones in speaker recognition" , Vol 57 *Artificial Intelligence Review* Article no. 58 (2024).

[37] Monika Saini and Anup Kumar Kapoor, "Biometrics in Forensic Identification: Applications and Challenges" Vol 1(2) *Journal of Forensic Medicine*, (2016).

noise, or codec signatures). In this digital age, the need for developing accurate detection frameworks and legal safeguards against the creation of such deepfakes is paramount.

8.3.3 Audio Enhancement and Forensic Signal Processing

Another key technological strand is signal processing, viz., cleaning, restoring, and isolating speech from noisy or degraded recordings. Audio evidence often comes from phone recordings with background noise, room echo, or low bit-rate compression, all of which complicate speaker identification. Forensic labs now use algorithms such as spectral subtraction, Wiener filtering, and even neural-network driven denoising to improve clarity. Some advanced tools perform blind source separation (in other words, isolating overlapping voices) or speech re-synthesis (in other words, reconstructing missing frequencies).[48]

These enhancements can make previously unusable tapes usable, but these also carry associated risks, which were previously unfathomable. If enhancement is undocumented or poorly logged, it may unintentionally alter evidentiary content or raise questions about reliability. Ethical guidelines insist that any processing may not add new speech and that the original recording be preserved.[49]

Thus, arguably, the convergence of AI-biometric speaker recognition, synthetic-voice generation, and advanced signal-processing tools has brought forensic speech science to a new frontier. Yet while the technology is advancing, so are the legal and scientific challenges. Courts will increasingly demand not only procedural compliance (chain of custody, voice-sample collection) but also rigorous scientific validation of the tools used including error-rates, dataset biases, and resistance to synthetic-voice attacks.

8.4 Case Studies and Global Best Practices

To appreciate how forensic speech evidence operates in practice, the following Indian illustrations followed by brief international context show how courts and investigators currently use voice analysis, together with the limitations that have emerged.

[48] Emmanual Vincent, Maria G Jafari, Samer A Abdallah et al, "Blind Audio Source Seperation" Technical Report, Centre for Digital Music, Queen Mary, University of London (2005).

[49] Helen Fraser, Vincent Aubanel, Robert C. Maher et al, "Forensic Speech Enhancement: Toward Reliable Handling of Poor-Quality Speech Recordings Used as Evidence in Criminal Trials," Vol. 72(11) *Journal of Audio Eng. Soc.* 748–753 (2024); https://doi.org/10.17743/jaes.2022.0176

8.4.1 Use of "Voice Evidence" in Indian Courtrooms: Some Illustrations

Retired Judge I. M. Quddusi Case (2020) [50] In the medical-college bribery investigation, the CBI submitted intercepted phone calls and obtained a Central Forensic Science Laboratory (CFSL) report concluding that the voice in the recordings matched Judge Quddusi's voice sample. Media reporting shows CFSL's confirmation strengthened the probe, and the defense later sought access to the spectrographic analysis to test it at trial. This episode demonstrates how CFSL voice-matching reports are operationally important in high-profile investigations, but it also illustrates the usual procedure: lab reports support investigations and remain subject to defense testing at trial.

Gujarat High Court, Domestic Violence Matter (2024) [51] The Gujarat HC held that a CD containing recorded calls, accompanied by a hash value and a Section-65B certificate, was admissible in domestic-violence proceedings. The court observed that a magistrate may, if necessary, direct a party to provide a voice sample for spectrographic comparison. This ruling underlines the practical interplay of electronic-evidence certification with judicial discretion to order scientific verification, signaling judicial willingness to use voice forensics in civil as well as criminal settings.[52]

CBI Collection of Voice Sample, Jagdish Tytler Case (2023) The CBI recorded a voice sample from political leader Jagdish Tytler while probing the 1984 anti-Sikh riots allegations; the collection took place at a CFSL facility and was reported in major outlets.[53] Investigative agencies now routinely obtain exemplars from high-profile persons when an intercepted recording is central to the probe, showing institutionalization of voice-sampling practice.

---

[50] Raghav Ohri, "Trouble for retired High Court Judge: CFSL verifies his voice Sample" THE ECONOMIC TIMES, (Oct 25, 2020), available at: https://economictimes.indiatimes.com/trouble-for-retd-hc-judge-cfsl-verifies-his-voice-sample/articleshow/79946204.cms? (last visited on Oct 22, 2025).

[51] "Verified Call recordings can be proof in DV cases" The Times of India, (Aug 2, 2024), available at: https://timesofindia.indiatimes.com/city/ahmedabad/verified-call-recordings-can-be-proof-in-dv-cases-gujarat-high-court-ruling-on-admissibility-of-voice-recordings-in-domestic-violence-act-cases/articleshow/112209088.cms? (last visited on Oct 25, 2025).

[52] JIL w/o Priyank Manubhai Choksi v State of Gujarat, Crl Rev. Application No.1243/2023 Gujarat HC.

[53] PTI "Jagdish Tytler summoned by CBI for recording voice sample in 1984 riots case" (Apr 11, 2023), available at: https://timesofindia.indiatimes.com/india/jagdish-tytler-summoned-by-cbi-for-recording-voice-sample-in-1984-riots-case/articleshow/99401257.cms? (last visited on Oct 22, 2025).

Family/Divorce Contexts and Other Magistrate Practice High courts and magistrates have accepted telephonic admissions and other recorded speech as evidence where certification and authenticity are shown, and trial courts have discretion to decide on verification methods, including judicially directed voice sampling. These examples demonstrate that voice evidence is not confined to narrow criminal contexts, and properly certified recordings are used across family and quasi-criminal proceedings.

8.4.2 International Perspectives

United States

Historically, many US courts have admitted spectrographic/voiceprint evidence where the method's reliability is established. The US Department of Justice's Criminal Resource Manual records that the majority of the courts that have considered the question of admissibility of voiceprints "have ruled that voiceprint evidence is admissible" while also noting the need for demonstrable reliability and methodology disclosure in court.[54] The US model demonstrates a gatekeeping approach, viz., courts admit voice-comparison evidence but subject methods to reliability scrutiny.

The admissibility of scientific evidence and specifically the issue of expert scientific evidence has been discussed in detail in the matter of *Daubert v. Merrell Dow Pharmaceuticals, Inc.*, 509 U.S. 579 (1993). Since this ruling in 1993 that overturned the earlier *Frye Standard* laid down in the judgment of *Frye v. United States*,[55] the *Daubert standard* remains as the primary "framework for a trial court judge to assess the reliability and relevance of expert witness testimony."[56] The court in *Daubert* prescribed that Federal Rules of Evidence, particularly Rule 702, provided the standard for admitting expert scientific testimony in a federal trial and supplemented the same with a list of factors that the judge must consider while determining the validity of the expert's methodology. The standard has been used by the US courts dealing with the question of admissibility and reliability of voiceprint evidence in cases such as *United States v Robert N. Angleton*[57] and many others.[58]

---

[54] Criminal Resource Manual, "258. Admissibility of Spectrograms," Archives, US Department of Justice, An official website of United States government, available at: https://www.justice.gov/archives/jm/criminal-resource-manual-258-admissibility-spectrograms-voice-prints? (last visited on Oct 25, 2025).

[55] 293 F. 1013 (D.C. Cir. 1923).

[56] See https://www.law.cornell.edu/wex/daubert_standard#:~:text=The%20%E2%80%9CDaubert%20Standard%E2%80%9D%20provides%20a,Supreme%20Court%20case%20Daubert%20v.

[57] 269 F. Supp. 2d 892 (S.D. Tex. 2003).

[58] For a detailed discussion on the use of 'Daubert Standard' by the courts in examination of forensic speech evidence, see, G.S. Morrison & W.C. Thompson, "Assessing the Admissibility of a New Generation of Forensic Voice Comparison Testimony" 18(2) *Science and Technology Law Review*, (2017) https://doi.org/10.7916/stlr.v18i2.4022

United Kingdom

In the United Kingdom, courts take a notably cautious and methodologically transparent approach to forensic voice identification. Voice evidence is not treated as a stand-alone fact but as a form of expert opinion, requiring the analyst to demonstrate the scientific basis, validation, and limitations of the method used. UK courts routinely direct experts to explain their comparative procedures, reliability metrics, and potential error rates so that opposing counsel can challenge the evidence through cross-examination. This emphasis on disclosure stems from judicial recognition that voice recognition whether auditory or spectrographic remains susceptible to bias, contextual influence, and technological variability.

Legal commentary underscores this cautious attitude. As Dr. J. Robson and Dr. H. Smith observe, "Identification by voice remains one of the most fragile forms of evidence... the sound of a voice is subject to distortion, imitation, and interpretation."[59] The UK's evidentiary model demands that forensic voice comparison experts disclose validation studies, acoustic parameters, and "uncertainty ranges," allowing courts to determine admissibility through methodological transparency rather than institutional trust. This mirrors the broader push within UK law for a "reliability-based" framework for expert testimony rooted in the recommendations of the Law Commission's 2011 Report on Expert Evidence in Criminal Proceedings in England and Wales.

In practice, appellate rulings such as *R v Flynn & St John*[60] have reaffirmed that voice evidence may be admitted if the court is satisfied as to its reliability, but the expert must provide clear justification for the analytical technique used. Overall, the UK model balances openness to scientific innovation with rigorous scrutiny of expert methodology—a balance increasingly relevant for jurisdictions like India as they modernize evidentiary frameworks for digital and forensic speech evidence.

International Best Practice and Standardization International guidance increasingly favors transparent, validated methods for speaker recognition. For example, NIST (National Institute of Standards and Technology)/OSAC (Organization of Scientific Area Committees for Forensic Science) and other forensic standard bodies urge documented protocols, proficiency testing, avoidance of discredited "voice-print" methods, and reporting of uncertainty (likelihood ratios and error-rates) in speaker recognition.[61] Global best practice recommends accredited labs, peer review, documented error rates, and combining human and automated analyses.

[59] J. Robson & H. Smith, "Identification by Voice (1)" *Counsel Magazine*, (December 2023). Available at: https://www.counselmagazine.co.uk/articles/identification-by-voice-%281%29

[60] [2008] EWCA Crim 970.

[61] Speaker Recognition Subcommittee, Standard Guide to the Forensic speaker Recognition landscape, Organization of Scientific Area Committee for Forensic Science (OSAC), 2023-N-0023, (Dec 2024), available at: https://www.nist.gov/system/files/documents/2024/12/02/OSAC%20 2023-N-0023%20Standard%20Guide%20to%20the%20Forensic%20Speaker%20 Recognition%20Landscape_REGISTRY%20VERSION%202.0.pdf

These principles are extremely relevant for India as it operationalizes CFSL and other forensic units.

Interestingly, for the handling of "digitally derived evidence" (DDE) in the proceedings of international criminal courts and tribunals, guidelines have been designed that are known as "The Leiden Guidelines on the Use of Digitally Derived Evidence in International Criminal Courts and Tribunals" as a part of a project headed by Dr. Emma Irving and the Director of Kalshoven-Gieskes Forum on International Humanitarian Law, Dr. Robert Heinsch.[62] The guidelines are based upon the three-limbed approach of the ICC toward evidence. In the three-part test laid down by the ICC in Prosecutor v. Bemba,[63] it has to be ensured, firstly, "that the evidence must be relevant to the case; second, that it has probative value; and third that it must be sufficiently relevant and probative as to outweigh any prejudicial effect its admission may cause." The guidelines prescribe specific instructions with respect to the handling of audio recordings as well as intercepted communications. This three-limbed approach to an extent establishes and inadvertently upholds position of Indian Court with respect to admissibility of electronic recording *qua* futuristic technologically advanced evidences.

In the case of intercepted communications, the guidelines lay down that the communications intercepted would not by themselves constitute a violation of privacy rights; however, the interception must be lawful, necessary, and proportionate under applicable law.

It stresses upon submission of audio recordings in full, rather than excerpts, so that the complete context can be assessed while determining the relevance and probative value of the same. Other important aspects include the need for demonstrating prima facie authenticity through verification of chain and custody and the exclusion of "opinion evidence" from audio recordings, focusing more on the factual content of "interviews" or "media broadcasts," which are sometimes tendered as evidence. What is interesting to note is that the guidelines prescribe that in case of weak authentication of the evidence, there is no automatic rejection of the evidence as inadmissible, rather the weakness of the authentication process would only impact the weight that the Court would accord to the evidence in such a case.

Thus, across varied jurisdictions, the pattern is consistent, that is, courts will admit voice recordings and expert speaker-comparison evidence so long as procedural safeguards (vis-à-vis chain of custody, device/certificate proof, analyst disclosure) and scientific reliability (method validation, error-rate reporting) are addressed.[64] India's recent decisions and investigative practice as cited above (CFSL

[62] See https://leiden-guidelines.com/assets/Leiden%20Guidelines%20on%20the%20Use%20of%20DDE%20in%20ICCTs_20220404.pdf

[63] Prosecutor v Bemba (Decision on the admission into evidence of items deferred in the Chamber's "Decision on the Prosecution's Application for Admission of Materials into Evidence Pursuant to Article 64(9) of the Rome Statute" (ICC-01/05–01/08–2299)) ICC-01/05–01/08 (27 June 2013).

[64] Geoffrey Stewart Morrison and William C. Thompson, "Assessing the Admissibility of a New Generation of Forensic Voice Comparison Testimony" Vol XVIII, *The Columbia Science and*

reports, magistrate directions for voice samples, etc.) show the country moving in this global direction; however, having said that, they also highlight the need for clearer lab standards, accreditation, and courtroom protocols when confronting new threats such as AI-generated synthetic audio.

8.5 Procedural, Ethical, and Privacy Considerations in Forensic Speech Evidence

The integration of technology into forensic analysis has significantly enhanced investigative capabilities. However, it concurrently introduces complex challenges concerning the integrity, reliability, and ethical handling of voice recordings. This section delves into the procedural, scientific, and privacy-related dimensions of forensic speech evidence, with a particular focus on Indian legal framework.

8.5.1 Chain of Custody and Verification

As has been mentioned before, for maintaining the integrity of forensic evidence, the existence of an unbroken chain of custody is essential. Section 65B(4) of the Indian Evidence Act, 1872 had clearly mandated the requirement of submission of the certificate in case of any electronic record, including audio recordings certifying the details of the device used for recording, its manner of storage, and the sequence of custody. This certification is imperative for the admissibility of such evidence in court.

Each step of the handling of the evidence, right from the stage of initial recording to its storage and analysis, must be meticulously documented so as to ensure the authenticity of evidence. Any lapse, such as unauthorized playback or unrecorded transfers, can jeopardize the evidence's admissibility. For instance, in the Gujarat Domestic Violence case (*Supra*), the prosecution's success was partly attributed to the meticulous preservation of the recording's integrity, including the use of cryptographic hashes and certificates to verify authenticity.

Furthermore, utmost transparency has to be maintained by the forensic experts in their analytical processes. Retaining original recordings and documenting each modification ensure that the analysis can withstand scrutiny and replication, thereby upholding the principles of scientific integrity.

8.5.2 Reliability and Scientific Standards

There are several factors that may affect the voice samples that have to be taken into consideration for accurate voice identification. Owing to these factors that include the emotional state and health of the speaker as well as recording conditions, voice

---

Technology Law Review, (Spring, 2017).

identification is seen to be inherently probabilistic, unlike other forensic evidence such as DNA profiling. Consequently, forensic analyses focus on assessing the degree of similarity between voice samples rather than asserting absolute identity.

To mitigate the risks of misidentification, the forensic community emphasizes the importance of validation studies and error rate disclosures. While India lacks a codified standard akin to the *Daubert* criteria in the United States, courts increasingly demand transparency regarding the reliability of forensic methods. The Supreme Court's decision in *Shafhi Mohammad v. State of Himachal Pradesh* (*Supra*) underscored the necessity of ensuring that scientific evidence adheres to accepted standards, even if formal procedural requirements are relaxed.[65]

International best practices advocate for a combined approach of aural and acoustic analyses, conducted by independent experts. Adherence to guidelines set by the International Association for Forensic Phonetics and Acoustics (IAFPA) can enhance the credibility of forensic analyses.[66] In India, establishing standardized protocols, possibly through the Bureau of Indian Standards or the DNA Profiling Board, could foster consistency and reliability in forensic voice analysis.

8.5.3 Ethical and Privacy Concerns

The collection and use of voice recordings intersect with fundamental privacy rights enshrined in Article 21 of the Indian Constitution. While the Supreme Court has affirmed that the right to privacy is not absolute, it can be reasonably restricted in the interest of public welfare and justice.[67] However, the manner of recording particularly in private settings raises significant ethical questions. Unauthorized recordings, even by one party to a conversation, can infringe upon privacy rights and may be contested in court.[68]

Moreover, voice samples constitute biometric data, which is subject to emerging data protection regulations. Under the Digital Personal Data Protection Act and the consequent Right to Privacy framework, such data must be handled with stringent safeguards to prevent misuse. Forensic laboratories are obligated to ensure that voice archives are used solely for legitimate investigative purposes and are securely deleted thereafter. Additionally, the potential for profiling based on voice characteristics such as age, health, or regional accent necessitates cautious interpretation. Analysts must refrain from making speculative assertions about a speaker's identity

---

[65] *Shafhi Mohammad* v *State of Himachal Pradesh*, (2018) 5 SCC 311. (SLP (Crl) No. 2302 of 2017 Supreme Court of India.)

[66] International Association for Forensic Phonetic & Acoustics, "Code of Practice" (2020), available at: https://www.iafpa.net/about/code-of-practice/? (last visited on Oct 15, 2025).

[67] *C.J. Christopher Signi* v. *State of Tamil Nadu*, 2025 SCC OnLine Mad 3214, decided on 09-07-2025.

[68] *S Pratap Singh* v *The State of Punjab*, AIR 1964 SC 72, where the Supreme Court accepted the tape-recorded conversation despite being obtained illegally.

beyond acoustically verifiable traits. Courts should be vigilant in excluding analyses that extend beyond the scientifically substantiated scope.

The integration of forensic speech evidence into legal proceedings necessitates a balanced approach that upholds scientific rigor while safeguarding individual rights. Adherence to established standards, transparent methodologies, and ethical considerations is paramount in ensuring that such evidence serves justice without compromising fundamental freedoms.

8.6 Conclusion and Forward-Looking Recommendations

Forensic speech science now occupies a genuinely consequential place within India's evidentiary landscape. The routine capture of human voice through telephony, messaging platforms, and omnipresent recording devices combined with improvements in automatic speaker recognition, anti-spoofing research, and digital-forensics practice has converted what was once an ancillary, dispute-specific exercise into a discipline with system-wide implications for investigation and adjudication. At the same time, the arrival of powerful machine-learning systems and generative audio technologies has transformed the stakes. The same methods that strengthen identification also create new avenues for error, bias, and invasion of privacy. These twin aspects and facets, viz., opportunity and risk, must shape any sensible public policy and judicial approach.

The aim going forward should therefore be twofold and mutually reinforcing: (a) to consolidate scientific maturity so that voice-forensic outputs meet recognizable standards of reliability and reproducibility and (b) to build legal, institutional, and privacy safeguards so that courts admit and rely on those outputs without eroding fundamental rights. The following integrated conclusions and concrete recommendations articulate how India can achieve that balance:

1. Scientific maturity before blanket judicial acceptance. Courts should admit algorithmic or statistical voice-forensic outputs only after the proponent demonstrates validation appropriate to the claimed use. Validation means (i) published performance on relevant test corpora that reflect India's linguistic diversity; (ii) disclosure of error characteristics (false-acceptance and false-rejection rates or calibrated likelihood ratios) for conditions approximating the case at hand; and (iii) peer review or independent replication where the method is novel. Judicial gatekeeping should focus on method and validation rather than brand. The issue is not whether a commercial product was purchased but whether its outputs have been meaningfully assessed for courtroom reliability.[69]
2. Codify admissibility and evidentiary procedure. India's new evidence architecture should explicitly recognize voiceprints and processed audio as scientific evidence while prescribing procedural safeguards. Legislative or rule-making measures (e.g., rules under the Bharatiya Sakshya Adhiniyam or directions to the

[69] *Daubert* v. *Merrell Dow Pharmaceuticals*, 509 U.S. 579 (1993).

subordinate judiciary) should set out minimum requirements for admissibility: an authenticated original or certified copy (or an explanation for absence), documentation of the chain of custody, a clear record of any enhancement, and indication that anti-spoofing checks were performed. Where a court orders a compelled voice exemplar, the process for obtaining it should be standardized—quiet environment, neutral phrasal prompts linked to disputed utterances, contemporaneous recording under supervision, and preserved in the record so experts may compare like with like.

3. National technical standards, accreditation, and quality assurance. Forensic voice work must be governed by published protocols covering sample collection, storage, enhancement, feature extraction, model testing, and reporting, and laboratories performing such work should be accredited to those standards. Accreditation should be coupled with inter-laboratory proficiency testing and periodic re-certification of analysts. Reports should state uncertainty measures and, where applicable, likelihood-ratio frameworks or other calibrated scores rather than categorical assertions that overstate certainty.[70]
4. Invest in indigenous datasets, research, and anti-spoofing capacity. Off-the-shelf models trained primarily on Western speech corpora risk lower performance and higher bias when applied to the many languages, dialects, and phonetic registers of India. Public investment (Department of Science & Technology (DST), Defence Research & Development Organisation (DRDO), Indian Council of Social Science Research (ICSSR), academic grants) should support multilingual corpora, open and privacy-preserving benchmarks for speaker recognition and deepfake detection, and collaborative testbeds linking forensic laboratories with engineering and linguistics departments. Locally validated models will reduce mismatch errors and give courts a firmer evidentiary basis for probabilistic claims.
5. Judicial and practitioner capacity building. The bench and the bar must be able to evaluate method, validation, and limitations. Judicial academies, bar councils, and forensic institutes should run modular training that combines (a) the scientific basis of speaker recognition and anti-spoofing; (b) common operational pitfalls in field collection and processing; and (c) practical checklists for admissibility and disclosure. Better informed judges and lawyers will sharpen adversarial testing and reduce miscarriages caused by procedural ignorance.
6. Integrate voice forensics into multidisciplinary digital workflows. Voice evidence gains probative traction when correlated with other digital traces—call detail records, device metadata, geolocation, message histories, and relevant IoT or CCTV audio/video. Standard operating procedures should require experts to situate their findings within this broader evidentiary matrix rather than presenting probabilistic matches in isolation.

---

[70] The European Network of Forensic Science Institutes (ENFSI) Guidelines for Evaluative Reporting in Forensic Science recommend using likelihood ratio framework or other calibrated scores rather than categorical assertions as the modern scientifically accepted method for reporting forensic evidence, which clearly communicates the uncertainty of the match to the court.

7. Transparency, limited disclosure, and procedural fairness. Where algorithmic systems are proprietary, courts should adopt measures that permit meaningful defense testing without publicizing trade secrets: protected disclosure to court-appointed experts, in camera inspection with protective orders, or secure re-analysis by accredited third parties. Reports must describe model class, general training corpus composition, and performance metrics in accessible language so that the trier of fact can meaningfully weigh probative value.
8. Robust privacy and governance safeguards. Voiceprints and exemplar recordings are biometric identifiers and deserve strict statutory controls. Rules should (a) require judicial authorization and case-specific necessity before compelling voice samples; (b) limit retention and secondary use of voiceprints to the specific investigation; (c) mandate secure storage, access logs, and auditability; and (d) prohibit repurposing forensic voice databases for non-judicial surveillance absent express statutory authority. These protections preserve investigatory utility while protecting dignity and informational privacy.
9. Oversight, ethics, and public accountability. A cross-disciplinary oversight body comprising forensic scientists, legal scholars, data-privacy experts, and civil-society representatives should review and update standards, commission periodic audits of forensic practice, and publish anonymized aggregate statistics on the use and outcomes of voice forensics. Public reporting builds trust and permits corrective action where systemic errors or disparate impacts are detected.[71]

The prospects for forensic speech science in India are real and significant. When properly validated and contextualized, voice analysis can materially strengthen fact-finding and can exonerate as readily as it can implicate. Yet the transition from promise to reliable practice requires more than technological acquisition; it demands an institutional ecosystem that privileges validation, transparency, and rights protection. If India adopts the combination of statutory clarity, laboratory accreditation, local research investment, judicial education, and privacy governance outlined above, voice forensics will become an asset to the rule of law rather than a liability.

Realizing this vision is an interdisciplinary project for which legal reformers, forensic scientists, engineers, linguists, and judges must cooperate. The immediate agenda is tractable: publish technical standards, institute accreditation and proficiency testing, fund Indian datasets and anti-spoofing research, and equip the bench and bar to perform rigorous gatekeeping. Doing so will ensure that the courtroom hears not merely novel technical outputs but robust, transparent, and legally defensible scientific testimony that advances both accuracy and justice.

---

[71] Rajesh Verma, "The Paradigm Shift in Forensic Voice Comparison" *SIFAS* (Aug 25, 2024), available at: https://www.sifs.in/events/blog-details/paradigm-shift-forensic-voice-comparison-evaluation-rajesh-verma (Last visited on Oct 15, 2025).

References

Jain P, Chinmayee P, Kaur K et al (2024) Advancement in forensic voice analysis: legal frameworks and technology integration. Asian J Adv Res 7(1):369–384

Probative force (n.d.) In Legal dictionary. Definition: The ability of evidence to prove or disprove a fact in a legal case

Zhang B, Cui H, Nguyen V, Whitty M (2025) Audio deepfake detection: what has been achieved and what lies ahead. Sensors 25(7):1989. https://doi.org/10.3390/s25071989

Indian Evidence Act, 1872; Information Technology Act, 2000; P.V. Anvar v. P.K. Basheer, (2014) 10 SCC 473; Arjun Panditrao Khotkar v. Kailash Kushanrao Gorantyal, (2020) 7 SCC 1.

Indian Evidence Act, 1872, Section 45 & 45A; Bharatiya Sakshya Adhiniyam, 2023, Section 39(1) & 39(2)

Spectral Data (n.d.) Technical definition regarding frequency content and spectrograms in forensic phonetics

State (through CBI/New Delhi) v. S.J. Choudhary, Supreme Court Appeal (Crl) 461 of 1987, AIR 1996 SC 491; Malay Kumar Ganguly v. Dr. Sukumar Mukherjee & Ors., (2009) 9 SCC 221, AIR 2010 SC 112

Bharatiya Sakshya Adhiniyam (2023) Section 63

Yusufalli Esmail Nagree v. The State of Maharashtra, AIR 1968 SC 147 (MANU/SC/0092/1967)

Arjun Panditrao Khotkar v. Kailash Kushanrao Gorantyal and Ors. 2020 (7) SCC 1

Sudhir Chaudhary v. State (NCT of Delhi), State (NCT of Delhi) Crl Appeal No. 700-701 of 2016, AIR 2016 SC 3772

Supra

R.M. Malkani v. State of Maharashtra, State of Maharashtra AIR (1973) SC 157; 1973 SCR (2) 417

Ritesh Sinha v. State of Uttar Pradesh, State of Uttar Pradesh (2019) SCC OnLine SC 855

Rahul Agarwal v. State of West Bengal & Anr, (2025) INSC 1223

AIR 2017 SC 4161.

Apoorva (2025) Privacy v evidence: supreme court allows secretly recorded spousal conversations as admissible evidence in matrimonial disputes. *SCC OnLine* Times. https://www.scconline.com/blog/post/2025/07/15/secretly-recorded-spousal-conversations-admissible-evidence-supreme-court/

Lexis Nexis (2025) Decoding Bharatiya Sakshya Adhiniyam, 2023: comparative insights & study with Indian evidence Act, 1872. Lexis Nexis Blog. https://www.lexisnexis.in/blogs/decoding-bharatiya-sakshya-adhiniyam-2023-comparative-insights-study-with-indian-evidence-act-1872/

Bharati RK, Nagarale S (2025) Digital forensic science and evidentiary standards in the Bharatiya Sakshya Adhiniyam 2023: a legal examination of admissibility. Indian J Nat Sci 15(88):53

Varghese J (2024) Evidentiary value of electronic form evidence, electronic and digital records under Bharatiya Sakshya Adhiniyam 2023 (Part VII). Judicial Vision

2018 INSC 75

Shafhi Mohammad v. The State of Himachal Pradesh, Special Leave Petition (Crl) 2302 of 2017, (2018) 5 SCC 311.

2020 INSC 453

(2014) 10 SCC 473

Police and Criminal Evidence Act 1984. https://www.legislation.gov.uk/ukpga/1984/60/contents

1993 AC 380: (1993) 2 WLR 102

1985 SCC (Supp) 611

R.M. Malkani v. State of Maharashtra 1973(1) SCC 471, AIR (1973) SC 157; 1973 SCR (2) 417

Singh, B. (2024) Family conversation secretly recorded by wife to prove domestic violence and cruelty admissible in evidence: Gujarat high court. Live Law. https://www.livelaw.in/high-court/gujarat-high-court/gujarat-high-court-family-conversations-wife-recorded-prove-domestic-violence-cruelty-admissible-evidence-family-matters-265833

2025 SCC OnLine SC 1421

Sharma R, Govind D, Mishra J et al (2024) Milestones in speaker recognition. Artif Intell Rev 57:58. https://doi.org/10.1007/s10462-023-10688-w

Saini M, Kapoor AK (2016) Biometrics in forensic identification: applications and challenges. J Forensic Med 1(2)

Khan AH, Aithal S (2022) Voice biometric systems for user identification and authentication—a literature review. Int J Appl Eng Manag Lett 6(1):198–209. https://doi.org/10.5281/zenodo.6471040

Mazaira-Fernandez LM, Alvarez-Marquina A, Gomez-Vilda P (2015) Improving speaker recognition by biometric voice deconstruction. Front Bioeng Biotechnol 3(126)

Gold E, Hughes V (2014) Issues and opportunities: the application of the numerical likelihood ratio framework to forensic speaker comparison. Sci Justice 54(4). https://doi.org/10.1016/j.scijus.2014.04.003

Central Forensic Science Laboratory, Chandigarh (n.d.) Research activities: automatic speaker identification

Garrett BL, Rudin C (2024) The right to a glass box: rethinking the use of artificial intelligence in criminal justice. Cornell Law Rev 109:561

Yi J, Wang C, Tao J et al (2023) Audio deepfake detection: a study. J arXiv., Cornell University 14(8). https://doi.org/10.48550/arXiv.2308.14970

Ajimah EN, Iloanusi ON (2024) Biometric voice recognition system in the context of multiple languages: Using traditional means of identification of individuals in Nigeria languages and English language. Res Stat 2(1)

Delfino RA (2023) Deepfakes on trial: a call to expand the trial judge's gatekeeping role to protect legal proceedings from technological fakery. Hastings Law J 74(2):293. https://repository.uclawsf.edu/hastings_law_journal/vol74/iss2/3

Vincent E, Jafari MG, Abdallah SA (2005) Blind audio source separation (technical report). Queen Mary, University of London, Centre for Digital Music

Fraser H, Aubanel V, Maher RC et al (2024) Forensic speech enhancement: toward reliable handling of poor-quality speech recordings used as evidence in criminal trials. J Audio Eng Soc 72(11):748–753. https://doi.org/10.17743/jaes.2022.0176

Ohri R (2020) Trouble for retired High Court judge: CFSL verifies his voice sample. The Economic Times. https://economictimes.indiatimes.com/trouble-for-retd-hc-judge-cfsl-verifies-his-voice-sample/articleshow/79946204.cms

The Times of India (2024) Verified call recordings can be proof in DV cases https://timesofindia.indiatimes.com/city/ahmedabad/verified-call-recordings-can-be-proof-in-dv-cases-gujarat-high-court-ruling-on-admissibility-of-voice-recordings-in-domestic-violence-act-cases/articleshow/112209088.cms

JIL w/o Priyank Manubhai Choksi v. State of Gujarat, Crl Rev Application No. 1243/2023 (Gujarat HC)

PTI (2023) Jagdish Tytler summoned by CBI for recording voice sample in 1984 riots case. The Times of India https://timesofindia.indiatimes.com/india/jagdish-tytler-summoned-by-cbi-for-recording-voice-sample-in-1984-riots-case/articleshow/99401257.cms

U.S. Department of Justice (n.d.) 258. Admissibility of spectrograms. Criminal Resource Manual https://www.justice.gov/archives/jm/criminal-resource-manual-258-admissibility-spectrograms-voice-prints

Frye v. United States, 293 F. 1013 (D.C. Cir. 1923)

269 F. Supp. 2nd 892 (S.D. Tex. 2003)

Morrison GS, Thompson WC (2017a) Assessing the admissibility of a new generation of forensic voice comparison testimony. Colomb. Sci. Technol. Law Rev. 18(2). https://doi.org/10.7916/stlr.v18i2.4022

Robson, J., Smith, H. (2023) Identification by voice (1). Counsel Magazine https://www.counselmagazine.co.uk/articles/identification-by-voice-%281%29

[2008] EWCA Crim 970

Speaker Recognition Subcommittee (2024) Standard guide to the forensic speaker recognition landscape (OSAC 2023-N-0023). NIST

Leiden Guidelines *on the Use of Digitally Derived Evidence in International Criminal Investigations and Trials* (2022). https://leiden-guidelines.com/
Prosecutor v. Bemba, ICC-01/05-01/08 (2013)
Morrison GS, Thompson WC (2017b) Assessing the admissibility of a new generation of forensic voice comparison testimony. Colomb. Sci. Technol. Law Rev. 18
Shafhi Mohammad v. State of Himachal Pradesh, SLP (Crl) No. 2302 of 2017, (2018) 5 SCC 311.
International Association for Forensic Phonetic & Acoustics (2020) Code of practice. https://www.iafpa.net/about/code-of-practice/
C.J. Christopher Signi v. State of Tamil Nadu, 2025 SCC OnLine Mad 3214
S. Pratap Singh v. The State of Punjab, AIR (1964) SC 72
Daubert v. Merrell Dow Pharmaceuticals, Inc., 509 U.S. 579 (1993)
European Network of Forensic Science Institutes (n.d.) Guidelines for evaluative reporting in forensic science
Verma R (2024) The paradigm shift in forensic voice comparison. SIFAS. https://www.sifs.in/events/blog-details/paradigm-shift-forensic-voice-comparison-evaluation-rajesh-verma

Stuttering, Stigma, and the Legal System

9

Samiksha Gaur, Emmanuel Kwaku Addo, Krittika Kunda, and Rodney Gabel

Abstract

This chapter provides a comprehensive understanding of stuttering and the diverse challenges experienced by people who stutter. Using the International Classification of Functioning, Disability and Health, it conceptualizes stuttering as a dynamic interplay of individual, social, and environmental factors. The chapter also investigates interactions between people who stutter and the legal system, using case studies to illustrate both obstacles and opportunities for equitable inclusion. Furthermore, it highlights community-based support and resources aimed at enhancing communication, social engagement, and overall quality of life of people who stutter.

9.1 Stuttering, Stigma, and the Legal System

Stuttering is a complex communication disorder characterized by moments of getting stuck and having no control over one's speech. It is not a matter of linguistic ability or cognitive capacity; a person who stutters knows exactly what they want to communicate but can have involuntary interruptions while articulating it (Tichenor and Yaruss 2019). Stuttering can manifest as part-word repetitions (he-he-he-hello), prolongations (ssssun), and blocks (g.irl) (Yairi et al. 2001; Lu et al. 2000). The exact cause of stuttering is unknown, but some risk factors include family history,

S. Gaur (✉) · E. K. Addo · K. Kunda
Department of Community Research and Action, Binghamton University, Binghamton, NY, USA
e-mail: sgaur@binghamton.edu; eaddo@binghamton.edu; kkunda@binghamton.edu

R. Gabel
Department of Speech, Language Pathology, Binghamton University, Binghamton, NY, USA
e-mail: rgabel@binghamton.edu

V. Kumar et al. (eds.), *Forensic Speech Sciences*, New Horizons in Forensic Science, https://doi.org/10.1007/978-981-92-1475-4_9

environmental influences, and biological factors (Guitar 2014). Stuttering is more prevalent in males than females, and 80% of the people who stutter recover naturally during childhood without intervention (Manning and DiLollo 2025). For those who continue to stutter, the impact of stuttering transcends the physical aspect of speech. It may lead to mental health problems, physical health issues, and poor quality of life (Boyle 2018; Boyle and Fearon 2018; Briley et al. 2021; Gerlach et al. 2021). People who stutter may encounter daily challenges, including persistent stigma and discrimination from both society and peers. Such negative experiences often lead to feelings of shame or embarrassment about their speech, prompting many to hide or conceal their stutter through various avoidance behaviors like steering clear of situations where they anticipate difficulty, substituting words or sounds to mask disfluency, or avoiding emotionally charged interactions that might trigger stuttering episodes (Boyle and Gabel 2020).

9.2 Multidimensional Nature of Stuttering Through the Lens of the International Classification of Functioning, Disability and Health (ICF)

The speaker's reactions are crucial in determining how much stuttering impacts an individual who stutters quality of life. Given the multidimensional nature of stuttering, ICF, as proposed by the World Health Organization, serves as an ideal framework for describing and understanding stuttering as a communication disorder and the lived experiences of people who stutter (Yaruss and Quesal 2004). The purpose of the ICF framework is to classify each disorder based on "components of health" rather than "consequences of diseases" (World Health Organization 2001). This focus describes stuttering not as a deficiency but instead highlights how people function in their daily lives. It also considers personal and environmental factors and their impact on the individual's life experiences caused by the disorder (Yaruss and Quesal 2004).

Now, let's examine how the four distinctive sections of the ICF can be applied explicitly to stuttering as explained in the studies conducted by Yaruss and Quesal (2004, 2006).

First, body functions and structures describe the physical signs of stuttering, including how it affects the rhythm, rate, and fluency of speech. Regarding structures, ICF has a separate section for the various oral structures involved in speech production, such as the nose, mouth, pharynx, and larynx. Any anatomical oral-structural deficit does not cause stuttering but may result from genetics and neurological differences in the brain, thus explaining the etiology of stuttering.

Second is the limitation of activities and participation: While body functions focus on observable and direct effects of stuttering, the limitation of activities and participation describes the communication challenges caused by stuttering. The primary focus is on communication, not just speech but communication as a whole. Activities can include, but are not limited to, initiating conversations, answering phone calls, and holding group discussions. This section explains how stuttering can affect a person in all these situations. Conversely, participation refers to the different contexts where these activities occur, such as domestic life, education, and employment, and how stuttering can influence their involvement in these areas.

Third, the ICF model describes the important environmental factors that influence the lived experiences of people who stutter. For example, when a person who stutters has supportive family and friends, their experiences with stuttering will be very different compared to someone who is denied a job promotion because of negative stereotypes their boss holds about stuttering. Since the environment is conducive to positive experiences, this section should be used to explain stuttering and to better understand the experiences of people who stutter.

Finally, personal factors describe how no two people who stutter will have the same experience. The personal factors are important to highlight the highly individual nature of each speaker's experience with stuttering. Personal factors include personal identifying factors like gender, race, age, and cultural background as well as psychosocial characteristics, especially the speaker's personal reactions to their stutter and how those reactions shape their lived experiences, including their feelings, behavioral struggles, and the thought process behind understanding their stuttering.

In addition to explaining the condition, the ICF framework can also be used to assess stuttering and develop intervention plans for people who stutter (Yaruss 2007). Using the ICF framework, a clinician can gain a more comprehensive understanding of stuttering, not just the surface symptoms but also the wider effects on the individual's quality of life. One example of an assessment tool is the OASES (Overall Assessment of the Speaker's Assessment of Stuttering), which targets each section of the ICF and is used to evaluate school-age children, adolescents, and adults who stutter, with the ICF serving as the foundational basis for this tool's development (Yaruss and Quesal 2006). In terms of intervention, the ICF helps the speech-language pathologist approach the treatment session from a well-rounded perspective, where the focus is not only on improving the client's fluency but also on overall communication, including psychosocial aspects like improving their attitude toward stuttering and fostering more positive emotions, leading to a healthy communication style (Beilby et al. 2012).

9.3 The Challenges for People Who Stutter

Based on the preceding discussion of the ICF model, it can be argued that the primary challenges experienced by people who stutter are not limited to bodily structures and functions. Although neurological, genetic, or environmental factors may contribute to the onset and persistence of stuttering, these factors alone do not determine how individuals participate in everyday activities. Rather, contextual factors, particularly environmental barriers and psychosocial responses, exert the greatest influence on participation restrictions faced by people who stutter. Environmental conditions can also shape personal attitudes and coping behaviors, reinforcing the psychological and social burden associated with stuttering.

To further understand how these contextual influences operate, let's draw on the seminal work of Erving Goffman from 1975 on stigma and the "spoiled identity" (Goffman 1975). Goffman asserts that society categorizes individuals as "normal" or "deviant" based on culturally valued characteristics. When an attribute, such as a disability or minority identity, marks someone as different or deficient, that individual becomes socially discredited. Such individuals may therefore attempt to conceal or minimize these attributes by developing what Goffman termed "disidentifiers" to avoid negative judgment or being excluded. However, even when concealment is possible, it frequently incurs significant personal costs, including stress, self-surveillance, and reduced social participation. For people who stutter, such concealments could mean using avoidance strategies such as not speaking in certain situations or not using certain words. As stated earlier, these strategies may come at a great cost.

Goffman's framework has been widely applied across health and social sciences to examine stigma and its consequences for marginalized groups (Şamar et al. 2024; Dew and Gabel 2025; Afroozeh et al. 2025; Vassenden et al. 2024; Borojevic and Söhner 2025; Castanelli et al. 2025). For instance, Borojevic and Söhner demonstrated that misunderstanding and suspicion toward medical cannabis users persisted even in contexts of legal acceptance (Borojevic and Söhner 2025). Similarly, Dew and Gabel found that inaccurate beliefs about stuttering can lead even individuals familiar with people who stutter to steer them toward restricted career paths based on observed communication behaviors rather than personal aspirations or abilities (Dew and Gabel 2025).

Together, these evidences highlight that the lived experience of stuttering is shaped less by the speech differences themselves and more by the stigmatizing social environments in which those differences are interpreted. The following section explores the specific challenges people who stutter encounter as a result of stigma, stereotyping, and public misunderstanding. Stigma profoundly influences the lives of people who stutter, affecting their mental health, emotional well-being, and overall quality of life, particularly when internalization is strong (Boyle 2018; Boyle and Fearon 2018; Gerlach et al. 2021).

The society we live in is shaped by misunderstanding, impatience, and persistent negative stereotypes toward stuttering and people who stutter. In many everyday interactions, people who stutter are confronted with subtle yet harmful behaviors such as being interrupted or talked over or having their sentences finished for them. While these actions may be intended as helpful, they frequently reflect a lack of respect for the speaker's autonomy. Rather than being given the time and space to express themselves fully, people who stutter are often placed in situations where their voice is minimized or dismissed.

9.4 Stuttering and Stigma

Stigma is defined as identifying and labeling certain individuals or groups by attaching negative assumptions to them, drawing attention to their perceived differences, and maintaining unequal power dynamics within society (Andersen et al. 2022). For people who stutter, stigma is a pervasive experience that can arise across various aspects of daily life, from strangers as well as family members, friends, or colleagues. This stigma can manifest in two principal forms: enacted stigma and felt stigma (Boyle 2018). Enacted stigma refers to overt behaviors or actions directed toward people who stutter, such as ridicule, exclusion, or discriminatory treatment leading to an increase in stress and anxiety. In contrast, felt stigma represents the internalized anticipation or fear of being stigmatized, which may persist even in the absence of recent negative encounters, as the anticipation of negative judgment can be as psychologically harmful as actual discrimination (Boyle 2018). Negative emotions and self-perceptions can become deeply ingrained in the identities of adults who stutter, especially among those who internalize stigma. Those with more severe stuttering may experience greater emotional distress and reduced quality of life, with frequent speech disruptions reinforcing a sense of difference and evoking feelings of shame (Gerlach et al. 2021).

Stuttering often presents significant barriers in educational environments, limiting participation in classroom activities such as reading aloud, presenting, or engaging in group work (Daniels et al. 2012). Fear of stuttering can disrupt concentration, reduce learning opportunities, and can contribute to lower academic performance (Daniels et al. 2012). Besides education and employment, stuttering also affects a person's social life, including friendships and romantic relationships. People who stutter are viewed as less desirable as a romantic partner and have a harder time forming friendships (Nang et al. 2018; Zeigler-Hill et al. 2020). Women who stutter often view their speech as a barrier to belonging and forming meaningful relationships. Many express fear of judgment and rejection, while others report limited support and feelings of being misunderstood or teased by family members, reinforcing stigma within close relationships (Nang et al. 2018). These experiences reveal how stuttering affects women's confidence, self-image, and participation in social and professional life. To quote a participant from the study:

> (stuttering) made study a lot more difficult, it made work a lot more difficult, it made socializing a lot more difficult, and together with that because your self-esteem goes lower as well, it impacts your assertiveness (Nang et al. 2018, p. 7).

In conclusion, stigma, whether enacted or internalized, shapes the lived experiences of people who stutter. Internalized stigma fosters anxiety, shame, and self-doubt, while both forms of stigma limit social participation and diminish quality of life by reinforcing psychological distress and social exclusion.

9.5 Stuttering and Mental Health

We now understand the psychosocial impact of stuttering, but what specifically does that include? Stuttering has long been linked to social anxiety (Iverach et al. 2017; Chu et al. 2020). However, the stereotype that an individual stutters "because" they are anxious has been repeatedly disproven (Smith and Weber 2017;

Frigerio-Domingues and Drayna 2017). While anxiety can worsen overt symptoms of stuttering, research has also shown that social anxiety develops in individuals because of their stuttering (Craig and Tran 2014).

Prolonged social anxiety can lead to depressive symptoms, including serious negative effects like fear, anger, hopelessness, and low self-esteem (Briley et al. 2021; Iverach et al. 2017; Alqhazo et al. 2016). There is a positive correlation between depression and anxiety in general, meaning that as anxiety increases, so does depression (Wang et al. 2025). There is also a significant difference in depressive mood and loneliness scores between people who stutter and their non-stuttering peers, notably 40% of the participants who stuttered reported *Global Severity Index* scores that were comparable to those typical of psychiatric outpatients (Tran et al. 2011). A higher global severity score signifies a greater negative effect on an individual's quality of life. It has also been found that people who stutter report more suicidal ideation, referring to the thoughts or behaviors associated with the intention of ending one's own life and associate these negative thoughts with their stutter (Tichenor et al. 2023). To illustrate the broader negative impact of stuttering on an individual's mental health, two participants from the study shared:

> These thoughts intensified in my 40s when I felt very alone and isolated (Tichenor et al. 2023, p. 2097).

> ...My suicidal thoughts passed once I reached college as I found people who accepted me and went to therapy. It returned in my third year of college as I faced a lot of sexism in my major and failed at getting an internship, which really hurt my self-esteem. [The suicidal thoughts] only worsened since the more anxious I was, the more I stuttered, and the more I stuttered, the worse my anxiety became. I felt suicidal again when I first thought to myself that I would never be able to hold a job with my stutter or gain respect from anyone I met (Tichenor et al. 2023, p. 2097).

Likewise, in another study, 33.9% of the people who stutter reported an attempt to commit suicide at least once, which paints a concerning picture regarding the mental health risks for people who stutter (Al-Ghamdi et al. 2022). Anxiety and depressive symptoms, along with experiences of bullying, mockery, or feeling ostracized, have led to a deterioration in the mental health and well-being of individuals who stutter (Türkili and Aydın 2022). Interestingly, this decline in emotional well-being and quality of life has been comparable to the decline experienced by individuals suffering from life-threatening diseases like neurotrauma, diabetes, and coronary artery disease (Craig et al. 2009). These numerous mental health challenges, when combined with other issues, create a sense of urgency and call for attention from speech therapists, researchers, policymakers, and society as a whole to develop a more empathetic and comprehensive support system for individuals who stutter.

One of the primary factors contributing to the decline in mental health for people who stutter is the discrimination they face. People who stutter report experiencing a major discrimination event at least once in their lives (Boyle and Cheyne 2024). Major discrimination, as described by the authors, refers to incidents that leave a lasting impact on an individual's life. The most significant discriminatory events for people who stutter include discrimination during the job hiring process and being discouraged from pursuing specific careers like those with high communication demands because of their stutter (Boyle and Cheyne 2024). Discrimination has also been strongly linked to lower job satisfaction (Plexico et al. 2019). Beyond the workplace, people who stutter encounter discriminatory behaviors from their communication partners, including family, friends, and therapists, such as being treated with "second-class status," having their privacy denied, or being patronized during therapy sessions, all because of their stutter (Coalson et al. 2021). These negative consequences of stuttering affect an individual in all aspects of their lives, and encounters with law enforcement are no exception. As emphasized through these two cases below.

Case 9.1

This case describes a highly capable and dedicated firefighter. For over a decade, he served his community with professionalism and skill, consistently demonstrating his ability to perform under pressure. Yet, when he applied for a permanent position within the city's fire department, he was denied the role solely because of his stutter. Despite a flawless service record, the decision-makers claimed that his stutter posed a risk to his colleagues in high-stress emergencies, even though they had no evidence to support this concern. Refusing to accept this injustice, he pursued legal action and sued the fire department for discrimination. Unfortunately, he lost the case. The decision left him not only without the promotion he had earned but also with a deep sense of defeat and disillusionment, both in his profession and in the legal system meant to protect him.

Case 9.2

In contrast to many stories of injustice, there are also moments of resilience and hard-won progress. One such story is of a determined and highly motivated professional working with a large international bank on Wall Street. Known for his strong work ethic and consistent performance, he excelled in a high-pressure environment and had proven his capabilities time and again. Yet despite his success, he was abruptly fired solely because of his stutter. His employers claimed he was unfit for a high-stress role, ignoring the evidence of his contributions and success. Refusing to accept this discrimination, he took legal action against the company. In a rare but powerful outcome, he won the case and received the compensation he deserved. More importantly, his victory became a reminder that unjust assumptions about people who stutter can and should be challenged and that change is possible through persistence and advocacy.

9.6 Stuttering and Interactions with the Law-Evidence Synthesis

In this section, we will explore the factors that could make it harder for people who stutter to achieve optimum quality of life, including their interactions with law enforcement. Everyday encounters with law enforcement, such as being stopped for a routine traffic check, questioned in public, or asked to verify one's identity, are typically brief and uneventful for most people. However, for a person who stutters, these same moments can provoke intense fear and anxiety. The sudden demand for clear, rapid, and fluent speech in a high-stakes context, may be misinterpreted by the officers. What is routine for fluent speakers may become an interaction fraught with potential misunderstanding and loss of dignity for individuals who stutter. These experiences demonstrate how everyday social systems, such as policing, can inadvertently amplify communication-based vulnerabilities, such as stuttering. It also highlights the need for increased awareness, empathy, and training among law enforcement officers.

Although the criminal justice system is designed to maintain a safe and just society, there is evidence to show that it is also a challenging path to navigate (Greenwald and Daniels 2024; Learoyd and Bryan 2023). STAMMA (the largest support group organization for people who stutter in the United Kingdom) shared an article on their Web site co-authored by Esther Pritchard, a person who stutters and a law professional, and Jennifer Short, a speech and language pathologist. This article focused on how the criminal justice system can be challenging for people with speech, language, and communication needs to navigate and how these challenges can be adequately addressed (Pritchard and Short 2022). According to the same authors, although there are no official statistics on the number of defendants who stutter within the United Kingdom's criminal justice system, the figure is likely to be considerable. Given that an estimated 1–2% of the adult population stutters and that around 60% of individuals in the Youth Justice System and 80% of adults in prison have been identified as having speech, language, and communication needs (SLCN), it stands to reason that a notable number of people who stutter are directly affected by this system. Ensuring equity and fair treatment for this population demands careful attention to the communication challenges that may shape their experiences and, ultimately, the outcomes of their interactions with law enforcement and the courts. Beyond recognition, meaningful change requires us to listen to the stories and examine the evidence, both lived and researched, about people who stutter and their encounters with the criminal justice system. Only by grounding policy and practice in such understanding can we move toward a justice process that is not merely procedural but genuinely inclusive and humane.

9.7 Law Enforcement Encounters

There is no doubt that people who stutter often face communication challenges in encounters with police and other first responders. Yet, few empirical studies examine this problem. People living with various forms of disabilities may have a harder time when they encounter emergencies, such as when interacting with law enforcement (Smith and Notaro 2009). Recent qualitative evidence indicates that adults with speech-language differences, including stuttering, describe stressful and sometimes adversarial interactions with law enforcement, where their communication differences can be misinterpreted as evasiveness or noncompliance (Greenwald and Daniels 2024). In this study, one of the participants described how his fear of being judged and misinterpreted by law enforcement could make it even harder to express themselves. He said:

> I think because I kind of feel like they're maybe evaluating me too…maybe they don't trust me totally. Like my speech could be something that causes an issue for them, you know, versus someone I've known a little while. They know it's a part of me, not something I'm choosing to do…So I guess in those types of situations where it's an acquaintance, I would feel more pressure to be fluent. Or like I'd feel more…like being observed. That way that I'm speaking would be observed under a closer microscope (Greenwald and Daniels 2024, p. 9).

This is not an isolated case finding, as another participant in the same study recounted his experience with a Transport Security Administration agent at the airport, which led to more stuttering due to the stressful encounter. Just like anecdotal evidence from other people who stutter, at the time of their interaction, they believed more stress could create a situation where their body language or stuttering (i.e., the core and secondary stuttering behaviors) could be misconstrued by their listener to either mean they are lying or trying to be evasive. He said:

> I just feel, like, whenever, you're not clear and concise with, like, law, T.S.A., especially them … They, like, right away, not like flag you but they, like, ask you questions more and more and, like, then, um, I stutter more because I have to worry about how comes across (Greenwald & Daniels 2024, p. 7).

Understandably, these experiences or reactions of people who stutter to law enforcement agents do not suddenly appear out of the blue. They often emanate from past traumatic events and experiences with the misinformed public (Boyle 2018). This suggests that people who stutter are constantly thinking of how their interactions with law enforcement agents are prone to being misjudged. The thought of these experiences repeating themselves, in itself, could cause more stress and social anxiety, consequently making them struggle more with speaking.

The Stuttering Foundation, a non-profit organization helping people who stutter, shared an article on their Web site that describes a hypothetical interaction between a local police officer and a person who stutters and possible outcomes (McCullough n.d.). The article written by McCullough, a senior social science analyst at the Office of Community-Oriented Policing Services, describes a scenario where a driver who stutters exceeds the speed limit and is stopped by a local police officer. The routine to ask for registration and a license is then followed by asking where the driver was heading. For a person who stutters, this stressful situation with law enforcement often leads to inaudible blocks, repetitions, and some inaudible sounds (Greenwald and Daniels 2024). The same question, when repeated again after a few seconds, leads the driver in this scenario to show physical struggles such as increased blinking of the eyes, an unnatural posture, and avoidance of eye contact during stuttering moments. Though these are typical core and secondary manifestations of stuttering, to the uninformed police officer, it may mean several things. For instance, the police could think the driver is driving under the influence, is hiding something, or may be simply trying to evade their questions. In this scenario, an informed police officer could make a good call and provide the necessary accommodations. However, an uninformed officer may escalate the situation, which may lead to other issues.

The importance of having an informed police officer cannot be overstated. The police may encounter people who stutter in a variety of contexts, including adults during traffic stops, victims or witnesses providing statements, or children experiencing bullying at school for their stuttering. A story was told by a female US citizen who claimed to have been questioned for several minutes and detained at the airport because she was flagged for faking her stutter as a coverup (see Fig. 9.1) (The Stuttering Foundation 2016). Given that intentionally lying to a law enforcement agent is a crime, whenever these agents, in the course of their lawful duties, misjudge people who stutter to be telling lies, the ramifications are great and an unpleasant situation for people who stutter. Developing practical strategies for mediating these interactions to ensure the safety of all is critical.

The problem is twofold. First, officers often receive little training about atypical speech, so they may misread hesitations, repetitions, or pauses as deception or nervousness. Second, the stress of a police encounter can exacerbate stuttering, producing a feedback loop that increases both communication difficulty and officers' misperception (Greenwald and Daniels 2024). The Stuttering Foundation's *I Stutter Card* and short guidance documents are low-cost, widely used mitigations for everyday encounters, a fact evidenced by the responses of some participants in the Greenwald and Daniels study. They work by providing an immediate, nonverbal cue about the person's communication difference and suggested accommodations (e.g., allowing extra time) (The Stuttering Foundation 2016). Refer to Fig. 9.1.

9.8 Courtroom Testimony and Witness Credibility

A growing empirical literature explores how stuttering affects witness testimony and juror perception. A recent study found that people who stutter can provide as accurate eyewitness accounts as their non-stuttering peers (Maras et al. 2025). However, in many contexts, jurors' credibility judgments may be negatively influenced by stuttering, even when the substance of testimony is equivalent. In other words, jurors perceive people who stutter as less confident, which correlates with a perception of low credibility. Furthermore, a witness who stutters may be tempted to alter their responses under oath by substituting challenging words with easier ones (StammeringLaw 2023). Stated otherwise, stuttering can create an extraneous credibility penalty for people who stutter. These findings suggest that while stuttering does not necessarily reduce the factual accuracy of eyewitness testimony, it does affect perceptions of witness confidence and credibility, which can influence legal outcomes.

How can we then support people who stutter in the courtroom? Scoping reviews of accommodations used in courts for people with communication and cognitive impairments identify several practical strategies that can improve access and protect evidentiary integrity. These include pre-trial meetings with legal professionals, the use of intermediaries or specially trained court staff to facilitate questions, simplified questioning, extra time, breaks, or the use of alternative modes of communication where appropriate (Turner and Hughes 2022). Furthermore, several jurisdictions

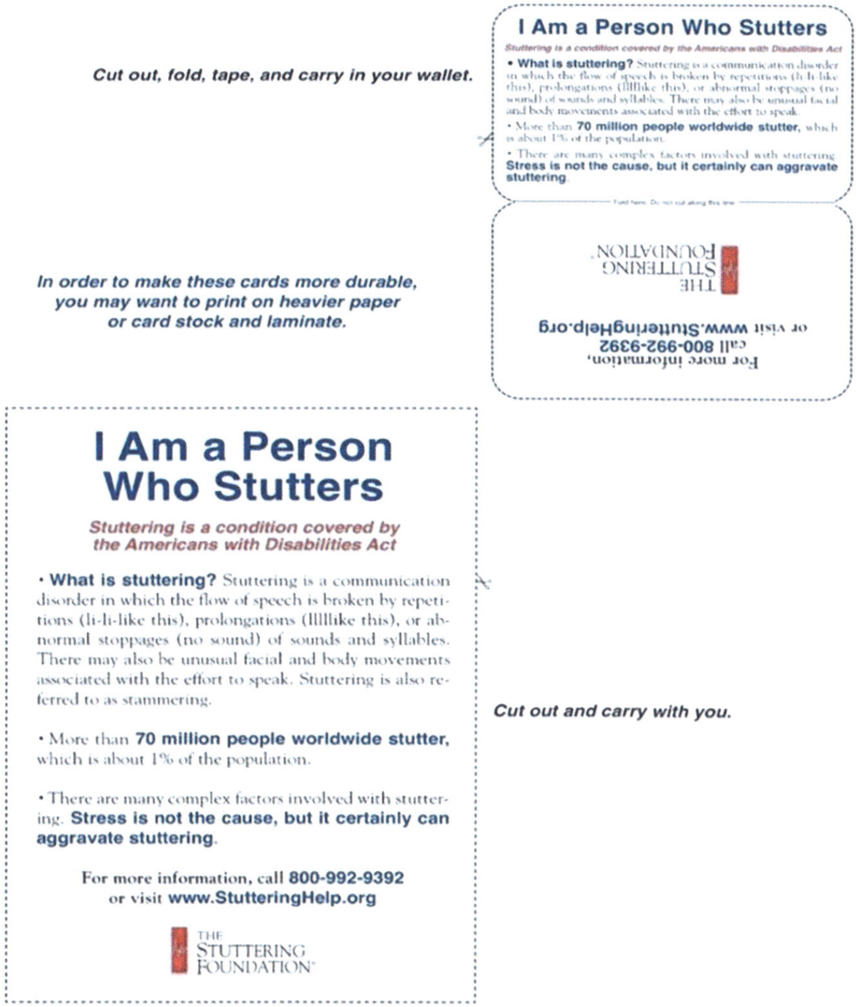

Fig. 9.1 The "I Stutter Card"
Note. From *I Stutter Card*, by The Stuttering Foundation (https://www.stutteringhelp.org/IDCard) Copyright 2016 by The Stuttering Foundation. Reprinted with permission

all over the world have developed specific judicial guidance and reasonable-adjustment pathways for people who stutter, ensuring jurors, judges, and legal practitioners are aware of how stuttering may affect testimony and how to mitigate potential prejudice (StammeringLaw 2023; Gordon 2018). As such, people who stutter are entitled to reasonable accommodations and should be empowered to demand such in situations where they perceive the lack of these supports could affect their liberty or affect the delivery of justice.

Additionally, to guard against the inadmissibility of a witness who stutters, procedural adaptations such as pre-trial familiarization, use of witness intermediaries, permitted pauses, and judicial instructions about fluency, as ways to uphold both witness rights and judicial fact-finding, should be encouraged in our criminal justice systems (Maras et al. 2025; Cooper and Mattison 2017). Although the use of witness intermediaries has been in practice in many countries, not much is known about their use in questioning or taking evidence from people who stutter. Nevertheless, if used among this population, who are likely to be rendered vulnerable due to having significant communication challenges (Gordon 2018; Department of Justice 2016), it could help reduce their stress and anxiety levels, especially those who may have symptoms of social anxiety disorder. Consequently, it will improve their comfort, which may reduce avoidance behaviors and, in turn, lead them to provide accurate and reliable witness statements.

9.9 Jury Service and Juror Participation

Jury service raises distinct issues for people who stutter who are summoned to serve. Organizations that support people who stutter emphasize that jurors who stutter often worry about reading verdicts aloud, asking questions during deliberation, or even speaking during voir dire (the jury selection process) (STAMMA n.d.). As discussed earlier, legal frameworks in many jurisdictions require reasonable adjustments for jurors with disabilities. Guidance materials outline practical steps such as allowing jurors to submit written questions, providing extra time to speak, or arranging for a support person to facilitate communication during breaks (Gordon 2018). Taking advantage of these accommodations could make a difference. However, two related risks must be balanced: first, the exclusion risk, where jurors are excused unnecessarily because of assumptions about their ability to speak, and, second, the exposure risk, where jurors are forced to perform (e.g., read aloud a verdict) without reasonable support. A suggested good practice is to provide options to the jurors to give them agency. For example, giving jurors advance notice of likely speaking requirements and the opportunity to request adjustments confidentially will enable participation and foster agency while protecting the integrity of the process (StammeringLaw 2023).

9.10 Defendants, Access to Justice, and Anti-discrimination Law

Just like witnesses and jurors, defendants who stutter may face compounded challenges. Communication barriers can affect their ability to ask questions, participate in their defense, and communicate with counsel. To reiterate, from a legal rights perspective, several jurisdictions recognize stuttering as potentially falling within disability protections (e.g., Americans with Disability Act in the United States and Equality Act in the United Kingdom), which can trigger duties to provide reasonable accommodations (StammeringLaw 2023; Weiner and Tetnowski 2016). However, case laws illustrate both successful claims of discrimination and unsuccessful cases due to the complexity of proving that stuttering has a significant impact on a person's daily functioning (Weiner and Tetnowski 2016). Since stuttering is variable in nature, and a person who stutters does not stutter the same way every time, it sometimes becomes challenging to provide sufficient evidence to prove a person is disabled by stuttering and to qualify for supportive accommodations. However, the literature on limited reasonable accommodation for people who stutter, while they navigate the criminal justice system, is grave enough that it warrants urgent and continuous discussions toward advocacy and policy change (Maras et al. 2025; StammeringLaw 2023; Turner and Hughes 2022; Gordon 2018). When these supports are absent, the risk increases that misunderstandings or perceived non-cooperation will influence bail decisions, plea negotiations, or sentencing.

9.11 Policy and Practice Recommendations

Enhancing access to justice for people who stutter requires systemic awareness, procedural adaptation, and a shift in how communication differences are understood within the legal system. Justice actors, including police officers, prosecutors, judges, and court staff, should receive targeted training on stuttering. Such programs should emphasize that stress often exacerbates disfluency, that stuttering does not signal deception or uncertainty, and that simple adjustments can make a profound difference in communication equity for people who stutter (Greenwald and Daniels 2024; StammeringLaw 2023). Likewise, judicial bench books and procedural manuals should include concise, actionable guidance describing what stuttering is and what it is not, along with templates for implementing reasonable accommodations. Also, when people who stutter are expected to give testimony, courts should allow pre-trial familiarization and, where necessary, appoint communication intermediaries or specialists to facilitate accurate and confident participation (Turner and Hughes 2022).

Furthermore, to promote consistency, standardized checklists of accommodations, such as accepting written responses to questions or avoiding timed reading aloud tasks, should be encouraged across police stations, courtrooms, and jury service settings (StammeringLaw 2023). Equally practical are nonverbal communication aids like the *I Stutter Card* and short explanatory scripts that individuals can use to self-advocate during stressful interactions. Beyond these procedural reforms, a comprehensive research agenda is warranted to systematically investigate juror bias toward people who stutter and to determine, through methodologically rigorous observational studies, which courtroom practices most effectively uphold evidentiary accuracy while safeguarding individual rights.

Importantly, proving a significant negative impact from stuttering should involve more than verification through assessments of stuttering severity. Justice systems must also value and incorporate the subjective experiences of people who stutter, how they perceive communicative barriers, and the conditions under which they can best express themselves, when determining accommodations. Recognizing these lived experiences, rather than relying solely on objective indicators, is essential for building a justice process that is both procedurally fair and genuinely inclusive.

9.12 Conclusion

In conclusion, stuttering is not merely a speech disorder, but it is shaped by psychological, social, and structural factors. People who stutter face multifaceted challenges, including stigma, reduced social participation, and potential disadvantages within the legal system. The current evidence base, combining qualitative reports, experimental investigations of witness credibility, legal analyses, and practical advocacy guidance, shows that people who stutter can be disadvantaged at multiple points in the justice system unless proactive accommodations are made. Fortunately, many adaptations are straightforward, inexpensive, and supported by advocacy organizations and a growing body of research. Embedding these practices into police training, court guidance, jury service protocols, and defendant support will reduce unfair outcomes and better align legal processes with principles of access to justice. Recognizing stuttering in this holistic way is crucial for fostering understanding, empathy, and meaningful inclusion for all individuals who stutter.

Disclosure of Conflict of Interest The Authors have no conflict of interest to disclose.

References

Afroozeh MS, Phipps C, Afrouzeh A, Alipour Asiri Z, Safari Jafarloo HR (2025) The sport and exercise experiences of physically disabled women in Iran: shame, stereotyping, and Goffman's stigma. Disabil Soc 40(4):1104–1126. https://doi.org/10.1080/09687599.2024.2328560

Al-Ghamdi S, Al-Ghamdi HA, Allarakia BM, Alshatri FA, Al-Ghamdi A, Al-Ghamdi M (2022) Association between stuttering and psychosocial complications in Saudi Arabian individuals: a pilot study. J Fam Med Prim Care 11(10):6087–6090. https://doi.org/10.4103/jfmpc.jfmpc_39_22

Alqhazo M, Blomgren M, Roy N, Awwad MA (2016) Discrimination and internalised feelings experienced by people who stutter in Jordan. Int J Speech Lang Pathol 19(5):519–528. https://doi.org/10.1080/17549507.2016.1209561

Andersen MM, Varga S, Folker AP (2022) On the definition of stigma. J Eval Clin Pract 28(5):847–853. https://doi.org/10.1111/jep.13684

Beilby JM, Byrnes ML, Yaruss JS (2012) Acceptance and commitment therapy for adults who stutter: psychosocial adjustment and speech fluency. J Fluen Disord 37(4):289–299. https://doi.org/10.1016/j.jfludis.2012.05.003

Borojevic V, Söhner F (2025) Detecting and understanding potential stigma among medical cannabis users in Germany. BMC Public Health 25(1):874. https://doi.org/10.1186/s12889-025-22084-w

Boyle MP (2018) Enacted stigma and felt stigma experienced by adults who stutter. J Commun Disord 73:50–61. https://doi.org/10.1016/j.jcomdis.2018.03.004

Boyle MP, Cheyne MR (2024) Major discrimination due to stuttering and its association with quality of life. J Fluen Disord 80:106051. https://doi.org/10.1016/j.jfludis.2024.106051

Boyle MP, Fearon AN (2018) Self-stigma and its associations with stress, physical health, and health care satisfaction in adults who stutter. J Fluen Disord 56:112–121. https://doi.org/10.1016/j.jfludis.2017.10.002

Boyle MP, Gabel RM (2020) Openness and progress with communication and confidence have all gone hand in hand: reflections on the experience of transitioning between concealment and openness among adults who stutter. J Fluen Disord 65:105781. https://doi.org/10.1016/j.jfludis.2020.105781

Briley PM, Gerlach H, Jacobs MM (2021) Relationships between stuttering, depression, and suicidal ideation in young adults: accounting for gender differences. J Fluen Disord 67:105820. https://doi.org/10.1016/j.jfludis.2020.105820

Castanelli DJ, Molloy E, Bearman M (2025) The stigma of underperformance in assessment and remediation. Adv Health Sci Educ Theory Pract 30(3):815–830. https://doi.org/10.1007/s10459-024-10382-8

Chu SY, Sakai N, Lee J, Harrison E, Tang KP, Mori K (2020) Comparison of social anxiety between Japanese adults who stutter and non-stuttering controls. J Fluen Disord 65:105767. https://doi.org/10.1016/j.jfludis.2020.105767

Coalson GA, Crawford A, Treleaven SB, Byrd CT, Davis L, Dang L, Edgerly J, Turk A (2021) Microaggression and the adult stuttering experience. J Commun Disord 95:106180. https://doi.org/10.1016/j.jcomdis.2021.106180

Cooper P, Mattison M (2017) Intermediaries, vulnerable people and the quality of evidence: an international comparison of three versions of the English intermediary model. Int J Evid Proof 21(4):351–370. https://doi.org/10.1177/1365712717725534

Craig A, Tran Y (2014) Trait and social anxiety in adults with chronic stuttering: conclusions following meta-analysis. J Fluen Disord 40:35–43. https://doi.org/10.1016/j.jfludis.2014.01.001

Craig A, Blumgart E, Tran Y (2009) The impact of stuttering on the quality of life in adults who stutter. J Fluen Disord 34(2):61–71. https://doi.org/10.1016/j.jfludis.2009.05.002

Daniels DE, Gabel RM, Hughes S (2012) Recounting the K-12 school experiences of adults who stutter: a qualitative analysis. J Fluen Disord 37(2):71–82. https://doi.org/10.1016/j.jfludis.2011.12.001

Department of Justice (2016) Northern Ireland registered intermediaries schemes pilot project phase II review. Department of Justice, Belfast

Dew CW, Gabel RM (2025) Relationship between familiarity with a person who stutters and vocational stereotyping. J Fluen Disord 85:106146. https://doi.org/10.1016/j.jfludis.2025.106146

Frigerio-Domingues C, Drayna D (2017) Genetic contributions to stuttering: the current evidence. Mol Genet Genomic Med 5(2):95–102. https://doi.org/10.1002/mgg3.276

Gerlach H, Chaudoir SR, Zebrowski PM (2021) Relationships between stigma-identity constructs and psychological health outcomes among adults who stutter. J Fluen Disord 70:105842. https://doi.org/10.1016/j.jfludis.2021.105842

Goffman E (1975) Stigma: notes on the management of spoiled identity. J Aronson, New York

Gordon SE (2018) The ADA'S effective communication requirements in state and local criminal justice settings. ADA National Network. https://www.adainfo.org/wp-content/uploads/imported/1.2-ADA-State-Local-Criminal-Justice-2-slides-per-page_0.pdf. Accessed 22 Oct 2025

Greenwald ML, Daniels DE (2024) When adults with speech-language impairment meet law enforcement: a qualitative analysis of client experiences. J Commun Disord 112:106471. https://doi.org/10.1016/j.jcomdis.2024.106471

Guitar B (2014) Stuttering: an integrated approach to its nature and treatment, 4th edn. Wolters Kluwer Health/Lippincott Williams & Wilkins, Philadelphia

Iverach L, Rapee RM, Wong QJJ, Lowe R (2017) Maintenance of social anxiety in stuttering: a cognitive-behavioral model. Am J Speech Lang Pathol 26(2):540–556. https://doi.org/10.1044/2016_AJSLP-16-0033

Learoyd J, Bryan K (2023) Working with adults with communication difficulties in the criminal justice system: a practical guide for speech and language therapists. Routledge, London

Lu Y, Wiltshire CEE, Watkins KE, Chiew M, Goldstein (2000) Characteristics of articulatory gestures in stuttered speech: a case study using real-time magnetic resonance imaging. J Commun Disord 97:106213. https://doi.org/10.1016/j.jcomdis.2022.106213

Manning WH, DiLollo A (2025) Clinical decision making in fluency disorders, 5th edn. Plural Publishing, San Diego

Maras K, Park S, Grafton P, Peat J, Toshniwal N, Haigherty A, Guo K, Franks M, Goodwin H, Grau Sainz V, Sharma A, Fridman A, Gordon-Ellis L, Howells K (2025) Eyewitness testimony by individuals who stammer: evidence, experience, and perceived credibility. Br J Psychol 116(1):1–28. https://doi.org/10.1111/bjop.70014

McCullough DC (n.d.) When police encounter persons who stutter. Stuttering Foundation. https://wwwstutteringhelporg/content/when-police-encounter-persons-who-stutter Accessed 22 Oct 2025

Nang C, Hersh D, Milton K, Lau SR (2018) The impact of stuttering on development of self-identity, relationships, and quality of life in women who stutter. Am J Speech Lang Pathol 27(3S):1244–1258. https://doi.org/10.1044/2018_AJSLP-ODC11-17-0201

Plexico LW, Hamilton M, Hawkins H, Erath S (2019) The influence of workplace discrimination and vigilance on job satisfaction with people who stutter. J Fluen Disord 62:105725. https://doi.org/10.1016/j.jfludis.2019.105725

Pritchard E, Short J (2022) Stammering and the criminal justice system. Your Voice. https://stamma.org/your-voice/stammering-and-criminal-justice-system. Accessed 20 Oct 2025

Şamar B, Taş M, Kayın M, Ünübol B (2024) Comprehensive analysis of social stigma of individuals with substance use disorder in Turkey in the context of Erving Goffman's stigma theory. J Ethn Subst Abus 23(4):679–698. https://doi.org/10.1080/15332640.2023.2176394

Smith DL, Notaro SJ (2009) Personal emergency preparedness for people with disabilities from the 2006-2007 behavioral risk factor surveillance system. Disabil Health J 2(2):86–94. https://doi.org/10.1016/j.dhjo.2009.01.001

Smith A, Weber C (2017) How stuttering develops: the multifactorial dynamic pathways theory. J Speech Lang Hear Res 60(9):2483–2505. https://doi.org/10.1044/2017_JSLHR-S-16-0343

STAMMA (n.d.) Stammering & jury service; stammering guidance for judges. https://stamma.org/get-help/help-speaking-situations/stammering-jury-service. Accessed 4 Nov 2025

StammeringLaw (2023) Appearing in court with a stammer. https://www.stammeringlaw.org.uk/services/court/. Accessed 31 Mar 2026

The Stuttering Foundation (2016) I stutter card. https://www.stutteringhelp.org/IDCard. Accessed 31 Mar 2026

Tichenor SE, Yaruss JS (2019) Stuttering as defined by adults who stutter. J Speech Lang Hear Res 62(12):4356–4369. https://doi.org/10.1044/2019_JSLHR-19-00137

Tichenor SE, Palasik S, Yaruss JS (2023) Understanding the broader impact of stuttering: suicidal ideation. Am J Speech Lang Pathol 32(5):2087–2110. https://doi.org/10.1044/2023_AJSLP-23-00007

Tran Y, Blumgart E, Craig A (2011) Subjective distress associated with chronic stuttering. J Fluen Disord 36(1):17–26. https://doi.org/10.1016/j.jfludis.2010.12.003

Türkili S, Aydın ZF (2022) Mental Well-being and related factors in individuals with stuttering. Heliyon 8(9):e10446. https://doi.org/10.1016/j.heliyon.2022.e10446

Turner K, Hughes N (2022) Supporting young people's cognition and communication in the courtroom: a scoping review of current practices. Crim Behav Ment Health 32(3):175–196. https://doi.org/10.1002/cbm.2237

Vassenden A, Handulle A, Orupabo J (2024) To confront or not to confront? Seeing minorities' responses to ethnoracial stigmatisation through Goffman's ritual interaction order. Sociol Rev 73(1):216–234. https://doi.org/10.1177/00380261241258613

Wang H, Wang M, Wang X, Feng T, Liu X, Xiao W (2025) Complex associations between anxiety, depression, and resilience in a college student sample: a network analysis. Front Psych 16:1502252. https://doi.org/10.3389/fpsyt.2025.1502252

Weiner C, Tetnowski JA (2016) Stuttering discrimination under the law. ASHA Leader. https://stuttering.okstate.edu/images/2016_Weiner_and_Tetnowski_Stuttering_Discrimination_Under_the_Law.pdf. Accessed 4 Nov 2025

World Health Organization (2001) International classification of functioning, disability and health: ICF. World health Organization. https://iris.who.int/handle/10665/42407. Accessed 14 Aug 2025

Yairi E, Watkins R, Ambrose N, Paden E (2001) What is stuttering? J Speech Lang Hear Res 44(3):585–592. https://doi.org/10.1044/1092-4388(2001/046)

Yaruss JS (2007) Application of the ICF in fluency disorders. Semin Speech Lang 28(4):312–322. https://doi.org/10.1055/s-2007-986528

Yaruss JS, Quesal RW (2004) Stuttering and the international classification of functioning, disability, and health (ICF): an update. J Commun Disord 37(1):35–52. https://doi.org/10.1016/S0021-9924(03)00052-2

Yaruss JS, Quesal RW (2006) Overall assessment of the speaker's experience of stuttering (OASES): documenting multiple outcomes in stuttering treatment. J Fluen Disord 31(2):90–115. https://doi.org/10.1016/j.jfludis.2006.02.002

Zeigler-Hill V, Besser Y, Besser A (2020) A negative halo effect for stuttering? The consequences of stuttering for romantic desirability are mediated by perceptions of personality traits, self-esteem, and intelligence. Self Identity 19(5):613–628. https://doi.org/10.1080/15298868.2019.1645729

Case Studies in Forensic Speech Sciences 10

Himanshi Sharma, Leena Bhardwaj, Kamal Chauhan, and Tirath Das Dogra

Abstract

Voice production is a complex physiological process. Its perception includes the recognition of speaker and understanding what the speaker means by a certain word or statement by accessing accents, specific speech habits and patterns, etc. Voice production and perception are an essential aspect of forensic speaker identification. Voice analysis has a significant role in speaker recognition for legal contexts. This analysis includes various scientific and technological aspects.

Keywords

Case studies · Forensic speaker identification · Judgment · Spectrographic analysis

10.1 Introduction

The dictionary definition of voice is sound formed in the larynx and uttered by mouth. Voice refers to sound produced by vibrations of vocal fold, known as voiced sound, in contrast to nonvoiced sound that is produced without the vibration of vocal fold. The voice source also conveys biological and paralinguistic information.

H. Sharma · L. Bhardwaj (✉)
Department of Chemistry, Biochemistry and Forensic Science, Amity University Haryana, Gurgaon, Haryana, India
e-mail: lbhardwaj@ggn.amity.edu

K. Chauhan
Central Forensic Science Lab, Department of Forensic Science Services, Ministry of Home Affairs, Govt of India, Bhopal, India

T. D. Dogra
All India Institute of Medical Science, New Delhi, India

V. Kumar et al. (eds.), *Forensic Speech Sciences*, New Horizons in Forensic Science, https://doi.org/10.1007/978-981-92-1475-4_10

The term biological information refers to the size of vocal tract, while paralinguistic information refers to speaker's social status, personal traits and emotional status. Voice production is the result of a complex fluid structured acoustic interaction process, which depends upon geometry and material properties of the lungs, larynx and the vocal tract. The vibration in vocal folds modulates the airflow and produces voice, which further gets modified into meaningful speech with the help of articulators such as the tongue, lip, soft palate etc (Zhang 2016).

10.2 Historical Context of Speech Sciences

The Indian philosophy describes the voice production as follows: The stimulated wind in brahmagranthi (located at the base of the spine Muladhara Chakra and Svadhisthana Chakra, where primitive brain functioning like fight or flight reflexes occurs) [Jivamukti Yoga] travels in the upward direction via three granthis (glands) located in the region of the stomach, chest and head. This upward travelling wind generates nāda at the levels of the stomach, heart, throat, head and tongue. These nādas produced at different levels are named according to their nature or audibility such as atisukshama (fine) at the stomach level, Sukshma (minute) at the heart level, apusta (soft) at the throat level, pusta (loud) at the head level and krtrima (artificial) at the tongue level.

The three Dosas in the human body—Vata, Pita, Kapha—of a healthy individual will be in an equilibrium state. The state of disease is defined as the disturbance in the equilibrium state of these three dosas. The deviation in the considered parts of speech such as pitch, clarity or loudness may be defined as voice abnormality of voice disorder. The type of speech has been explained as normal, abnormal or disordered voice such as speech of children have lisping, (aspstavarnasamyukta); change in voice quality can be perceived just after the sleep, repetition of same meanings; speech of old people have hesitant or halting voice with misarticulations; speech of a dying person shows relaxed and heavy sound, and the voice is associated with heavy breathing, hiccups and repetition and seems like stammering or halting.

Perception of any sensory stimulus/object as vision, hearing, touch, taste and scent is processed by the five sensory organs such as the eyes, ears, skin, tongue and nose. The seven pitch forms that link with the musical notes are Sadja, rsabha, Gandhara, Madhyama, pancama, dhaivata and nisada. Three pitch forms accepted by other sources are udatta (high), anudatta (low) and svarita (high-low). The **time taken** during/at the time of the utterance of speech is measured on the basis of the time taken to produce/speak the vowels as short (Hrasva, i.e., one matra), long (dirgha, i.e. two matras) and prolated (pluta, i.e. three matras). According to the locations of articulation, the seven places are the palate, root of the tongue, lips, nose, chest, throat and teeth. The Sanskrit speech sounds were explained on the basis of the place of articulation. The studies of West, Annsberry and Carr (1956) ascribed that the production of sounds is due to the muscular actions caused by the impulses from nerve endings. However, studies infer that the production of sound is caused due to the venal plexus present in different regions.

10.3 Production of Speech Sounds

There are internal and external efforts primarily while producing the speech (Story 2019). The internal efforts refer to the actions made before speaking that are described as the contact between the articulator and the location of articulation and the degree of opening between these. The stop and nasal consonants are produced by the action of contact between articulator and articulation location, called the Sprsta effort (Savithri 1987). The semivowels are produced when articulator reaches the place of articulation and slightly touches it; this produces sound, and the effort is called isatprsta. The sibliants and vowels are produced by the opening of mouth; this effort is called vivrta. The production of the sound of 'a' requires contraction of mouth, and this effort is called samvrta. The external efforts include the production of sound encompassing the different movements, contractions and vibrations of vocal cords. The stiffening or loosening of vocal cords are termed and considered under the secondary efforts, called anupradana. It involves intonations and pauses (Raphael et al. 2007) (Casserly and Pisoni 2010). **Intonation** is the rise and fall of the voice when one speaks. Intonations can be of different styles. These are identified by understanding the different pitches involved with different conditions such as joyous conditions that may be evaluated by high, excited and fast intonations.

10.4 Forensic Voice Analysis

The previous inventions and researches provide an overview of how the researchers developed different tools and techniques to understand how the vocal folds move and vibrate during the process of phonation or sound production. The development of a laryngeal mirror in 1854 was made possible by Garcia. During 1878, Stroboscopic techniques were given by Max Jospeh Oertel. Albert Musehold combined stroboscopic and photographic techniques to comprehend how individual voice production is done and voice physiology. In 1958, to diagnose various voice disorders, Beck and Schönhärl used stroboscopy. Technologies such as laryngostroboscopy, high-speed video laryngoscopy (HSV) and trans-nasal endoscopy have been employed. Magnetic resonance imaging (MRI) has been utilized for visualizing voice physiology, acoustic properties and laryngeal configurations, although it does not allow to visualize voice onset changes in vocal cords (Richter et al. 2024; Jessen 2018). Formant analysis can also be used for speaker identification in forensic speech sciences (identification and comparison) (Jain et al. 2024). The analysis of formants can be done by measuring midpoint measurements (including capturing questioned vocalic segment from the centre), dynamic measurements (including multiple timepoints in the segment) and long-term formant (LTF; includes all formants that contain speech in a segment) analysis (Hollien et al. 2014) (Fairclough et al. 2023).

10.5 Case Studies

10.5.1 State (N.C.T. Of Delhi) vs Navjot Sandhu@ Afsan Guru (Indian Kanoon n.d.)

Date of judgement: 4 August 2005
Bench of P. Venkatarama Reddi & P.P. Naolekar

The case reported was the incident where five heavily armed men tried to attack the Parliament at noon on 13 December 2001, with the intent to seize the building. On Dec 14, at 20:09 h, an incoming call to 9,810,081,228 was intercepted by S. I. Harender Singh. Voice samples from phone call (from Kashmir) conversations in Kashmiri language have been used for forensic analysis. There were voices of two individuals. After the auditory and spectrographic analysis of these samples, it was revealed that the male voice in the conversation was of the accused Shaukat Hussain, and that of the female voice was his wife (accused no. 4). On the same day, at 12:22 h, the conversations between Gilani and his brother Shah Faizal were also recorded. Both intercepted calls were analysed and considered by Inspector M.C. Sharma. He drew an inference that the people who were conversing on two mobile phones had knowledge about the attack on the parliament and two persons, Shaukat and Chotu, who were connected with the case were in Srinagar.

On the night of Dec 14, Shaukat called up from Srinagar and spoke to his wife, Afsan, the receiving number which was later recovered from the house of Shaukat. Voice samples recorded from the conversations were sent to the senior scientific officer of CFSL, Delhi. Voice samples of Afsan Guru and Shaukat were also sent for comparison with the intercepted conversation.

Auditory and spectrographic analysis was conducted for the voice samples. He submitted the report and testified that on comparison, the voice was found to be the same. The high court doubted the authenticity of the intercepted conversation on the ground as the duration noted by the expert in his report was 2 min, 16 s, which was at variance with the duration of 49 s noted in all call records. Still no question was raised in this regard. The telephonic conversation between Gilani and his brother Shah Faizal on 14 December 2001 at 12:22 h was intercepted and recorded on tape. The conversation was in Kashmiri language, which was translated in Hindi. Translator revealed that it was an ordinary colloquial conversation. Only inference made from the conversations was that Afsan was scared and that she was aware that Shaukat and Afzal did something that attracted police surveillance.

Judgement The appeal filed by Mohd. Afzal was terminated, and the court confirmed the death sentence upon him. The appeal filed by Shaukat was partly permitted. He was convicted under Section 123 IPC, i.e. ‘Concealing a plan to wage war against the Government of India’, and sentenced to RI (rigorous imprisonment) for 10 years with a fine of Rs 25,000.

10.5.2 Nilesh Dinkar Paradkar vs State of Maharashtra (Indian Kanoon n.d.)

Judgement date and court: 9 March 2011
Bench of B. Sudershan Reddy, Surinder Singh Nijjar

According to the prosecution, there were four accused numbered as 1, 2, 3 and 5, who were active members of the organization crime syndicate of Chhota Rajan. Accused no. 4 had assisted, encouraged and conspired with accused nos. 1, 2, 3 and 5 in committing various offences under the Maharashtra Control of Organized Crime Act (MCOC Act). Police noticed that these people were planning to kill Bharat Shah, a Mumbai-based businessman. The plan was to kill him near a pan shop near 'Mehta Bhuvan' where his office was situated at Charni Road, Mumbai. His office timings were communicated to the accused via telephone by Bharat Nepali. The information about the plan was received by D. C. P. Mr. Dhananjay Dattatraya Kamlakar on 14 October 2004. Taped telephone conversations have been intercepted between the accused Bharat Nepali and accused persons including Nilesh Paradkar (A5). On 28 October 2004, the phone call was intercepted and recorded, which was about 9.16 min. During the conversation, the plan to assassinate a businessman was discussed. With the recordings and conversations, police presented these as evidence to prove the presence of accused in the conspiracy. These recordings were played before the police officers who had already met the accused; they identified Bharat Nepali's voice and Nilesh Paradkar's voice.

Court Admissibility Voice identification is less reliable in comparison with visual identification. No forensic, spectrographic and scientific voice analysis was conducted in the case. Only the police officers identified the accused with the help of voice recordings. The Supreme Court discredited the voice identification as weak and improperly handled, and the prosecution failed to prove the accused's involvement based on the voice evidence as it was not properly examined with forensic protocols.

10.5.3 Sunil Singla vs State of Maharashtra (Casemine n.d.)

Judgement date and court: 23 July 2018
Bench of Prakash D. Naik, J.

The prosecution case is that of Mr. Venkoba Gujjal, the deputy general manager of Punjab National Bank, Corporate Branch, New Delhi, who received illegal gratification in conspiracy with co-accused Vinit Kumar (A2) and accused no. 4. A2 is the managing director of M/s. temptation Foods Limited. The voice sample recordings of accused nos. 1, 2, 3 and 4 were forwarded to the CFSL. The voice samples of accused nos. 3 and 4 were identified by Santosh mane, the IT manager. The report of voice analysis is admissible in the court of law under section 65 B of the Indian Evidencce Act. The chargesheet contains certificate of Shailendra Kumar Singh, Inspector of Police, CBI Special Unit, Mumbai, under Section 65 B of IEA. This certificate gave complete details of computer system on which the phone calls were recorded during 29 October 2009 to 26 April 2010. The CD of the recordings were forwarded to CFSL, Delhi. The recorded conversations between accused no.1 and Alka Gujral were admissible evidence.

The prosecution case was based on documents and electronic evidence.

On 10 May 2011, voice identification panchnama of accused no.1 was drawn, wherein his voice was identified by Sudarshan Vadhwa, AGM Punjab National Bank, Circle Office, Mumbai. On 22 April 2011, voice identification panchnama of accused no. 2 was drawn, and his voice was identified by Mr. Chandan, manager of M/s Temptation Foods Limited, Mumbai. On 03 September 2011, voice identification panchnama of accused nos. 3 and 4 was drawn, and their voices were identified by Santosh Rane, IT manager of M/s. Portfolio Financial Services Limited, Mumbai.

Voice samples were forwarded to CFSL for expert opinion. The prosecution relied on the forensic voice examination report of CFSL, New Delhi, dated 03 July 2013.

CBI had filed certificate and thereby compiled by the condition prescribed under section 65 B (4) of the Evidence Act. It was the case of prosecution that accused no.1 had accepted bribe from accused nos. 3 and 4 for providing finance to M/s. Temptation Foods limited, Mumbai. A3 and A4 were directors of M/s. Portfolio Financial Services Limited and submitted the proposal to Punjab National Bank.

From the CD conversation, it was clear that there is prima facie case against accused nos. 1 to 4. Statements of witnesses were recorded. The investigating officer had recorded statements of witnesses under Sections 161 and 164 of CrPC. Thus, there were sufficient evidence to proceed against the applicant. Refer to Fig. 10.1.

10.5.4 Natvarlal Amarshibhai Devani vs State of Gujarat (Indian Kanoon n.d.)

Judgement date and court: 18 January 2017 at Gujarat High Court
Bench of J.B. Pardiwala

The case was on the writ applicant Natvarlal Devani, a superintendent of the Prohibition and Excise Directorate, charged under Section 7, 13 (1)(d) and 13 (2) of the Prevention of Corruption Act, who asked and demanded an amount of Rs 4000 as an illegal gratification for renewing the permit issued in favour of the original complainant. There was a recorded telephone conversation between the two. Investigating Agency prepared a quotation for these recorded conversations. This led to the Anti-Corruption Bureau (ACB) to lodge an FIR. He applied for a writ to restrain the police from compelling him to provide a voice sample against him according to Article 20 (3) of the Constitution of India.

The telephone conversations were recorded and submitted as evidence against the accused. These recordings were to prove the involvement of the accused in the conspiracy and were sent to the FSL with the voice samples of the accused for comparison. The spectrographic analysis was performed to compare voice samples in the forensic science laboratory. A unique voiceprint was generated, which represented frequency, pitch, formants and articulation patterns for the individual.

FSL reports showed that the voice recordings matched the accused's voice samples.

The voice samples were considered credible and admissible with the significant forensic expert opinion in the court of law. The forensic voice analysis was accepted by the court and considered legally valid and reliable evidence. As the voice spectrograph technique is not a psychiatric or testimonial compulsion, it does not violate Article 20 (3).

The final verdict is based on voice samples, previously voice spectrograph analysis is not considered as testimonial under the article 20(3) of Constitution of India. The court also clarified that forensic voice spectrography analysis doesn't fall under any psychiatric or any other kind of treatment.

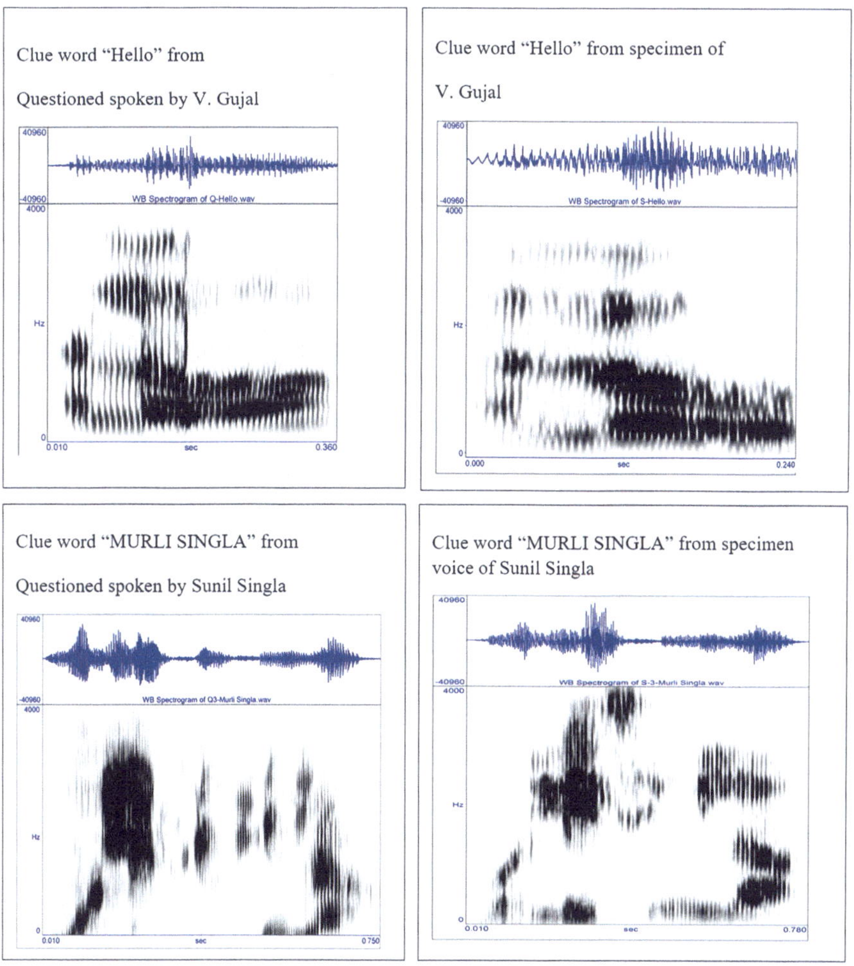

Fig. 10.1 Spectrogram of speech sample of case 3

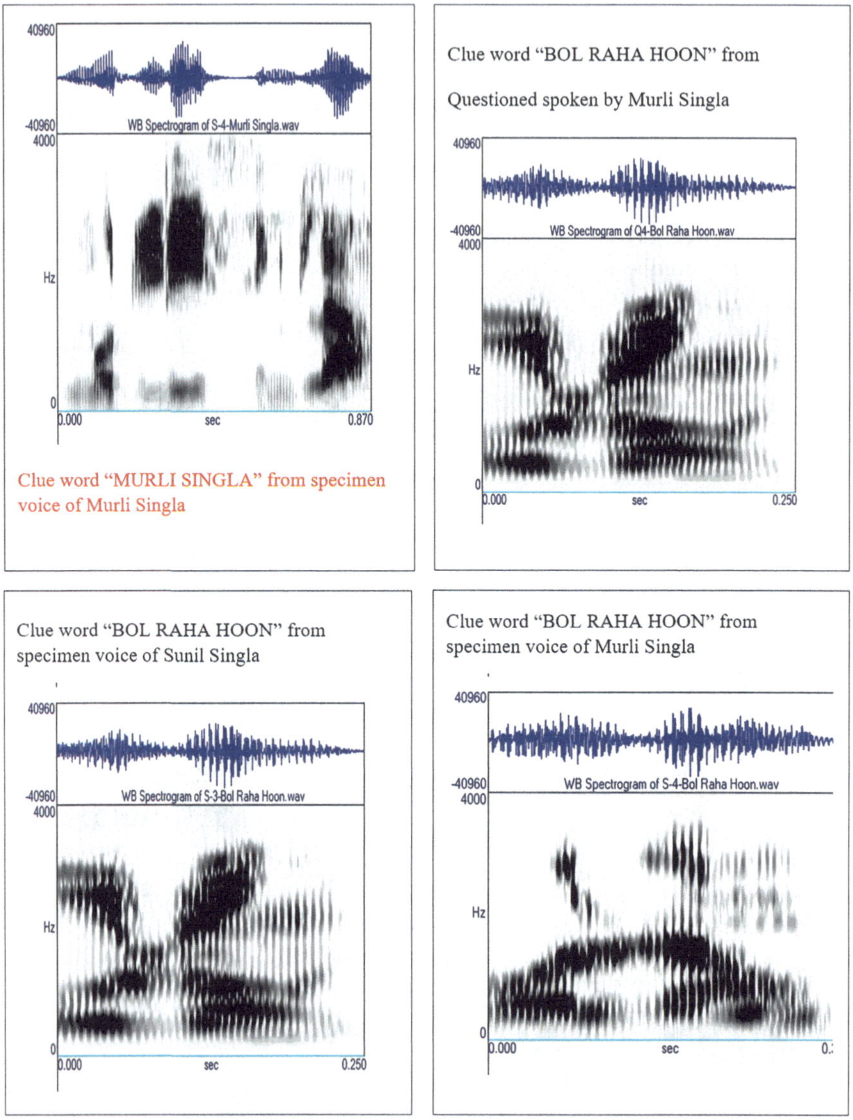

Fig. 10.1 (continued)

10.5.5 CBI vs. Suresh Kr. Lakra, etc. Judgement Dt… (Indian Kanoon n.d.)

Judgement date and court: 7 May 2016

This case was registered against MCD officials for demanding and accepting bribe as illegal gratification, in exchange of permitting unauthorized construction, allowing illegal commercial activities in residential areas. The case was that the officials of MCD and its middlemen were running a racket to extract money from building owners in Karol Bagh in exchange of them claiming that their buildings are illegally made. The information came across CBI unit, and after taking the authority orders, the conversations of the accused were recorded from November 2008 to April 2009 on the concerned mobile numbers. The recorded telephone conversations were collected and analysed during the investigation.

VOICE Analysis

CBI investigated the case of criminal conspiracy that involved bribing. There were recorded conversations between the accused and the complainants about the demand and acceptance of bribe money. These conversations were secretly recorded and submitted as evidence.

The voice samples of the accused were recorded during the investigation, and these were used for comparison with the recorded conversation evidence. CFSL conducted voice analysis by using the voice spectrographic technique for speaker identification. The forensic experts gave their opinion that the recorded voice of the accused matched with the voice samples. The experts' opinion was submitted under Section 45 of IEA as testimony. Voice samples were considered admissible in court only if they were collected and recorded following proper protocol. Voice evidence was considered as a corroborative evidence and served as link in proving the above case of bribe and criminal conspiracy.

Voice analysis was conducted to compare the questioned audio samples with reference samples. Forensic experts examined voice parameters including pitch and intonation and linguistic parameters to provide scientific opinions. The audio recordings were admissible under Section 65B of the Indian Evidence Act.

Based on the forensic voice examination results, the court convicted Suresh Kumar Lakra and Mukesh Gupta with violation of the Prevention of Corruption Act. Suresh Kumar Lakra was convicted under 120 B IPC with Sections 7, 12 and 13 (1) (d) of the Prevention of Corruption Act and sentenced to 3 years of rigorous imprisonment. A fine of Rs 10,000 was imposed upon him.

Mukesh Gupta was convicted under Section 120 B IPC with Sections 7, 12 and 13 (1)(d) with rigorous imprisonment for 3 years, and a fine of Rs 1,00,000 was imposed upon him.

10.5.6 Ritesh Sinha v. State of Uttar Pradesh (2019) (Indian Kanoon n.d.)

Judgement date and court: 2 August 2019
Bench of Sanjiv Khanna, Deepak Gupta, Ranjan Gogoi

The case was registered against Dhoom Singh and appellant Ritesh Sinha for demanding and accepting different sums of money from people in exchange of the promise to give them jobs in the police. The FIR was lodged by an In-charge of Electronics Cell of Sadar Bazar Police Station, Saharanpur, UP. Police arrested and recovered a mobile phone from Dhoom Singh. The authorities wanted to verify that the voice recordings of the conversations in the mobile were between Dhoom Singh and the appellant Ritesh Sinha.

A sample of Ritesh Sinha's voice was required for the above verification, and after submitting an application to CJM, he was summoned to court for recording his voice samples. The magistrate had an implied power under Section 53 of CrPC to pass an order permitting taking voice samples for criminal investigation and also to order any person, either an accused or other, to give their handwriting and signature specimens for the purpose of criminal investigation or proceeding under the CrPC.

The above case summarizes that voice sample collection for case investigation is not considered the exploitation of Article 20 (3) of the Constitution of India.

The court defined that the voice/audio evidence can be admissible in the court of law for the purpose of voice comparison. It was also noted that asking or taking voice/audio samples doesn't violate the human rights under the article 20 (3) of the constitution of India. The voice evidence certainly acts as physical evidence rather than any communicated statement of self-incrimination against an individual. The court implies that forensic examinations are considered a valuable testimony in the court of law for analysing voice samples, audio recordings and telephone call recordings by implementing scientific technologies to provide strong evident results to prove a conviction or disprove an innocence. The judgement includes that the magistrate has the power given by the judicial interpretation to order an individual to provide his voice samples for the purpose of investigation of crime.

10.5.7 Research Study on Forensic Voice Analysis

Researchers explored the role and importance of voice analysis and spectrography for crime investigation and solving crimes involving biological relatives. The study includes the identification and differentiation of voice samples from two or more biological sisters, by using telephonic conversations. Approximately 40 voice samples were included in the study. The samples were taken from the siblings from Himachal Pradesh and Punjab region. The researchers used the application of voice biometrics software to analyse certain words and intricate acoustic parameters for speaker identification. Formant comparison is also performed and studied by using spectrograms (*J Pharm Negat Results* 2022).

Finally, the researchers concluded the relevance and reliability of voice evidence in forensic analysis. Speech analysis was performed by careful auditory listening, extraction (Kushwaha et al. 2024) of specific clue words and spectrographic analysis by using multi-speech.

The results revealed that even if there is close similarity between the voice characteristics of biological relatives/siblings, there is also certain individuality between them that requires careful examination. Refer to Figs. 10.2 and 10.3.

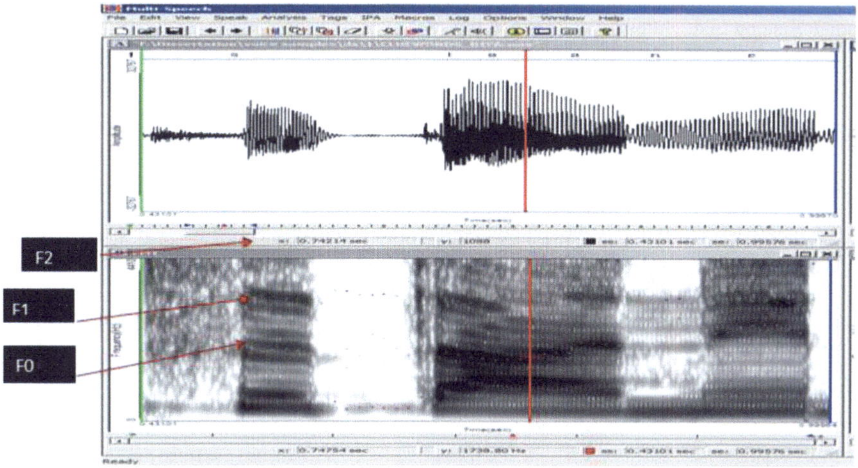

Fig. 10.2 Band and formant formation of speaker A

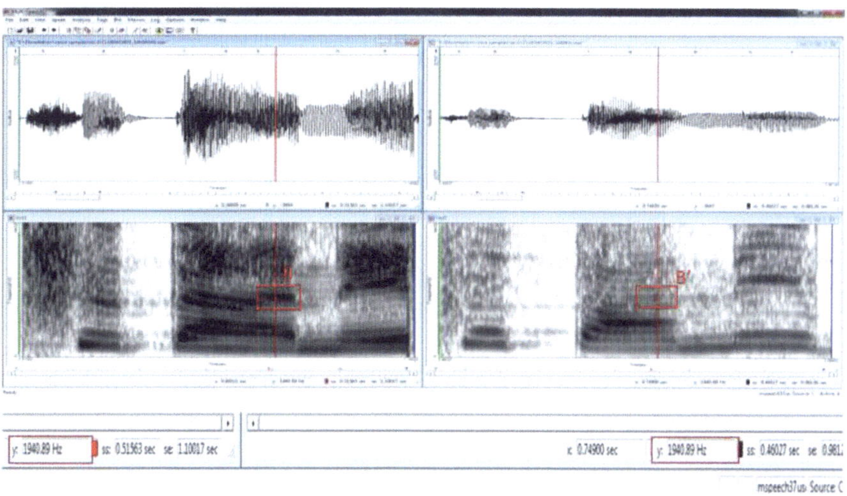

Fig. 10.3 Spectrographic results for wide-band frequency in speech data of speaker B

References

Casemine (n.d.). https://www.casemine.com/judgement/in/5d9199bb714d587fe94ea7b0

Casserly ED, Pisoni DB (2010) Speech perception and production. Wiley Interdiscip Rev Cogn Sci 1(5):629–647

Fairclough L, Brown G, Kirchhübel C (2023) Reviewing the performance of formants for forensic voice comparison: a meta-analysis of forensic speech science research. In: Proceedings of the 20th international congress of phonetic sciences, pp 3834–3838

Hollien H, Bahr RH, Harnsberger JD (2014) Issues in forensic voice. J Voice 28(2):170–184
Indian Kanoon (n.d.). https://indiankanoon.org/
(2022) Forensic voice characterisation and comparison of female siblings using multi-Speechsoftware (2.7.0). J Pharm Negat Results:1739–1746. https://doi.org/10.47750/pnr.2022.13.S10.199
Jain P, Chinmayee P, Kaur K, Chaudhary S, Kaur K, Karunya S (2024) Advancements in forensic voice analysis: legal frameworks and technology integration. Asian J Adv Res 7(1):369–384
Jessen M (2018) Forensic voice comparison. In: Handbook of communication in the legal sphere, pp 219–255
Kushwaha N, Mishra N, Lalawat RS, Jaswal G, Gupta VK, Padhy PK (2024) Voice signals feature extraction and classification of bedridden patients. In: 2024 International conference on communication, control, and intelligent systems (CCIS). IEEE, pp 1–5
Raphael LJ, Borden GJ, Harris KS (2007) Speech science primer: physiology, acoustics, and perception of speech. Lippincott Williams & Wilkins
Richter B, Echternach M, Traser L (2024) Investigation methods for vocal onset—a historical perspective. Bioengineering 11(10). https://doi.org/10.3390/bioengineering11100989
Savithri SR (1987) Speech pathology in ancient India—a review of Sanskrit literature. J Commun Disord 20(6):437–445
Story BH (2019) History of speech synthesis. In: The Routledge handbook of phonetics. Routledge, pp 9–33
Zhang Z (2016) Mechanics of human voice production and control. J Acoust Soc Am 140(4):2614–2635

Challenges and Future Research in Forensic Speech Sciences

11

Vikas Madukar, Leena Bhardwaj, Monika Arora, and Vijay Kumar

Abstract

Forensic speech science has evolved from subjective listener-based judgments to a multidisciplinary, data-driven field grounded in acoustics, aerodynamics, linguistics, psychometrics, and artificial intelligence. Contemporary forensic practice integrates cepstral and spectral measures, aerodynamic indices, and automatic speaker recognition systems to evaluate voice evidence with greater objectivity, transparency, and reproducibility. Despite these advances, significant challenges remain, including variability in speech due to health, emotion, recording conditions, language diversity, and intentional disguise, as well as limitations in database availability and legal admissibility. Emerging AI and machine learning techniques, big data infrastructures, and next-generation instrumentation promise to enhance evidential robustness, particularly through probabilistic reasoning, validation frameworks, and explainable models suitable for courtroom scrutiny. This chapter highlights current challenges, psychometric considerations, and the urgent need for novel speech science measures that can better

V. Madukar
Amity University Haryana, Gurugram, Haryana, India

L. Bhardwaj
Department of Chemistry, Biochemistry and Forensic Science, Amity University Haryana, Gurgaon, Haryana, India

M. Arora (✉)
Amity Business School, Amity University Haryana, Gurugram, Haryana, India
e-mail: marora@ggn.amity.edu

V. Kumar (✉)
Department of Audiology and Speech-Language Pathology, Amity Medical School, Amity University Haryana, Gurgaon, Haryana, India
e-mail: vkumar@ggn.amity.edu

V. Kumar et al. (eds.), *Forensic Speech Sciences*, New Horizons in Forensic Science, https://doi.org/10.1007/978-981-92-1475-4_11

capture voice uniqueness, improve reliability under real world forensic conditions, and strengthen the scientific foundations of forensic speech evidence within legal systems.

Keywords

Psychometrics · Novel markers of voice · Speech evidence reproducibility · Voice uniqueness

11.1 Psychometrics of Forensic Speech Science Tools

Psychometrics in forensic speech science concerns the reliability, validity, sensitivity, specificity, calibration, and fairness of tools used for speaker identification and forensic voice comparison (Rose 2002; Nolan 2013; Basu et al. 2022). Reliability refers to the consistency of measurements across time, speaking tasks, examiners, and recording conditions. Traditional auditory-perceptual judgments have repeatedly demonstrated limited inter-examiner reliability due to listener bias, variation in expertise, and contextual influences (Morrison 2011; Meuwly et al. 2017). In contrast, acoustic and automatic approaches based on standardized protocols show improved test–retest reliability and reproducibility (Künzel 2001). Validity addresses whether a tool measures speaker-specific characteristics rather than task-dependent, linguistic, or channel-dependent artifacts. Construct validity is particularly critical in forensic contexts, as speech features must reflect relatively stable anatomical and physiological properties of the speaker rather than transient states such as emotion, illness, or intoxication (Jessen 2008). Criterion-related validity is commonly evaluated through likelihood-ratio frameworks that compare system outputs against known same-speaker and different-speaker conditions (Morrison et al. 2016; Sveinsdottir et al. 2020). Sensitivity and specificity are essential psychometric properties, as forensic tools must accurately discriminate between speakers while minimizing false inclusions and false exclusions (Brümmer and de Villiers 2013). Calibration represents another key psychometric concern, especially for likelihood-ratio-based systems presented in court. Proper calibration ensures that numerical values correspond to real-world probabilities and that evidential strength is neither overstated nor understated (Sveinsdottir et al. 2020; Juola 2019). Explainability and transparency further influence legal admissibility, as courts increasingly require forensic conclusions to be interpretable, reproducible, and resistant to cognitive bias (Edmond et al. 2022; Eriksson n.d.). Overall, psychometric rigor is fundamental for ensuring that forensic speech science tools meet scientific standards and withstand judicial scrutiny (Basu et al. 2022; Zhang and JHL 2007).

11.2 Identification of Novel Speech Science Measures

The identification of novel speech science measures is motivated by the inherent complexity and variability of human speech, which limits the discriminatory power of traditional acoustic parameters (Titze 2000). Classical measures such as fundamental frequency, formant frequencies, jitter, and shimmer are highly sensitive to recording quality, phonatory instability, and channel effects, making them insufficient for many forensic scenarios involving short, noisy, or telephonic recordings (Dehak et al. 2011).

Emerging directions include advanced cepstral and spectral representations, voice source dynamic measures, articulatory coordination metrics, and integrated aerodynamic–acoustic indices that jointly capture phonatory efficiency, control, and stability (Snyder et al. 2018). Deep-learning-based speaker embeddings, such as x-vectors, represent another class of novel measures capable of encoding high-dimensional speaker information beyond human perceptual limits (Wall 2021). However, these measures must be accompanied by interpretable descriptors and empirical validation to meet forensic transparency and legal admissibility requirements (Juola 2019; Edmond et al. 2022). There is also a growing need for measures capable of distinguishing natural human speech from synthetic or AI-generated voices, detecting intentional disguise, and remaining robust across languages, dialects, and sociophonetic variation (Hughes and Wormald 2020). Population-specific normative databases and longitudinal voice profiling are particularly important for addressing inter-speaker and intra-speaker variability in multilingual contexts such as India (Morozova et al. 2025; Hansen and Hasan 2015).

In essence, novel speech science measures are required to bridge the gap between laboratory-controlled research and real-life forensic conditions. Their development, validation, and standardization are central to enhancing evidential strength, reducing bias, and ensuring the continued scientific credibility of forensic speech science (Basu et al. 2022; Zhang and JHL 2007).

11.3 Cepstral and Spectral Measures

Cepstral peak prominence (CPP) is a cepstral-domain measure that quantifies the strength of harmonic structure in the voice by calculating the amplitude of the dominant cepstral peak relative to the surrounding noise floor, typically expressed in decibels (French and Stevens 2018). Lower CPP values indicate increased aperiodicity and breathiness, and CPP has been shown to be more reliable than perturbation measures such as jitter and shimmer, particularly in severely dysphonic or highly aperiodic voices (Belin et al. 2004). Because CPP can be derived from continuous speech, it is well suited for clinical screening, monitoring therapeutic change, and distinguishing normal from pathological phonation in connected discourse (Pavlidis et al. 2012). Mel-frequency cepstral coefficients (MFCCs) are computed by filtering the short-time magnitude spectrum through a mel-scaled filter bank, applying a logarithmic transformation, and performing a discrete cosine transform to obtain a compact representation of the spectral envelope (Altayari et al. 2022). MFCCs approximate human auditory frequency resolution and are widely used in automatic speech recognition, speaker identification, and forensic voice comparison because they encode speaker-specific vocal tract and spectral characteristics (Wall 2021; Bertovsky et al. 2021). Spectral centroid, defined as the amplitude-weighted center of mass of the spectrum, provides an index of spectral brightness and varies systematically with changes in phonation, articulation, and resonance (Ferrazzano et al. 2020).

Composite acoustic indices such as the Dysphonia Detection Index integrate multiple features, including cepstral, spectral, and perturbation measures, into a single score optimized for classifying normal and disordered voices (Pavlidis et al. 2012). By combining source-related and filter-related information, composite indices offer a more robust representation of vocal function and reduce susceptibility to recording variability and task effects (Belin et al. 2004).

11.4 Aerodynamic and Power-Based Measures

Phonatory power refers to the aerodynamic power required to initiate and sustain vocal fold vibration and is commonly operationalized as the product of subglottic pressure and airflow (Snyder et al. 2018). At the minimum level required for oscillation, this is termed phonation threshold power. Phonation threshold measures are sensitive to changes in vocal fold tissue properties, hydration, and glottal configuration and can reveal early glottal insufficiency not evident in purely acoustic analyses (Snyder et al. 2018). Glottal resistance, defined as subglottic pressure divided by mean airflow during phonation, quantifies the degree to which the glottis resists airflow. Elevated resistance is associated with hyperfunctional phonation, whereas reduced resistance reflects glottal incompetence such as vocal fold paralysis or atrophy (Snyder et al. 2018). Phonatory flow measures provide sensitive indicators of posterior glottal gaps, bowing, and surface dehydration and are widely used to evaluate surgical and therapeutic outcomes (Snyder et al. 2018).

Mean subglottic pressure during sustained phonation or connected speech is the primary aerodynamic correlate of vocal intensity and contributes to fundamental frequency control and overall voice quality. Clinically, it is often estimated noninvasively using intraoral pressure during bilabial plosives (Snyder et al. 2018). Peak subglottic pressure, particularly during phonation onset or high-intensity voice use, reflects maximal vocal fold loading and is relevant for assessing phonotrauma risk in professional voice users (Snyder et al. 2018).

11.5 Contribution to Voice Uniqueness and Clinical Application

When considered together, cepstral, spectral, and aerodynamic measures form a multidimensional profile capturing both source and filter characteristics unique to individual speakers (Titze 2000; Wall 2021). Stable patterns across these measures contribute to perceived voice uniqueness and support applications in forensic speaker identification, personalized speech technologies, and characterization of inter-speaker variability (Basu et al. 2022). In clinical speech-language pathology, integrating these measures enhances sensitivity to early dysphonia, enables objective monitoring of therapeutic change, and strengthens links between physiological mechanisms and signal-level outcomes (Pavlidis et al. 2012).

11.6 Consideration of Speech Science Evidence in the Courtroom Conviction

Forensic speech evidence was primarily used for forensic voice comparison (FVC), where unknown or questioned voice recording was compared with the known or reference recording from a suspect to identify or distinguish between the two individuals. The order of court relies on the expert testimony. Historically, the voice identification or comparison results were only based on human listeners and their experience in the field; no scientific or technological approach were followed. Later, it was devised that the court has to make their decisions based on the factual, scientific information provided by the forensic experts. The court must measure the probative value of the forensic speech evidence in the courtroom. One of the few challenges in the field is that voice prints or voice's uniqueness may not remain rigid as if affected by factors such as illness, emotional encounter while speaking, background noise, etc.

The role of forensic speech sciences in legal context has come a long way from individuals listening and guessing the speaker to the incorporation of objective, scientific, highly sophisticated technology-driven forensic approaches for voice/speaker identification. The highly skilled voice experts implement the use of advanced Automatic Speaker Recognition (ASR) technologies such as x-vector-based systems, which are proved to give better results and accuracy than "earwitnesses" or listeners of the recorded samples. Implementing the technologies in the real case scenarios has proved valuable as human listeners may possess intrinsic biases at some levels. Also, there are chances of human errors. The forensic voice experts utilize the auditory-phonetic analysis where they examine similar sounding voice patterns, voice quality, and articulation. Acoustic analysis is examined by the data of spectrographs. The likelihood ratio of the evidence's results is also assessed. There are a few challenges faced by the examiners and researchers in the field. There are mostly telephonic recorded audio evidence available for examination that have a high noise level, and limited bandwidth in telephone transmissions makes it problematic to compare speaker voices. Unsolicited disguises like whispering or faking an accent can hinder the voice examination. The lack of databases and local language and accent familiarity make it quite challenging in speech understanding and identifying. As we previously discussed the shortcomings faced by the researchers in this field especially in India where the many local languages are used. Here, we have future ahead with implementation of integrating technologies of artificial intelligence and machine learning in generating valuable databases, understanding unique and individual voice features. These can be useful in mitigating biases due to human listeners/experts in the results that may probably influence the results. The future of forensic speech sciences lies in refining the deep neural network (DNN) embeddings as in x-vectors. These systems are expected to provide higher accuracy in handling the short voice recording evidence, which is a case of real-life forensics. Developing technologies and systems are making their way to reduce mismatched conditions. There is further need for empirical evidence in the legal context that require proper validation and calibration of forensic voice comparison especially for real-life case conditions. Emerging technologies involve the use of neurophysiological detection of deception by voice recordings. Recent experiments reveal the application of functional magnetic resonance imaging (fMRI) for deception detection and analyzing neurophysiological differences between true or falsified statements. Another technique is neural correlation with voice perception that includes monitoring brain functioning and response when one listens to familiar voice and its comparison with non-familiar voice. Thermal imaging with high resolution may be explored for detection of changes in the blood flow in the facial region; it can be a noninvasive method to detect stress, fear, or deception of an individual during speaking. Future aspects will be focusing on identifying or differentiating between the original human voice and synthetic or AI-generated voice. There will be a need for massive databases providing updated information about the certain speech or vocal traits of a particular population. Further developments and improvements of real-time voice authentication for the prevention of call frauds and other related crimes (Hansen and Hasan 2015).

11.7 Role of AI and ML and Big Data Management in Forensic Speech Science

The various upcoming technologies such as AI and ML are used for the data collection and recovery. The cybercrime timeline reconstruction will help get the accurate prediction and usage to help in robust big data analysis. The pattern recognition is used to safeguard the chain of custody and helps in hacking incidents. The use of artificial intelligence (AI) and machine learning (ML) in forensic speech science is a transformative technology in the dynamic of digital forensics (Altayari et al. 2022). The various AI tools are integrated with software applications for facial and speaker recognition. There are many challenges as there is an increasing database size and evolving criminal tactics that necessitate ongoing research and refinement within the digital forensics profession. AI's acts as a potential tool in forensic evidence include enhancing causation establishment, meeting laboratory standards, interpreting evidence, and removing coincidental matches (Bertovsky et al. 2021). AI's applications extend to crime scene reconstruction and understanding complicated forensic findings.

However, there are concerns regarding algorithmic transparency and the need for explanation in court, as well as the potential for manipulation and the need for continuous research on AI applications (Ferrazzano et al. 2020). AI's use in forensic evidence presentation includes facial comparison, DNA analysis, and digital forensics investigations (Jain 2024). While AI presents opportunities in forensic science, the challenges of managing large databases and evolving criminal tactics necessitate continual research and refinement within the digital forensics profession. The role of artificial intelligence in forensic sciences is to enhance the effectiveness in terms of improving the accuracy, consistency, and efficiency in evidence analysis, particularly for high-dimensional and pattern-based data such as DNA profiles, speech signals, and digital traces. AI-driven automation reduces human bias and supports large-scale forensic data processing (Singh 2018; Jain et al. 2025). AI helps in causation and strengthening forensic standards. ML models will help minimize coincidental matches and improve reproducibility and increasing the robustness of models for future use (Dunsin et al. 2024; Endres 2023). There are numerous studies that are focused on the non-availability of AI-based evidence, and that is a gap at this industry especially DNA and speech evidence—in judicial contexts (Berutu and Multazam 2022). There is always a bias recognition in identifying the forensic speaker identification (Geradts 2020; Vásquez-Correa and Álvarez-Muniain 2023).

There is always an emergence of AI forensics as a subfield where the focus of AI is to identify the malicious AI behavior, causation, and accountability. This evolution represents a critical expansion of traditional digital forensics (Reedy 2023). Legal, ethical, and professional implications in AI into forensic science and criminal justice necessitates updated legal frameworks, enhanced forensic literacy, and ethical safeguards to ensure responsible, fair, and admissible use of AI-generated evidence (Juola 2019; Meuwly 2009).

AI, including agentic and generative AI, plays a significant role in forensic speech science through data management, evidence presentation, and establishing causation. AI improves forensic science's effectiveness by automating tasks and providing insights, enabling better understanding of complex forensic findings (Muda 2014).

The growing need of integration of AI with forensic science will be transformative shift where the forensic evidence is generated, interpreted, and presented within criminal justice system particularly in DNA profiling and forensic speech science (Singh 2018). The literature emphasizes that forensic science depends on human expertise specially identifying the pattern for voice comparison, handwriting analysis, and evaluation of language, which raises a concern related to reproducibility, reliability, and cognitive biases. AI and ML techniques are used for the emergence of tools capable of enhancing objectivity, accuracy, and standardization for forensic processes (Singh 2019). This contribution of AI has given the solution and ability to process large data in significant way and strengthening evidentiary robustness in legal contexts. The application of AI in DNA analysis supports accurate estimations and will reduce the error and risk (Schneider and Breitinger 2023). DNA evidence interpretation in forensic practices can also be accepted by courts as evidence.

AI-driven automatic speaker recognition (ASR) systems are used to trained human experts. Traditional forensic voice comparison has long faced criticism due to the lack of fixed discriminatory speech features, susceptibility to contextual bias, and variability caused by recording conditions, emotional states, and linguistic diversity (Sveinsdottir et al. 2020). AI-based systems address many of these limitations by extracting high-dimensional acoustic and spectral features from speech signals and analyzing them using machine learning models trained on extensive datasets. Such systems can objectively assess speaker similarity even in challenging forensic conditions involving short, noisy, or degraded recordings, which are common in real-world investigations. Importantly, the literature underscores that AI does not merely automate existing forensic practices but fundamentally reconfigures them by introducing probabilistic reasoning, performance validation, and reproducibility as core principles of forensic speech analysis (Wall 2021).

Based on the AI modelling complex relationships between variables, AI systems assist forensic experts in establishing clearer causal links between evidence and alleged criminal events. AI-supported evidence presentation allows experts to communicate likelihood ratios, confidence measures, and alternative hypotheses in a manner that is scientifically grounded and legally defensible, thereby enhancing judicial decision-making. Explainable AI (XAI) highlights the importance of forensic contexts (Neustein and Patil 2012). AI models offer superior analytical power, as a "black box" that poses challenges for legal acceptability and expert deposition (Osmëni and Ali 2023). Cloud-based database systems help access the data anywhere and everywhere. It also helps provide standardized algorithms and performance metrics; AI supports the development of unified forensic standards that align with international best practices and address long-standing critiques raised by scientific and legal bodies.

The criminal activities increasingly involve AI-generated speech, deepfakes, and algorithmic manipulation; forensic science must evolve to address these novel threats. AI is catalyzing the emergence of new subfields such as AI forensics and digital forensic intelligence, which focus on detecting, interpreting, and attributing AI-mediated crimes and synthetic evidence. AI in forensic science enhances scientific rigor, reduces subjectivity, and reshapes evidence presentation to create an ethical governance, legal adaptation, and interdisciplinary collaboration to ensure its responsible and effective use. There is a great future of incorporation of AI and ML in forensic studies. The role of AI in forensic science, emphasizing scientific rigor, explainability, and legal compatibility as essential pillars for its effective adoption.

11.8 Synergy Among Speech Scientists, Forensic Experts, and Lawmakers

Forensic speech sciences can be considered as a part of forensic linguistics that include analysis of text messages, individual characteristics, recorded messages and speech, e-mails, languages and their structure, letters, etc. for the administration of justice. Forensic linguistics compiles the application of scientific knowledge and practice of language analysis, textology, speech-act theories, and criminalistics for legal matters (Leonard et al. 2024). Voice evidence is acceptable in many countries as a significant identification source considered for data analysis, particularly in European countries, North America, Australia, etc. The most common practice performed for the analysis of voice and speech is forensic voice comparison (FVC), also called forensic speaker identification. The forensic voice examiners identify and compare the questioned voice recording samples with the known/reference samples by instigating various scientific principles and techniques including hardware and software devices. The scientific and technical applications provide a significant evidentiary value to the voice samples in legal aspects by identifying certain similarities between the samples or identifying the differences. Forensic speech sciences include voice and speaker identification and community-specific speech features identification. Voice evidences have distinct characteristics as they are mostly recorded without the knowledge of the speaker on telephones. Telephone signals cause a lot of disturbance in the speech signals that leads to uneven, hinged, and broken voice outputs that become a task for the examiner to analyze the sample in its raw condition. In Europe, the componential approach for vocal, auditory, and acoustic analysis has been done predominantly. The research widely involves the use of automatic speech recognition systems or ASRs in Germany, Spain, Sweden, and England. ASRs utilize voice recordings as signal and extract data from the samples. The voice/speech recordings as valuable evidence in the courts require proper validation and data-driven efficiency. Previously, the examination was primarily based on the examiner's experience. Some examiners relied on the older data recorded per se a few decades prior and compare them with the current data. This time frame shift may also lead to visible changes in the voice of an individual that act as a biasing factor in voice identification. These days, courts mandate the use of scientific and technical approach to analyze evidence. The main challenges faced by forensic speech experts are primarily the lack of available data for reference and comparison purposes. Additionally, limited information is available for sociophonetics and the evolution of languages and dialects across the country (Hughes and Wormald 2020).

Voice recordings have an essential role in cases of bribery, threat, and extortion via phone calls or recorded voice messages; forensic speech recognition plays a role in identifying the unknown speaker. This could be incorporated with other fieldwork forensic linguistics and phonetical analysis. That may help in identifying the dialect, culture, and geolocation of an individual. Countries like India, multilingual with around 2220 dialects, widely require forensic linguistics and voice experts to examine, identify, and interpret voice evidence for the purpose of justice. The study and applications of forensic linguistics become an essential component for the Indian justice system. The court of law demands to conduct the trials in the accused's known language to prevent falsification of information under section 277 of CrPC. India is developing in the speech sciences field with the application of artificial intelligence. For example, court proceedings have been transcribed using Nomology Technology's Natural Language Processing (NLP) technology. Another example is SUPACE, a data management portal that uses machine learning. AI systems like SUVAAS help in translating English court rulings into their dialects/local languages. Yet there is a further need for development in India. Traditionally, acoustic analysis and auditory perception methods were performed for voice and speech recording recognition. The "voiceprint" method, an analogue to fingerprints, had also been incorporated for legal purposes in some countries of the United States but proved to be unreliable due to dynamic nature of speech and low accurate results.

Speech recognition involves various strategies of auditory and acoustic characteristics, phonetics analysis, and linguistics analysis of the recorded evidence. These techniques include the application of different hardware and software tools (Altayari et al. 2022). Unlike countries as Russia and Brazil, India is tad behind the line in voice and speech recognition and research. There is a need for further development and exchange of methodological strategies between the countries to conduct valuable research in Indian scenario.

11.9 Present Scenario of Forensic Speech Sciences and Future Aspects

Forensic speech evidence has traditionally been applied primarily in forensic voice comparison, where questioned recordings are compared with known reference samples to determine speaker identity (Jain 2024). Historically, courts relied heavily on expert auditory judgments, resulting in subjective and potentially biased conclusions (Nolan 2013; Singh 2018). Over time, legal systems increasingly emphasized the need for scientifically validated evidence, prompting greater scrutiny of reliability, validity, and probative value (Rose 2002; Basu et al. 2022).

Speaker characteristics are inherently variable and influenced by health, emotional state, stress, intoxication, and recording conditions, complicating forensic interpretation (Dehak et al. 2011; Dunsin et al. 2024). Contemporary forensic practice has therefore shifted toward objective, technology-driven approaches, particularly automatic speaker recognition systems based on deep neural networks and x-vector embeddings, which consistently outperform listener-based methods (Wall 2021; Geradts 2020). Despite these advances, real-world forensic casework remains challenging due to noisy telephonic recordings, bandwidth limitations, and deliberate disguise strategies (Dehak et al. 2011; Vásquez-Correa and Álvarez-Muniain 2023). Limited population-specific databases and linguistic diversity further complicate analysis in multilingual regions such as India (Morozova et al. 2025).

Future developments will focus on improving AI-based systems for short and mismatched recordings, enhancing calibration and validation for courtroom use, and addressing emerging threats such as AI-generated and synthetic voices (Hughes and Wormald 2020; Hansen and Hasan 2015). Research into neurophysiological and thermal indicators of deception remains exploratory and requires careful ethical and legal consideration (Reedy 2023; Schneider and Breitinger 2023; Neustein and Patil 2012).

References

Altayari W, Kamalrudin M, Jaber MM (2022) The role of artificial intelligence in forensic evidence presentation. Int J Health Sci 16(Suppl II):5649–5662

Basu N, Bali AS, Weber P, Rosas-Aguilar C, Edmond G, Martire KA, Morrison GS (2022) Speaker identification in courtroom contexts—part I: individual listeners compared to forensic voice

comparison based on automatic speaker recognition technology. Forensic Sci Int 341:111499. https://doi.org/10.1016/j.forsciint.2022.111499
Belin P, Fecteau S, Bédard C (2004) Thinking the voice: neural correlates of voice perception. Trends Cogn Sci 8(3):129–135
Bertovsky LV, Burmistrova NS, Shapovalov YN, Petukhov EN, Vilgonenko IM (2021) Artificial intelligence in criminal law and forensic profiling. Adv Res Russ Bus Manag:383–389
Brümmer N, de Villiers E (2013) The speaker partitioning problem. Comput Speech Lang 27(2):385–402
Dehak N, Kenny P, Dehak R, Dumouchel P, Ouellet P (2011) Front-end factor analysis for speaker verification. IEEE Trans Audio Speech Lang Process 19(4):788–798
Dunsin D, Ghanem MC, Ouazzane K, Vassilev V (2024) Artificial intelligence and machine learning in digital forensics and incident response. Forensic Sci Int Digital Investig 48:301675
Edmond G, Towler A, Growns B, Ribeiro G, Found B, White D, Ballantyne KN, Searston RA (2022) Thinking forensics: cognitive science for forensic practitioners. Sci Justice 62(3):233–245
Eriksson A (n.d.) Tutorial on forensic speech science: Part I—Speaker identification. Int J Speech Lang Law
Endres K, Hillygus DS, DeBell M, Iyengar S (2023) A randomized experiment evaluating survey mode effects for video interviewing. Political Sci Res Methods 11(1):144–159
Ferrazzano M, Brighi R, Saporiti L (2020) Legal issues in AI forensics: understanding the importance of humanware. I-LEX 13:19–42
French P, Stevens L (2018) Forensic speech science. Routledge, London
Geradts Z (2020) The application of artificial intelligence in digital forensic science. Proc Am Acad Forensic Sci 26:C17
Hansen JHL, Hasan T (2015) Speaker recognition by machines and humans: a tutorial review. IEEE Signal Process Mag 32(6):74–99. https://doi.org/10.1109/MSP.2015.2462851
Hughes V, Wormald J (2020) Sharing innovative methods, data and knowledge across sociophonetics and forensic speech science. Linguistics Vanguard 6(s1). https://doi.org/10.1515/lingvan-2018-0062
Jain A (2024) Enhancing forensic analysis of digital evidence using machine learning. Int J Innov Res Multidiscip Perspect Stud 18:1–8
Jain S, Narne VK, Bharani Valayutham H, Madan T, Ravi SK, Jain C (2025) Speech recognition in noise: analyzing phoneme, syllable, and word-based scoring methods and their interaction with hearing loss. Diagnostics 15(13):1619
Jessen M (2008) Forensic phonetics. Lang Linguist Compass 2(4):671–689
Juola P (2019) Artificial intelligence and pattern evidence: a legal application for AI. In: Proceedings of the XX Simposio Argentino de Inteligencia Artificial (ASAI)
Künzel HJ (2001) Beware of the telephone effect: the influence of telephone transmission on speaker recognition. Int J Speech Lang Law 8(1):80–99
Leonard MK, Gwilliams L, Sellers KK, Chung JE, Xu D, Mischler G,... & Chang EF (2024) Large-scale single-neuron speech sound encoding across the depth of human cortex. Nature 626(7999):593–602
Meuwly D (2009) Forensic speaker recognition. Wiley Encyclopedia of Forensic Science 1–5
Meuwly D, Ramos D, Haraksim R (2017) A guideline for the validation of likelihood ratio methods used for forensic evidence evaluation. Forensic Sci Int 276:142–153
Morozova J, Papoyan N, Upadhyay NK (2025) Forensic linguistics: identification of individuals by written and oral speech as evidence in criminal cases in BRICS countries. BRICS Law J 12(4):119–146. https://doi.org/10.21684/2412-2343-2025-12-4-119-146
Morrison GS (2011) Measuring the validity and reliability of forensic likelihood-ratio systems. Sci Justice 51(3):91–98
Morrison GS, Zhang C, Enzinger E, Ochoa F (2016) Relevant data, relevant models and relevant validation: using the principle of empirical validation in forensic voice comparison. Speech Comm 79:54–69
Muda LB (2014) Speech recognition for connected word using cepstral and dynamic time warping algorithms

Neustein A, Patil HA (2012) Forensic speaker recognition. Springer, New York
Nolan F (2013) The phonetic bases of speaker recognition. Cambridge University Press, Cambridge
Osmëni T, Ali M (2023) Generative AI: Impactful considerations to responsible data practices in business execution. In 2023 International conference on computing, networking, telecommunications & engineering sciences applications (CoNTESA) (pp. 75–82). IEEE
Pavlidis I, Levine J, Baukol P (2012) Thermal imaging for anxiety detection. IEEE Eng Med Biol Mag 21(6):56–63
Reedy P (2023) Artificial intelligence in digital forensics. In: Encyclopedia of forensic sciences, 3rd edn. Elsevier, pp 170–192
Rose P (2002) Forensic speaker identification. Taylor & Francis, London
Schneider J, Breitinger F (2023) Towards AI forensics: did the artificial intelligence system do it? J Inf Secur Appl 76:103517
Singh D (2018) Artificial intelligence in forensics and criminal investigation: Indian perspective. Int J Innov Sci Res Technol 7(7):142–144
Singh S (2019) The role of speech technology in biometrics, forensics and man-machine interface. IJECE 9(1):281–288
Snyder D, Garcia-Romero D, Sell G, Povey D, Khudanpur S (2018) X-vectors: Robust DNN embeddings for speaker recognition. Proc IEEE ICASSP:5329–5333
Sveinsdottir T, Troullinou P, Aidinis S, Delipalta A, Finn R, Loukinas P, Wieltschnig P (2020) The role of data in artificial intelligence. AI Ethics 1(2):151–165
Titze IR (2000) Principles of voice production. National Center for Voice and Speech, Iowa City
Vásquez-Correa JC, Álvarez Muniain A (2023) Novel speech recognition systems applied to forensics within child exploitation: Wav2vec2. 0 vs. whisper. Sensors 23(4):1843
Wall J (2021) A conversational AI approach to detecting deception and tackling insurance fraud. Proc ICICIS
Zhang C, JHL H (2007) Analysis and classification of speech mode: Whispered through shouted speech. Proc Interspeech:2289–2292

The manufacturer's authorised representative in the EU is Springer Nature Customer Service Centre GmbH, Europaplatz 3, 69115 Heidelberg, Germany. If you have any concerns regarding our products, please contact ProductSafety@springernature.com

Printed and bound by CPI Group (UK) Ltd, Croydon, CR0 4YY
21/09/2026
02219991-0002